GIOVANNI BOCCACCIO

ON FAMOUS WOMEN

GIOVANNI BOCCACCIO

ON FAMOUS WOMEN

TRANSLATED, WITH AN INTRODUCTION AND NOTES, BY
GUIDO A. GUARINO

SECOND, REVISED EDITION

WITH BIBLIOGRAPHICAL NOTE AND NEW BIBLIOGRAPHY

ITALICA PRESS
NEW YORK
2011

ITALICA PRESS, INC.

595 Main Street, Suite 605
New York, New York 10044
inquiries@italicapress.com

Library of Congress Cataloging-in-Publication Data

Boccaccio, Giovanni, 1313–1375.
[Concerning famous women.]
On famous women / by Giovanni Boccaccio ; translated, with an introduction
and notes , by Guido A. Guarino.
p. cm.
Includes bibliographical references.
Summary: "This first collection of biographies exclusively of women, both
mythological and historical, was written by Giovanni Boccaccio, author to the
"Decameron," between 1361 and 1362. It includes 106 biographies ranging from
Eve to Boccaccio's contemporary, Queen Giovanna I of Naples"--Provided by
publisher.
ISBN 978-1-59910-265-8 (alk. paper) -- ISBN 978-1-59910-266-5 (pbk. : alk. paper)
-- ISBN 978-1-59910-267-2 (e-book)
1. Women--Biography. I. Guarino, Guido A., 1925- II. Title.
PQ4274.D5E5 2011
858'.107--dc23   2011025365

Images: Woodcut illustrations from *Ioannis Boccatii insignie opus De claris
mulieribus.* Bern: Mathias Apiarius, 1539.
Cover art: Marcia, the daughter of Varro, paints her self-portrait (chapter
LXIV), 1402/3. Paris, Bibliothèque National, MS Français 598.

FOR A COMPLETE LIST OF ITALICA PRESS TITLES
VISIT OUR WEB SITE AT:
WWW.ITALICAPRESS.COM

CONTENTS

·· (v) ··

CONTENTS

CONTENTS

CONTENTS

INTRODUCTION

BOCCACCIO'S fame today rests on his masterpiece, the *Decameron*. From the moment it was published this work forced everyone to be aware of its existence but was not always praised by Boccaccio's contemporaries and the men of the Renaissance; at times it was attacked together with its author. To the men of the Renaissance Boccaccio was primarily a Latin scholar: the Humanist who had brought Tacitus back to life, the scholar who had embraced the wisdom and knowledge of the ancients, the lover of poetry who had been the first, after so many centuries, to commune with the divine Homer. The great artist had to give way to the learned scholar, whose fame rested on his Latin works. With his *De Casibus Virorum Illustrium, De Montibus, De Claris Mulieribus*, and other works, Boccaccio was the great propagator of classical history, literature, and mythology, and his *Genealogia Deorum Gentilium* in particular became the textbook and font of inspiration for generations of poets.

When these works had fulfilled their historical role and helped bring new life to the ancient world, they were slowly relegated to oblivion. The world had come a long way from the time when adventurous Humanists searched every corner of Europe for lost treasures. Men who could easily buy Latin and Greek classics in the original and in translation as they came off the Aldine and other presses no longer needed Boccaccio to synthesize the learning of antiquity for them. Thus, the Latin works of Boccaccio slowly went out of use, print and fashion, and are today condemned to live among cobwebs in the lowest stacks of libraries and in the minds of a few scholarly professors.

Boccaccio's *De Claris Mulieribus* is a remarkable treatise which contains the lives of one hundred and four women. It is the first collection of women's biographies ever written, as the author proudly points out in the preface. It is very fitting that this honor should belong to Boccaccio, who took such pains to please and entertain women, and whose answer to those who criticized him for it was that yes, he liked women indeed. He was also among the first men of his age to turn his attention seriously to biography, a genre which was to become so popular. Boccaccio looked for glory in this world, not in the next, and believed that it was here that man affirmed himself and achieved fame, and that it was the writer's duty to preserve the deeds and achievements of great men for posterity. It was for this reason that he turned to biography.

Boccaccio's *De Claris Mulieribus* follows in the tradition of the medieval didactic and moralizing works. It has many characteristics of the encyclopedia and the *speculum* which were very popular in the Middle Ages. It shares with them the concern to instruct and strengthen the reader. Yet, there are many differences. His moralizing is not always of the medieval type; his attitude toward women and the ideals he asks them to follow are quite different, as we shall see. Above all, we notice a change in his attitude toward the ancient world, and in his reasons for writing this work and the treatises on mythology and geography. His motive is not simply compiling facts to make them more easily available, nor is it a mere show of erudition. He is filled with the desire to accumulate new knowledge to be added to that of the Christian Middle Ages. He wants to show that the ancient myths, which the Middle Ages had misinterpreted, contain much truth, and that under the veil of poetry there are universal sentiments, ideals, and beliefs. He places the myths of the ancients on a par with Holy Writ as teachers of mankind. In the preface to the *Genealogy of the Gentile Gods*, the soldier Donino, speaking on behalf of King Hugo, asks Boccaccio to write about the ancient gods, and refuses to listen to his objections:

I can well believe that those nations you mention are inaccessible, and that such records as they possess are wholly unknown to the Latins. But whatever has passed by way of Greek literature among the Latins, or whatever can be found in Latin writers themselves, who in early times won no little distinction and glory in literature, let it all be brought to light. . . .[1]

[1] Charles G. Osgood, ed. *Boccaccio on Poetry*, by Giovanni Boccaccio, 2nd ed. (New York, 1956), p. 7. Copyright © 1956, by The Liberal Arts Press, Inc., and reprinted by permission of The Liberal Arts Press Division of the Bobbs-Merrill Company, Inc.

Boccaccio, then, sees his mission in life as that of dispelling the gloom of centuries and restoring the knowledge of the ancient world. In accepting King Hugo's invitation, he stresses the difficulties that lie ahead and shows the awe and reverence with which he approaches his task:

At your behest, then, I leave behind the mountain snails and barren soil of Certaldo, and, raw seaman that I am, embark in my frail little craft on a stormy sea all involved with reefs, little knowing whether my voyage will be worth the trouble. For I may trace every shore and traverse every mountain grove; I may, if need be, explore dyke and den afoot, descend even to hell, or, like another Daedalus, go winging to the ether. Everywhere, to your heart's desire, I will find and gather, like fragments of a mighty wreck strewn on some vast shore, the relics of the Gentile gods. These relics, scattered through almost infinite volumes, shrunk with age, half consumed, well-nigh a blank, I will bring into such single genealogical order as I can, to gratify your wish. . . . Who in our day can penetrate the hearts of the Ancients? Who can bring to light and life again minds long since removed in death? Who can elicit their meaning? A divine task that — not human! The Ancients departed in the way of all flesh, leaving posterity to interpret according to their own judgment. What wonder? There are the words of Holy Writ, clear, definite, charged with unalterable truth, though often thinly veiled in figurative language. Yet they are frequently distorted into as many meanings as there are readers. This makes me approach my own task with less misgiving. Where I do not perform it well, at least I shall arouse a wiser man to do it better.

It is, therefore, my plan of interpretation first to write what I learn from the Ancients, and when they fail me, or I find them inexplicit, to set down my own opinion. This I shall do with perfect freedom of mind, so that men who are ignorant and fastidiously despise the poets whom they do not understand, may see that the poets, though not Catholics, were so gifted with intelligence that no product of human genius was ever more skilfully enveloped in fiction, nor more beautifully adorned with exquisite language, than theirs. Whence it is clear that they were richly imbued with secular wisdom not often found in their jealous accusers. And these interpretations will enable you to see not only the art of the ancient poets, and the consanguinity and relations of the false gods, but certain natural truths, hidden with an art that will surprise you, together with deeds and moral civilization of the Ancients that are not a matter of every-day information.[2]

Boccaccio is concerned with the "human genius" of the ancients, their "secular wisdom," and the "natural truths" their works contain. This "moral civilization" of antiquity is definitely set apart from the Christian world. Boccaccio does not attempt to find Christian truths in the works of the ancients, as the men of the Middle Ages and Petrarch himself had done. He does not try to redeem the pagans by finding similarities with Christian thought and doctrine in their works. His work is a celebration of the ancient world for the human and secular values it contained, and for those "natural truths" which are part of every man's world, whether pagan or Christian.

In his defense of poetry in his *Vita di Dante* and in the *Genealogia Deorum Gentilium*, Boccaccio expresses his life-long love for this art, which he places on the same level with theology. In his views on poetry we find the reason for his concern with ancient myths and his efforts to place all this material at the disposal of other poets. In his *Vita di Dante* he states that primitive men shared with us the natural desire for knowledge. Seeing the order which reigns in Nature, they thought there must be a power or force from which this order emanates. This they called "deity." They decided that this deity was to be venerated by other than ordinary means. They appointed priests for this purpose, built statues, and invented poetry in order to express their devotion in words different from their everyday speech. Poetry, then, finds its origins in theology. But poetry did not content itself with the deification of the sun, the moon, Jupiter and the other planets; it also showed that everything which was useful to man was a deity, no matter how earthly. It sang the praises of those men who rose above others through their intellect and strength, and who, because of their excellence, were deemed gods rather than men. Thus poetry celebrated battles and notable events in which both men and gods played a role. Boccaccio strives to give a rational explanation

[2] *Ibid.*, pp. 10-12.

INTRODUCTION

of religion and poetry, and at one point states that they are the same thing. Theology is the "poetry of God" and its purpose is to instruct men in divine mysteries so that one day they may reach the kingdom of heaven. With their myths, the ancient poets instruct men in the things of this world and show them the virtues they must pursue and the vices they must flee. The myths and the gods of the poets may be false, but under the veil of fiction they explain the world of man, or, as he says, the "natural truths."[3]

In giving equal importance to the secular myths of the poets and to Holy Writ, Boccaccio does not intend to lessen the importance of the spiritual values of man; he was a believer like his contemporaries, although, unlike his friend Petrarch, he did not allow religion to torture him. He insists, however, that this earth is part of man's world. In re-telling the myths of the ancients and interpreting them, Boccaccio wishes to present a different concept of life on this earth. He sees man as having certain "natural" powers and capacities which he must develop fully in order to play an active role in this world. Man is not to abandon God, but he must no longer renounce the world. Like Petrarch, he believed that the ancients had found a way of life and certain values proper to man. This concept of life was to be found in the works of the poets. By collecting and interpreting their myths, Boccaccio was making this material available to future generations of poets, for in his view there could be no poetry without myths. But more important, he was undertaking the "divine task" of bringing "to light and life again minds long since removed in death"; he was taking a world which the Middle Ages had distorted and was attempting to restore it to its original state. In many works of the Middle Ages, the ancients appear as men who have the same ideas and feelings and speak in the same way as the author and his contemporaries. In the *Novellino*, Hercules, Socrates, Trajan and others do not differ at all from Christian heroes. Boccaccio knew they were different and tried to learn what they and their world were like. As an historian and as a critic Boccaccio did not equal Petrarch.

[3] Giovanni Boccaccio, *La Vita di Dante*, ed. Francesco Macrì-Leone (Firenze, 1888), pp. 48-56.

His reconstruction of the ancient world is not very accurate or successful, and he lacks Petrarch's objectivity and critical resources. Yet in some ways he seems to approach it more closely through his love and admiration, which are evident in every line. It is a world peopled with heroes who, because of their "natural abilities," have become representatives of the civic and secular virtues which form the basis of Boccaccio's new world. They allow him to indulge in his love for the magnificent and the extraordinary, for the deed or word which symbolize man's greatness.

The stories and myths of the ancient world also give Boccaccio the opportunity to moralize, which was one of his favorite occupations. His moralizing is often highly conventional. At times, when he moves away from tradition, he shows doubt and even defends ideals which seem to clash. This is especially true of the ideals he proposes as models for women. An example of his ambivalent attitude is found in Chapter V, where he discusses the results of civilization. In itself civilization is good, for it has brought man from the condition of an animal to that of a human being; he has become refined and has acquired high spiritual values. Yet civilization is also evil. In his primeval state of bliss man knew no vice and lived without fear or wants, envy or greed. Civilization has changed him into a being who cannot live in peace with other men for he is never satisfied with his possessions. Boccaccio felt these questions very deeply and personally. If we know something about this man who was given the name of *Giovanni della tranquillità*, which he bitterly resented, we can easily see how serious and sincere he was even in his ambivalent attitude to civilization. His ideal life was one of peace and quiet, devoted to scholarly pursuits and to poetry, a simple life in which everyday necessities do not intrude. His personal life was quite different from this ideal, and we can easily understand his dreams of an age of gold. He loved heroic deeds, but was not of heroic temper. All this appears in his moralizing and in his interpretation of ancient myths.

In all his works on classical poetry, Boccaccio uses the fourfold medieval system of interpretation. Any given myth has four meanings: literal, moral, allegorical, and anagogical. In his *Genealogy of the Gentile Gods*, he gives an explanation of this system:

According to the poetic fiction, Perseus, son of Jupiter, killed the Gorgon, and flew away victorious into the air. Now, this may be understood superficially in its literal or historical sense. In the moral sense it shows a wise man's triumph over vice and his attainment of virtue. Allegorically it figures the pious man who scorns worldly delight and lifts his mind to heavenly things. It admits also an anagogical sense, since it symbolizes Christ's victory over the Prince of this World, and his Ascension ... But it is not my intention to unfold all these meanings for each myth when I find one quite enough.[4]

Usually Boccaccio resorts to the moral and allegorical interpretations. As for the literal or historical meaning of myths, Boccaccio adheres to the rationalistic system of Euhemerus, with which he was acquainted through Lactantius. An explanation of euhemerism is found in the *Life of Dante*:

Afterwards, various men in various places began to rise above the ignorant multitudes in their regions through their excellence in different things. They judged disputes not according to written laws, for they still did not have them, but through a certain natural sense of justice, which some had more than others. They gave order to their lives and customs, for they had been enlightened by Nature itself. They resisted adverse events with bodily strength, and took precautions against those which might happen. They called themselves kings and appeared before the people followed by servants and wearing ornaments which men had not used until that time. They made others obey and finally worship them. This happened without difficulty, if they but dared demand it, for they seemed gods rather than men to these primitive people who saw them in that guise. These men did not put all their trust in their strength, but began to multiply the number of religions. Through them they cowed their subjects, and bound to obedience through sacraments those whom they could not have subjected through force. In addition, they began to deify their fathers, grandfathers, and ancestors so that they would be feared and revered more by the people. These things could not be done without the aid of the

[4] Giovanni Boccaccio, *Boccaccio on Poetry*, p. xviii. See p. x, n. 1.

poets, who . . . with various masterly myths made the people believe what the princes wanted. In the service of these new gods and the men for whom they claimed divine origin, they used the same style which the first poets had reserved only for the worship of the true God.[5]

Boccaccio was conscious of living in a new age. However, he was still in what may be called a transitional period in which new values were making themselves felt but had not yet displaced the old. Thus, as he moved in new directions, he carried along a number of medieval traditions and practices. One of these was *exemplarism,*[6] that is, the use of the *exemplum* whereby the author expresses his ideas and discusses various topics. For instance, to demonstrate the power of Grace and to show that God's mercy is infinite, a writer presents the example of a man who has committed many offenses against God and men, repents and is then saved through God's Grace. This is one of the three basic patterns which are found in medieval sermons and the *Vitae Sanctorum.* Boccaccio uses this method, but his stories no longer demonstrate God's love, as was the case for the Christian *exemplum,* but the operation of Nature and the human intellect: the method is the same, but the purpose differs greatly.

Boccaccio makes use of this method in the *Decameron* as well as in *Concerning Famous Women.* Both these works can be divided into categories which exemplify vices and virtues, and celebrate man's ability to live in this world. For instance, in the *Decameron* lust is exemplified by Masetto da Lamporecchio (III, 1), Brother Puccio (III, 4), Rustico and Alibech (III, 10), and the village priest of Varlungo (VIII, 2). Fidelity in love is illustrated by Ghismonda (IV, 1), Isabetta (IV, 5), the wife of Guglielmo Rossiglione (IV, 9), and Federigo degli Alberighi (V, 9). For the power of love and its results there are Cimone (V, 1), Gerbino (IV, 4), and Federigo (V, 9). Adventure and the ways of Fortune are represented by Landolfo Ruffolo (II, 4), Madonna Beritola (II, 6), Andreuola (IV, 6), and Simona and Pasquino (IV, 7).

[5] Giovanni Boccaccio, *La Vita di Dante,* p. 50.
[6] Cf. Enrico de' Negri, "The Legendary Style of the *Decameron*," *The Romanic Review,* XLIII (October, 1952), pp. 166ff.

Examples of intelligence and stupidity are don Felice and Brother Puccio (III, 4), Ferondo (III, 8), and Brother Alberto (IV, 2). Generosity and magnanimity may be found in Natan (x, 3), Ansaldo (x, 5), and King Charles (x, 6), and naive belief in saints and miracles in Ser Ciappelletto (I, I), Brother Alberto (IV, 2), and Brother Cipolla (VI, 10), to cite only a few.

These same categories may be used for *Concerning Famous Women*: lust is exemplified by Venus (VII), Clytaemnestra (XXXIV), Helen (XXXV), and Faustina Augusta (XCVI); fidelity in love may be found in the chapters on Penelope (XXXVIII), Dido (XL), Nicaula (XLI), Artemisia (LV), and Portia (LXXX); the power of love and its results is shown by Iole (XXI), Aemilia (LXXII), and Triaria (XCIV); adventure and the ways of Fortune are illustrated by Polyxena (XXXI), Cassandra (XXXIII), Hypsipyle (XV), and Thisbe (XII); the chapters on Amalthea (XXIV), Thamyris (LIV), Irene (LVII), and Paulina (LXXXIX) contain examples of intelligence and stupidity; generosity and magnanimity are portrayed in Busa (LXVII), Aemilia (LXXII), and Camiola (CIII); naive belief in gods and miracles is shown in Minerva (VI), Isis (VIII), Flora (LXII), and Paulina (LXXXIX).

The similarities between the *Decameron* and *Concerning Famous Women* do not end here. Almost all the *novelle* of Boccaccio's masterpiece have their counterpart in his later volume on women, and the comments found in the latter work may well serve as an explanation of the author's thought in the *Decameron*. His handling of the subject is often similar in both works: the story of Ser Ciappelletto in the *Decameron* and Flora; Isabetta and Artemisia; Cimone and Triaria. Perhaps the best illustration, however, can be found in the *novella* of Brother Alberto and Lisetta (IV, 2) and the story of Paulina (LXXXIX). Alberto was a scoundrel who was forced to leave his city when his crimes became public knowledge. He went to Venice, where, in order to cloak his hypocrisy more successfully, he became a friar, and then a priest. He played his role of a humble and devoted priest so well, even crying during the sacrifice of the Mass, that his fame as a holy man spread throughout the city. Now, it happened that among the many women who flocked to Alberto's church to be edified by his holiness there was a certain Lisetta, who was both beautiful and foolish. After she had confessed her sins, Brother Alberto asked her whether she had any lovers. She answered that she had a husband, and he was more than she needed. How could he think she had a lover? Did he not realize that she was too beautiful to let another mere mortal caress her? Alberto now thought that the occasion had arrived to start reaping the rewards of the saintliness he had shown during the Venetian interlude. He convinced the naive woman that the Angel Gabriel had come to him during the night and had asked him to let Lisetta know that he had been captivated by her extraordinary beauty and would like to spend a night with her. On receiving this message Lisetta's joy knew no bounds, and she told Alberto that she would be delighted to receive the Angel at night, if he promised he would never abandon her for the Virgin Mary. Then Alberto let her know that angels are not of the same substance as men; therefore, Gabriel would have to assume a man's body to visit her. She agreed to this. Now, Alberto had a favor to ask: could the angel assume Alberto's body for his visit with her so that Alberto's soul might dwell in heaven for a few hours? Thus the woman spent the night with Alberto's body, and the following day Alberto told her of the joys of heaven, which his soul had experienced.

Paulina's story is very similar to that of Lisetta. She was a Roman woman who had great devotion for the god Anubis, whose temple she visited every day. She too was beautiful, and a young man, Mundus, fell in love with her. His advances were harshly rejected by Paulina, who proclaimed her fidelity to her husband. Thus the young man was forced to resort to subterfuge. He gave a great deal of money to the priests of the temple of Anubis to secure their help. The following day, when she arrived at the temple, Paulina was met by the most venerable of Anubis' priests, who had a message for her from the god. He told her that Anubis was very pleased by her long devotion to him and wanted to reward her for it. That night she was to sleep in the temple, and Anubis would come to her. Paulina went home and told her husband, who expressed surprise and delight at so signal an honor and gave her his permission. That night Paulina slept in the temple, where Mundus came to her in the regalia of the god Anubis and shared her bed. Before leaving he told her that she could expect the birth of a son who would be a god.

The similarity in plot and technique in both these stories is striking. In both cases an outrageous and ridiculous fraud is perpetrated on a foolish and simple woman. Both these women are devout: one lights a candle before every image of the Angel Gabriel, and the other visits the temple of Anubis every day to honor him with sacrifices. Both women are beautiful; both are inordinately proud, one of her beauty, the other of her saintliness. It is because of this pride that they refuse to accept the attentions of mortal lovers. One, madonna Lisetta, believes and finds it most natural that she has been noticed by the Angel because of her most marvelous body, which was not to be defiled by the touch of common lovers: "I am not the sort to be loved by anyone who comes along! How many women can you quote me, who can hold a candle to me? Why, I'd be considered good-looking even in Heaven!"[7] The other, Paulina, adores Anubis with great affection and thinks it only just that her saintliness be rewarded with his love. Both take great pride in being singled out among women by a divine being. Both are apprised of this divine love by hypocritical intermediaries of the gods. Blinded by their ridiculous vanity, both women fall prey to their lovers' wiles, and afterwards one waits impatiently for the return of her angel, and the other, together with her husband, awaits the birth of a god. Boccaccio delights in the foolishness of the women, the slyness of their deceivers, and the duplicity of the priests, whom everyone considered saintly. In both cases the perpetrators of the fraud are punished, but this is a minor detail. However, even in this there are similarities: the two women are ridiculed by everyone because of their credulity; the punishment meted out to the false Anubis is lighter and less cruel than that of Brother Alberto, but this is

---

[7] Giovanni Boccaccio, *The Decameron*, trans. Frances Winwar (New York, 1955), p. 238.

explained by the fact that Alberto belonged to a religious order, thus deserving harsher treatment, just as the deceitful priest of Anubis did. All the basic ingredients of the *novella* of the *Decameron* can be seen in Paulina's story, which could easily have found a worthy place in Boccaccio's masterpiece.

The story of Paulina is one of the very few in *Concerning Famous Women* where the spirit and humor of the *Decameron* retain some of their brilliance. But a significant relationship between these two works is to be found elsewhere. From an artistic point of view, or in respect to humor and satire, they are very different. *Concerning Famous Women* does not have the lightness of touch and the sparkle of the prose of the *Decameron*. It was not meant to have these qualities. Many chapters are somewhat dull because Boccaccio was more interested in moralizing than in telling a story. Yet, this concern for moralizing provides the strongest link with the *Decameron*. In the light tales of the latter work, Boccaccio is guided primarily by artistic, rather than pedagogical reasons. But beneath all his laughter he remains a moralist. This becomes very clear if we compare the *novella* of Masetto da Lamporecchio (III, 1) and the life of Rhea Ilia (XLIII). Artistically these two stories have nothing in common. The Masetto story is one of the most successful in the *Decameron*; Rhea is the mere retelling of an event without any artistic distinction, wit, or life. In both of these, however, we find the same moral.

Masetto was a shrewd young man, completely alive and full of animal vigor. He was a lustful man, whose only purpose in life was to gratify his senses. One day, an old man, who had been employed as general handyman in a convent, told him that he had left his job because there were too many young women in that place, who, having nothing else to do, spent their time devising ways and means of annoying him. Masetto said nothing, but immediately made his way to the convent. Once there, he pretended he was mute and was immediately hired, since the mother-superior felt that his handicap was a valuable asset in that he would not be able to reveal any of their secrets. Boccaccio portrays the young nuns who dwelt in this convent very skillfully. They were not in the cloister because of their overpowering love of God. Their convent was a prison for them, and their thoughts were not of God but of the pleasures of life which other women enjoyed in the outside world, and which were denied to them. Now, to these young women Masetto's arrival seemed a godsend, for here was the opportunity to enjoy the love they desired without any danger, since Masetto, being mute, could not reveal the secret. Thus Masetto's stratagem met with success, and the forces of Nature triumphed once more, for Masetto spent the rest of his life bringing little monks into the world, as Boccaccio puts it.

The story of Rhea Ilia is a well-known one. For political reasons, she was forced to become a Vestal Virgin, incurring the obligation of eternal chastity. Again the forces of Nature are too powerful, and she cannot fulfill her obligation. When this becomes known through the birth of Romulus and Remus, she is put to death. Boccaccio makes little or no effort to give this biography distinction of style or bring the tragic figure of Rhea to life. He uses her story simply as a framework on which to hang the moralistic comments he has to offer. He protests vehemently against the practice of forcing young girls to enter the cloister against their wishes, and at an age when they cannot know what life has to offer and what they are sacrificing. Those who force them to become nuns, thinking that they are dedicating them to a holy life, do not realize that the flesh will claim its own:

So, when I consider this woman and see the sacred bands and vestments of nuns hiding furtive love, I cannot help laughing at the madness of some. . . . They say that they have dedicated those virgins to God so that with their prayers their own affairs will prosper more, and after death they will gain eternal life. This is ridiculous and foolish. They do not know that an idle woman serves Venus and that these nuns greatly envy public prostitutes, whose chambers they think preferable to their own cells. . . . Wretched are parents and other relatives if they think that others can endure what they themselves avoid and cannot bear.[8]

[8] Giovanni Boccaccio, *De Claris Mulieribus*, ch. XLIII.

Is this not the same theme that appears in the *novella* of Masetto?
And is this *novella* not an *exemplum* of the power of Nature and
of an injustice to women, according to Boccaccio? Of course, the
shift in emphasis in the two works is clear. In the *Decameron*
Boccaccio does not preach. We can read Masetto simply as a delightful and droll story. The author does not point out the moral
of the story at length as he does in his other work. But in the
Decameron too he cannot escape the temptation to make sure
that his point is understood, as can be seen at the beginning of
Masetto's story:

Loveliest Ladies, there are many people foolish enough to believe that,
once a girl has a white band tied around her head, and a black cowl
hanging down her back, she is no longer a woman, with a woman's
desires! As though by becoming a nun, she had turned to stone! If those
fools happen to hear anything contrary to their belief, they fly off the
handle as though an execrable, unnatural sin had been committed,
unmindful of their own personal experience — they whom even license
cannot satisfy, and disregarding the great temptations of idleness and
brooding.[9]

Yet, some critics have found it difficult to believe that the
Decameron and *Concerning Famous Women* could have been
written by the same man. Their misconception of the author's
masterpiece made them see a dichotomy which does not really
exist. They saw a libertine in the author of the earlier work and
a moralist in the biographer of women. Many attempted to find
an explanation for this difference. For Hortis the solution lay in
the fact that a period of ten years had passed between the writing
of the *Decameron* and *Concerning Famous Women*. Boccaccio
had become old, he could no longer enjoy the pleasures of life, and
so he became a severe judge condemning them for others.[10]
Landau faced the same problem. He stated that the treatise on women was
a "good" book, which could have been written by a pious monk

[9] Giovanni Boccaccio, *The Decameron*, p. 144.
[10] Attilio Hortis, *Studj sulle Opere Latine del Boccaccio* (Trieste, 1879), pp. 88ff.

who had never left his cell.[11] The truth is that Boccaccio always remained a moralist. In all his works, including the *Decameron* and *Concerning Famous Women*, he places great stress on man's condition in this world, his freedom, his duties and obligations, and the bonds which enslave him. The difference between his *novelle* and his lives lies in a change of emphasis. In the *Decameron* the moral and the *exemplum* can be found just as well as in the later book, but the purpose of these works is different. In the *Decameron* the author's first desire was to entertain, while in the biographies of women it was to teach. The same moral, therefore, which in Boccaccio's *novelle* appears in a subtle fashion, to be found by the reader himself, is clearly stated in *Concerning Famous Women*, an historical and pedagogical work which presents the author with a greater opportunity for his comments. Thus even if we compare Rhea, one of the dullest chapters in the latter work, to Masetto, one of those stories which have caused a number of critics to call Boccaccio a libertine, we cannot escape the conclusion that both of these were indeed written by the same man. Both have the same basic morality.

It is clear that Boccaccio adopted the form which the *Vitae Sanctorum* and medieval legends offered him. However, while the Christian *exemplum* was focused on Grace, Boccaccio, as I have said, substituted "Nature" and the human intellect for it. Moreover, he used this same form to ridicule the Christian legends. We find instances of this in both the works we have been discussing, and again they show striking similarities. The first story of the *Decameron* fires the initial salvo against Christian legends. Boccaccio proceeds to create a "saint" out of Ser Ciappelletto, a worse scoundrel than any the world will ever see. As the story opens, Ciappelletto is on his death-bed in a strange city. His hosts are worried, for they find themselves in an impossible situation: if Ciappelletto dies without having seen a priest, they will be accused of having harbored a heretic; if he does see a priest, they will suffer just the same, for no priest can give absolution to a man

---

[11] Marcus Landau, *Giovanni Boccaccio Sein Leben und Seine Werke* (Stuttgart, 1877), p. 211.

who has committed every crime conceivable and shows no repentance. Ciappelletto, however, comforts them; he will see a priest and no harm will come to them. The priest who finally comes to minister to him is a very old and holy man, who is revered by everyone in the neighborhood. Ciappelletto's confession consists in the very opposite of his sins: every vice becomes a virtue, and this master criminal seems to be as innocent as a child. The simple priest is moved by the rogue's false tears and by his professions of faith and repentance and believes he has finally encountered a really good man. Ciappelletto dies after having received absolution. At the funeral, the old priest extols the virtues of good Ciappelletto in a sermon to the assembled people, and offers his life as an "example" to follow. His enthusiasm and admiration are contagious; everyone rushes to kiss Ciappelletto's feet and secure a piece of his clothes as a relic. He is finally buried in a marble sepulcher, which became a shrine, and soon everyone begins to tell of the miracles performed by Saint Ciappelletto. Thus this scoundrel became a saint with a last sacrilegious act, when the flames of hell were already burning him.

One saint is not enough for Boccaccio; he also presents the goddess Flora (LXII) in similar fashion and for the same purpose. Flora was a prostitute who plied her trade and accumulated great wealth over the years. As death approached, a desire for glory and immortality seized her. To be remembered forever, she left her wealth to the Roman people, with the proviso that it be used for yearly games in her honor. The Romans were delighted to accept. They were a lusty lot and insisted on properly honoring Flora by hiring prostitutes to perform at her festival. As the years passed, Rome became ruler of the world, and dignified senators began to feel that to hold games in honor of a prostitute was a blot on their great city's name. They attempted to put an end to these games, but unsuccessfully, for the people clamored for them. The people's will could not be thwarted, and yet Rome's honor had to be safeguarded. What was to be done? Finally the senators found a solution. They foisted a legend upon the people: Chloris had once been a beautiful nymph loved by the god Zephyrus. He married her and as a wedding gift he made her an immortal goddess, whose duty it was to adorn the world with flowers in the spring. And he called her Flora. Now, since flowers are a harbinger of new life and the fruit which will follow, the ancient Romans had established a festival in her honor to propitiate her. At this festival prostitutes had been employed to symbolize fertility. The people believed this legend, and thus a prostitute was metamorphosed into a goddess.

Boccaccio, then, ridicules the Christian legends by creating saints and gods, and by using the very form of the legends to do so. He felt that the authors of the *Vitae Sanctorum* had lost their sense of proportion and that their fantastic claims were an insult to man's intelligence. He has very little patience with the miraculous or the supernatural and states his skepticism bluntly. He makes this quite clear when dealing with myths or with the pagans. He shows greater care in dealing with Christianity, but does manage to show his disbelief, as can be seen from some of the parenthetical remarks in the life of Eve. His reluctance to deal with the Middle Ages and the Christian era in general is quite apparent, for the vast majority of the figures treated in *Concerning Famous Women* belong to classical times. He tries to explain his neglect of the Christian era by affirming that he does not wish to offend Christians by placing them next to pagans. Some critics have accepted Boccaccio's statement, seeing in it a sign that the author still belonged to the Middle Ages, and stating that later in the Renaissance writers no longer showed such scruples.[12] Boccaccio's affirmation, however, cannot be accepted at face value, and as for having scruples, he has amply expressed his ideas on the subject in all his works. He did not write of saints and martyrs simply because he was not drawn to them, while classical antiquity held him enthralled with its charms.

The condition and place allotted to women in the Middle Ages is well known. They and their beauty were seen as tools of Satan devoted to man's perdition. Their faults and weaknesses were many, and they were mercilessly reminded of them. They were

[12] E. Rodocanachi, *Boccace* (Paris, 1908), p. 158.

inferior beings, incapable of understanding, and were to be restrained and ruled with an iron hand, not guided, by their fathers and brothers at first, and then by their husbands. They were chattels rather than individual human beings: a necessary evil for the continuation of the species. The knight's lady-love and the *donna angelicata* of the *Dolce Stil Novo* may have been placed on a pedestal, but were not granted independence of will and action. The fact that their love may have been idealized and exalted by the knights of the Age of Chivalry, by Andreas Capellanus, and by the poets of the *Dolce Stil Novo* does not alter the basic position of women in that period, for reality showed itself in everyday life with all its brutality in spite of the poetic allegory of love. In a theological encyclopedia of the thirteenth century by the Dominican Nicolas Byard we find the following assertion:

"A man may chastise his wife and beat her for her correction; for she is of his household, and therefore the lord may chastise his own, as it is written in Gratian's *Decretum*, under the gloss *judicari*."[13] And in a much later period, Thomas More states in his *Utopia*: "The husbandes chastice theire wyfes; and the parentes theire chyldren."[14] And in speaking of the position of each member of the family he affirms: "The eldeste (as I sayde) rueleth the familie. The wyfes bee ministers to theyr husbandes, the chyldren to theyr parentes, and, to bee shorte, the yonger to theyr elders."[15] Woman's condition was to change slowly during the Renaissance, and the beginning of her metamorphosis may be observed in Boccaccio's works.

In the preface to his *Concerning Famous Women*, the author stated that the biographies of illustrious men had been written often by a number of excellent writers, and he cited Petrarch as an example. No one, however, had ever done the same for women. Boccaccio's surprise at this lack, and the fact that he set about writing a book on women shows the author's different attitude towards

[13] MS Royal 6E. VI, f. 214a. This quotation is taken from G. G. Coulton, *Medieval Panorama* (New York, 1955), p. 615.

[14] Thomas More, *Utopia*, trans. Ralph Robynson, ed. J. H. Lupton (Oxford, 1895), p. 230.

[15] *Ibid.*, p. 156.

them. He recognized that women can live and achieve glory just as men do. But once again he shows that he is in a period of transition, where the new clashes with the old. Women can become great scholars, rulers, painters and poets, if they but put their minds to it. But this requires a greater effort on their part since Nature has not made them the equals of men. Nature has given them frail bodies and sluggish minds, and to achieve glory they must first overcome these handicaps. Many of them have done so, and therefore deserve greater praise than men, according to Boccaccio. This is a sort of left-handed compliment, which he uses repeatedly. To lavish praise on a woman, Boccaccio can think of no better adjective than "manly," and his greatest condemnation of sluggish and insignificant men is to call them women. Yet he has taken a step forward, for he grants them the right of independent will and action. In fact, he often exhorts them to lay aside the traditional tasks of women and turn their minds and energies towards greatness of thought and action. Indeed, the overt scope of his treatise is to inspire them to do so. Yet he also seems to fear that women may encroach on the rights of men. In speaking of the honors and rewards heaped by the Roman Senate on Veturia for having saved the country, he states in his inimitable fashion that the senators outdid themselves in generosity, their minds befuddled by gratitude. Veturia and the Roman women would have been satisfied with the temple erected in their honor. Why then did the Senate have to grant them so many other rewards and prerogatives, which women have tenaciously held on to over the centuries to the discomfort and inconvenience of men? As always, Boccaccio moves forward instinctively towards a new era, but his progress is hindered by the *impedimenta* of traditions and prejudices of a former age.

In *Concerning Famous Women*, Boccaccio's comments and digressions give a picture of the world as he saw it, and as he would have preferred it to be. There are few facets of life that he does not touch upon in his commentaries and in his comparison of the customs of his and previous ages, usually to the detriment of the former. He discusses education, monastic life, politics, and morals, as well as the temperament and clothing of women. In these comments we find many problems which were afterwards developed and discussed fully by the men of the later Renaissance: fame and earthly glory; Fortune's role in the affairs of men; the individual's duties and obligations towards his fellow men; the place of the Church in everyday life; Man and Nature. From these lives, which are a blend of mythology, history and fantasy, there emerges the picture of Man as Boccaccio saw him. He is basically good when in his natural state. Civilization has brought about many changes. Some of these are good in themselves, but have had a detrimental effect on his character. They have prevented the individual from attaining the utmost fulfillment of his powers. The idea of property has prevented both rich and poor from pursuing ideals worthy of a human being: the rich, to become wealthy, turn all the powers of their minds to the acquisition of wealth, and the poor have to struggle for the basic necessities for themselves and their families. Thus both lose their independence. Wars destroy Man's character. He is born good but becomes cruel and harms his fellow creatures. Envy makes friendship impossible. Some of the practices of the Church are against Nature and deprive human beings of their natural rights. These are the evils Boccaccio struggles against. He believes they are the bonds which have enslaved humanity and he strives to burst them because he believes that Man is good and worth saving. It is his environment and the society in which he lives that bring out evil in him. To these evils he opposes those qualities which we should hold dear, and which he himself admired and cherished: peace of mind, goodness, mercy, friendship, and love of Man. Yet, because his concern is often hidden by a smile, Boccaccio has been accused of superficiality, immorality, and selfishness. Being not only Italian but Tuscan, he smiles and is amused by the stupidity of others and by the spectacle they offer as they make themselves ridiculous while pursuing their folly. But beneath this there is a deep love for his fellow creatures and a desire to improve their lot. His smile cloaks his great concern for man's welfare and a love deeper, perhaps, than that of his accusers who were always ready to offer man fire and damnation.

For the sources of his lives Boccaccio depends mainly on Latin authors, with the exception of Flavius Josephus, whose work, however, had been translated into Latin, Eusebius in Jerome's translation, and Homer, whose poetry he struggled to read in Greek. Valerius Maximus, Livy, Hyginus, and Tacitus are his most frequent sources. The following authors are consulted with less frequency: Pliny, Vetruvius, Suetonius, Ovid, Sallust, Cicero, Virgil, Justinus, Servius, Annaeus Florus, Macrobius, Paulus Orosius, Lactantius, Pomponius Mela, and the Augustan Historians, Julius Capitolinus, Vulcatius Gallicanus, Aelius Lampridius, Trebellius Pollio, and Flavius Vopiscus.[16]

To understand Boccaccio's way of handling his sources, we must not forget the nature of his work. He is interested in telling the story, of course, but even more interested in presenting an example of vice or virtue. When the source of his example is very brief, Boccaccio weaves out the story to a suitable length for a chapter. He does this by putting in details which help him create the atmosphere he desires. He provides a background, writes speeches for the characters and discusses their motivation. These additions fit in quite well with the stories or characters he presents. When historical sources do not come to his aid, Boccaccio feels justified in using his imagination, for after all he must write the story, give the example, and make it palatable. A good illustration of this technique is the chapter on Megullia Dotata. The author found only two or three lines on Megullia in Valerius Maximus, but expanded them into an entire chapter. Valerius Maximus states only that Megullia brought a large dowry to her husband, and was then given the name of Dotata (richly dowered). Boccaccio provides a background by discussing the simplicity and frugal life of the Romans at that time. He speaks of the results of her action.

[16] Cf. Hortis, op.cit., pp. 363ff.; Laura Torretta, "Il Liber De Claris Mulieribus di Giovanni Boccaccio," Giornale Storico della Letteratura Italiana, XXXIX (1902), pp. 273ff.

He then praises the simplicity of the Romans, compares it to the love of luxury of his own time and moralizes on the vices of his contemporaries.

At times Boccaccio reverses this procedure. If his source is lengthy and contains matters which are not essential to his purposes, he shortens it considerably. In the chapter on Niobe, Boccaccio wants to present an example of the foolishness of pride and the harm it can cause. He uses as his source Ovid's account of this queen in the *Metamorphoses* (vi. 146-312), but reduces the part devoted to the queen to about one-fifth the length of the original. He does this by deleting Ovid's description of the sacrifices to Latona, the description of the queen's robes, her speeches, Latona's complaints to the other gods, and the manner in which Niobe's children died. He does not speak of Niobe's continued defiance as some of her children died, and her ultimate despair and entreaties to the goddess to spare her youngest son at least. He gives just the bare outline of the story, and in this case his reasons are obvious. The essential part for him is the example and he does not want it to become lost in details. To make doubly sure of this, he allots about one-third of the chapter to comments of a moralistic nature.

At times Boccaccio uses more than one author as his sources for the same chapter. In the majority of cases he simply uses details given by one author in order to expand or complete the story he has taken from another. In the cases where his sources are at variance, the procedure is somewhat different. When he is able to determine critically which version is correct, he will invariably use it. When this cannot be determined, he uses the version which lends itself more to his moralistic purposes. He often mentions the fact that there are other versions of the story, and gives his reasons for choosing one over the other. His methods of criticism may seem very simple and unsophisticated to us; yet he does make an attempt at criticism, at times with excellent results. He has a very suspicious attitude towards his sources and constantly seeks confirmation for his facts. He is greatly annoyed by discrepancies in chronology or identity and does his best to arrive at the truth. He relies heavily on etymology but without a great degree of accuracy. Whenever possible he reads his sources in the original rather than in translations, which he regards with suspicion. He rejects supernatural explanations of events. Instead he makes an effort to find an explanation based on the psychology of the men he is discussing and in accordance with their times and culture. He does not accept blindly even the most respected authorities. Above all, he had a genuine love of poetry and scholarly studies. As Osgood observed, his methods were a little better than those of his day; we cannot ask more of anyone.

Boccaccio's *De Claris Mulieribus* was written and revised over a period of years, from 1355 to at least 1359. Extant codices present two versions which are quite dissimilar. The earlier of these includes a smaller number of chapters, which are shorter than those in the final version. The present translation is based on the edition of Mathias Apiarius, printed in Berne in 1539,[17] which reproduces all the biographies of women written by Boccaccio.

The eternal question of what a translation should be has been kept in mind by the translator throughout this work. Of course, his first preoccupation must necessarily be to render the author's thoughts and meaning into English as faithfully and precisely as possible. Several questions arise: What sort of English? Shall it be contemporary English? Shall an attempt be made to remain faithful to form as well as content? These are important matters at all times, but when we deal with an author whose style became the model of literary prose in Italian, these questions loom large in reference to his Latin works as well. Then, there is the peculiar tone of this particular book. It has a quaint air all its own, which is certainly not that of our century, and which could not be adequately expressed in contemporary English. It would be incongruous to have a goddess speak as if she were chatting while

[17] For a discussion of the text see: Guido Traversari, "Appunti sulle redazioni del *De Claris Mulieribus* di Giovanni Boccaccio," *Miscellanea di Studi Critici Pubblicati in Onore di Guido Mazzoni*, ed. A. Della Torre and P. L. Rambaldi (Firenze, 1907), pp. 225ff.; Hortis, *op.cit.*, pp. 89 n. 2, 110; Henri Hauvette, *Boccace* (Paris, 1914), pp. 397ff.

INTRODUCTION

holding a glass at a cocktail party, or noble Lucretia proclaim her determination and love of chastity as if she were a secretary reading the minutes at a board meeting. For these reasons the translator has attempted above all to render Boccaccio's work accurately into readable English, and at the same time to use a language which would be in conformity with the author's style and would not destroy the author's thoughts by making them ridiculous.

I wish to express my gratitude and offer my thanks to Prof. Joseph Chierici of Rutgers University, Prof. Mills F. Edgerton, Jr. of Bucknell University, and Dr. Wade C. Stephens of the Lawrenceville School, who read the manuscript and made many valuable suggestions. I also wish to thank Prof. Enrico de' Negri of the University of California (Berkeley), and Profs. Jack Undank, Edward Nagy, and Serge Sobolevitch of Rutgers University for their helpful suggestions and comments on the introduction. My thanks go also to Prof. Remigio U. Pane of Rutgers University, who did everything possible to facilitate the completion of this work.

· · ·

EDITORIAL CONSULTANTS:

Joseph Chierici
Mills F. Edgerton, Jr.
Wade C. Stephens

TO THE MOST GRACIOUS LADY
ANDREA ACCIAIUOLI OF FLORENCE,
COUNTESS OF ALTAVILLA

SOME time ago, illustrious lady, while away from the crude multitudes and almost free of other concerns, I wrote a little book in praise of women, more for the pleasure of my friends than as a service to humanity. While considering to whom I should first send it, so that it would not languish uselessly in my possession and so that aided by someone else's favor it could appear in public with greater safety, I realized that since it speaks of women it should not be dedicated to a prince but to some illustrious lady. As I sought one more worthy than any other, there came to my mind that radiant splendor of Italy, unique glory not only of women but of rulers, the Most Serene Joanna, Queen of Sicily and Jerusalem.[1] I considered the great fame of her family, the splendor of its forebears, and the new praises won by the vigor of her own spirit, and I wished to offer my work humbly and devotedly before her Majesty's throne. At last, however, since her royal splendor is so bright and my little book almost a semi-extinct spark, I gradually changed my mind, fearing that the greater would altogether eclipse the lesser light.

After carefully considering many other women, I finally re-dedicated my work to you instead of that illustrious queen, and not undeservedly. For when I meditated on your gentle and renowned character, great honesty, lofty womanly dignity, and elegance of speech, and when I considered the generosity of your soul and the powers of your intellect, in which you far surpass the endowments of womankind, and when I saw that what Nature has taken from the weaker sex God in His liberality has granted to you, instilling marvelous virtues within your breast, and that He willed you to be known by the name you bear (since in Greek *andres* means 'men'), I felt that you should be set equal

---

[1] Joanna's story is told in Chapter CIV.

·· (xxxiii) ··

to the worthiest of men, even among the ancients. Since through your many splendid and honorable deeds in our times you are a shining example of ancient virtue, I should like to present you this little book, well-deserved by your splendor, thinking that with this humble work I may add for posterity no less of an ornament to your name than at one time the Count of Monteodorisio did, and now the Count of Altavilla, through whom Fortune has made you illustrious.[2] To you, therefore, I send and to your name I dedicate what I have thus far written about famous women.

Illustrious lady, I beg you in the holy name of modesty, for which you are prominent among mortals, to accept with favor this small gift from a scholarly man. And if you are to believe me in anything, I urge you to read it some time, for with its aid you will sweeten your leisure, and you will rejoice in the virtues of women and the charm of the stories. Nor will the reading have been in vain, I believe, if by emulating the deeds of ancient women you spur your spirit to loftier things. If at times you find wantonness intermingled with purity, as accuracy has compelled me to do, do not pass over it and do not be terrified. Rather persevere, just as on entering a garden you put out your ivory hands for the flowers after moving the thorns aside. Thus, putting aside offensive matters, consider the praiseworthy ones. Whenever you read of a pagan woman having qualities which are worthy of those who profess to be Christians, if you feel that you do not have them, blush a little and reproach yourself that although marked by the baptism of Christ you have let yourself be surpassed by a pagan in integrity, chastity, or virtue. Call on the powers of your intellect, in which you excel, and do not allow yourself to be surpassed but strive to outdo all women in noble virtues. Just as you are remarkable for your youth, beauty, and bodily charm, be preeminent in spiritual excellence not only among your contemporaries, but even

---

[2] Andrea Acciaiuoli was the sister of Niccolò Acciaiuoli, Grand Seneschal of the kingdom of Naples. She married Carlo d'Arto, Count of Monteodorisio, and when the latter died, she became the wife of Bartolomeo di Capua, Count of Altavilla. Boccaccio was on friendly terms with Niccolò, who invited him to the court of Naples. However, his feelings changed because of the cold welcome he received.

when compared to the women of antiquity. Remember that beauty should not be enhanced by cosmetics, as the majority of women are wont to do, but adorned with honesty, sanctity, and pious deeds, so that while you please Him Who granted it to you, you will not only be glorious in this mortal life, but on dying you will be received into eternal splendor by the Giver of all blessings.

If you deem it worthy, most excellent lady, you will give this book courage to appear in public. Under your auspices it will go forth, I believe, safe from the insults of malicious people, and it will make your name and those of the other illustrious women glorious on the lips of men. As you cannot be present everywhere, this book will make you and your virtues known to our age and will render you eternal for posterity.[8]

[8] Although the tone of this dedication may seem too humble and servile to the modern reader, it must be remembered that this was the common style for dedications in that period. Boccaccio was always a proud and independent person.

BOCCACCIO'S PREFACE

ALONG time ago some ancient authors wrote brief works on the lives of famous men, and in our own times that renowned man and great poet, my master Petrarch, is writing a fuller work in a loftier style.[1] This is fitting. For assuredly, those who have given all their energy, substance, and (when the occasion required it) their life's blood in order to surpass other men with their illustrious deeds have deserved that their names be forever remembered by posterity. But I have been quite astonished that women have had so little attention from writers of this sort that they have gained no recognition in any work devoted especially to them, although it can be clearly seen in the more voluminous histories that some women have acted with as much strength as valor. If men should be praised whenever they perform great deeds (with strength which Nature has given them), how much more should women be extolled (almost all of whom are endowed with tenderness, frail bodies, and sluggish minds by Nature), if they have acquired a manly spirit and if with keen intelligence and remarkable fortitude they have dared undertake and have accomplished even the most difficult deeds?

Lest, therefore, they be cheated of their just reward, the idea came to me to honor their glory by bringing together into one book those women whose memory is still alive, adding to them some of the many whom daring, intellectual power, perseverance, natural endowments, or Fortune's favor or enmity have made noteworthy. To them I have added a few who, although they performed no action worthy of remembrance, nevertheless offered very great inducements for the performance of mighty deeds.

Nor do I want the reader to think it out of place if together with Penelope, Lucretia, and Sulpicia, who were very chaste matrons, they find Medea, Flora, and Sempronia, who happened to have very strong but destructive characters. For it is not my intention to give the word 'famous' so strict a meaning that it

---

[1] Boccaccio is referring to Petrarch's *De Viris Illustribus*.

will always seem to signify 'virtuous,' but rather to give it a wider sense, if the reader will forgive me, and to consider as famous those women whom I know to have become renowned to the world through any sort of deed. For I remember reading about the Leonidas, the Scipios, the Catos, and the Fabricii, who were splendid men, often together with the seditious Gracchi, sly Hannibal, treacherous Jugurtha, Sulla and Marius stained with the blood of civil war, Crassus as avaricious as he was rich, and others of similar character. But since I have extolled with praise the deeds deserving of commemoration and have condemned with reproach the crimes, there will sometimes be not only glory for the noble, but opprobrium for the wicked. I have pulled back the reins a bit from evil but I have restored[2] what seems to be missing from the disgrace of certain women's loveliness. I have also thought that at times I would include among these stories some pleasant exhortations to virtue and add inducements to avoid and detest wickedness, so that by adding pleasure to these stories their value would enter the mind by stealth.

Lest it seem that according to ancient custom I have touched only on the high points of what I could learn from trustworthy authors, I have lengthened them and broadened them into more extensive histories because I think it both useful and necessary that the accomplishments of these women please women no less than men. For as women for the most part are not acquainted with history, they need and enjoy a more lengthy discussion. It will also seem that with the exception of our first mother I have neglected to include almost all Hebrew or Christian women among these pagans. But this was done because it seemed that they could not very well be placed side by side and that they did not strive for the same goal. In order to attain true and eternal glory Hebrew and Christian women did indeed steel themselves to endure human adversities, imitating the sacred commandments and examples of their teachers. But these pagans through some

[2] The Latin is very difficult here. The words *but I have restored* do not appear in the 1539 Latin text which is the basis of this translation but have been added from the Latin edition published at Louvain in 1487 by Egidius van der Heerstraten.

natural gift or instinct, or rather spurred by desire for this fleeting glory, reached their goal not without great strength of mind and often in spite of the assaults of Fortune, and they endured numerous troubles. Moreover, not only do Christian women, resplendent in the true, eternal light, live on, illustrious in their deserved immortality, but we know that their virginity, purity, saintliness, and invincible firmness in overcoming carnal desire and the punishments of tyrants have been described in special books, as their merits required, by pious men outstanding for their knowledge of sacred literature and for their venerable greatness. The merits of pagan women, on the other hand, have not been published in any special work up to now and have not been set forth by anyone, as I have already pointed out. I have, therefore, begun to describe them in order to give them some reward. May God, the Father of us all, be present during this pious work, may He lavish His favor on what I am about to write and grant that I write to His true glory.

CONCERNING FAMOUS WOMEN

CHAPTER I

EVE, OUR FIRST MOTHER

SINCE I am going to write about the glories for which women have become famous, it will not seem inappropriate to begin with Eve, who was the mother of us all. She was, in fact, our original mother and was likewise famous for her distinguished honors. She was not born into this vale of misery and tears into which we other mortals are born to labor. She was not made with that same hammer or anvil or even by the same smith, and she did not come to life like others, weak and tearfully bewailing her original sin. When the good Creator of all things had formed Adam from clay with His own hand (something which is known to have happened to no one else) and had taken him to the garden of delights from that field which was later called Damascene, He made him fall into peaceful slumber. With a skill known only to Himself, God fashioned Adam a mate from his side while he was sleeping. She was ripe for marriage and joyful at the beauty of the place and at the sight of her Maker.

·· (I) ··

She was the immortal mistress of all things, companion of the man who, already awake, called her Eve. Could anything greater and more glorious ever happen to one at birth? Moreover, we can imagine how marvelously beautiful her body was, for what can be created by God's own hand that does not surpass everything else in beauty? Beauty perishes with old age and even in the flower of youth it may vanish from a slight attack of illness. Nevertheless, since women count it among their foremost endowments, and since through the poor judgment of mortals many have achieved glory because of their beauty, it is not unfitting that so great a splendor was placed foremost among their attractions, and it will be so placed in the following pages.

In addition to these things, Eve was made a citizen of paradise as much by right of her creation as of her dwelling in it, and she was cloaked in a splendor such as is not known to us. She was eagerly enjoying the garden's pleasures together with her husband, when the Enemy, envious of her happiness, with execrable counsel instilled in her the thought that she could reach greater glory if she disobeyed the one law which God had imposed upon her. With a woman's fickleness she believed him more than was good for her or for us. Before doing anything else, she brought her pliant husband to her way of thinking with enticing suggestions, foolishly thinking that she was about to rise to greater heights. With heedless daring, they broke the law and tasted the apple of the tree of knowledge.

Thus they brought themselves and all their future descendants from peace and immortality to dire labor, suffering, and death, and from a delightful country to thorns, clods, and rocks. For, when the gleaming light which clothed them disappeared, the punished ones, dressed in leaves, were driven by their angry Creator from the site of pleasures, and they came as exiles to the fields of Ebron. There, while her husband tilled the soil with the hoe, this distinguished woman, famous for her above-mentioned deeds, discovered the art of spinning with the distaff, as some believe. She often felt the pangs of childbirth, and her soul was tormented with the grief felt at the death of children and grandchildren. Likewise, she endured in misery both cold and heat and other sufferings. She reached old age, tired out by her labors and waiting for death.

CHAPTER II

SEMIRAMIS, QUEEN OF THE ASSYRIANS

SEMIRAMIS was a glorious and very ancient queen of the Assyrians, but time has denied us knowledge of her parents. Moreover, since the ancients liked myths, they said that she was the daughter of Neptune, who was the son of Saturn and god of the sea, and they persisted in this false opinion. Although this story should not be believed, it is an indication that she was born of noble parents. She married Ninus, the noble king of the Assyrians, and bore him their only son, named Ninus after his father. When he had subjected all Asia to his rule and finally conquered the Bactrians, Ninus died of an arrow wound, while Semiramis was still quite young and her son a boy. She thought it unsafe to entrust the reins of such a great and growing kingdom to so young a child. She was so spirited that she, though a woman, dared undertake to rule with skill and intelligence those nations which her valiant husband had subjugated with arms and governed by force.

Having conceived a great stratagem, she first proceeded with feminine wiles to deceive her late husband's army. Semiramis' face looked very much like her son's; both were beardless; her woman's voice sounded no different from her young son's; and she was just a trifle taller, if at all. Taking advantage of this resemblance, she always wore a turban and kept her arms and legs covered so that in the future nothing might disclose her deceit. At that time it was not the custom of the Assyrians to dress in this guise. Lest the novelty of her garb shock her countrymen, Semiramis decreed that everyone should dress in this fashion. And so this woman, who had been Ninus' wife, masqueraded as a man and pretended to be her own son. Having assumed royal majesty, she preserved it and the rule of the armies, and by pretending very carefully to be a man she achieved many things which would have been great and noble even for the strongest of men. She spared herself no labors, feared no dangers, and with her unheard-of deeds overcame the envy of all men. Finally she did not fear to reveal to everyone who she really was and how with womanly deceit she had pretended to be a man. It was almost as if she wanted to show that in order to govern it is not necessary to be a man, but to have courage. This fact heightened that woman's glorious majesty as much as it gave rise to admiration in those who looked upon her.

To narrate her deeds in a little greater detail we shall state that after that marvelous subterfuge she took up arms with manly spirit, and not only did she maintain the empire acquired by her husband, but added to it Ethiopia, which she attacked and conquered in a bitter war. Then she turned her powerful arms against India, where up to that time no one had gone except her husband.[1] In addition to this she restored the city of Babylon, Nimrod's ancient work, which at that time throve in the fields of Sennaar. She surrounded it with walls of marvelous height, thickness, and length, made of baked bricks cemented with sand, pitch, and tar. Of her many deeds we shall single out the one which is most worthy of remembrance. The story is reported as fact that one day,

---

[1] Boccaccio's sources do not state that Ninus had undertaken an expedition to India, but mention only Alexander the Great.

after she had pacified her domains and was resting at leisure, she was having her maids comb her hair with feminine care into braids as was the custom of the country. Her hair was only half combed when the news that Babylon had rebelled was brought her. This so angered her that she threw aside her comb and immediately abandoned her womanly pursuits. She arose in anger, took up arms, and led her forces to a siege of that powerful city. She did not finish combing her hair until she had forced that mighty city to surrender, weakened by long siege, and brought it back into her power by force of arms. A huge bronze statue of a woman with her hair braided on one side and loose on the other stood in Babylon to bear witness to this brave deed for a long period of time. She also built many new cities and performed great deeds, but time has consigned them to oblivion, so that almost nothing pertaining to her praise has come down to us except what we have mentioned.

But with one wicked sin this woman stained all these accomplishments worthy of perpetual memory, which are not only praiseworthy for a woman but would be marvelous even for a vigorous man. It is believed that this unhappy woman, constantly burning with carnal desire, gave herself to many men. Among these lovers, and this is something more beastly than human, was her own son Ninus, a very handsome young man. As if he had changed sex with his mother, Ninus rotted away idly in bed, while she sweated in arms against her enemies. Oh, what a wicked thing this is! For this pestilence flies about not only when things are quiet, but even among the fatiguing cares of kings and bloody battles, and, most monstrous, while one is in sorrow and exile. Making no distinction of time, it goes about, gradually seizes the minds of the unwary and drags them to the edge of the abyss, staining every honor with disgraceful infamy. It is said that Semiramis, tainted by this infamy, thought that her cleverness could lessen the blot of her lasciviousness and decreed that notorious law which allowed her subjects to do as they pleased in sexual conduct. According to some, because she feared that the women of her household would deceive her and seduce her son, she was the first to invent chastity belts. She forced all her court ladies to wear them and locked them with keys. They say that this custom is still in use in the lands of Egypt and Assyria.

Others, nevertheless, write that after she had reigned for thirty-two years, she fell in love with her son who was already an adult. But when she attempted to bring him to her desires, he killed her. Some others do not agree with this, saying that she mixed cruelty with her lust. They claim that to hide her sins she was accustomed to order the death of the men she had called to satisfy her lust, immediately after copulation. But they say that at times, when she became pregnant, her concupiscence was disclosed by the fact that she gave birth. And they add that she proclaimed the above-mentioned law in order to be excused. Although she seemed to keep her shameful sin with her son somewhat hidden, she was not able to avoid his indignation. Either because he could not bear seeing her with many other lovers, or because he thought that his mother's dishonor brought him shame, or perhaps because he feared that children might be born to succeed to the throne, he killed the wicked queen in anger.

CHAPTER III

OPIS, WIFE OF SATURN

IF WE believe the ancients, Opis, or Ops or Rhea, also called Cybele, was very famous in both prosperous and adverse times. She was the daughter of Uranus, a very powerful man among the then uncultured Greeks, and of his wife Vesta. She was both sister and wife of the ruler Saturn, and she was not famous for any deeds which have come down to us except for the fact that through feminine cleverness she saved her children, Jupiter, Neptune, and Pluto, from a death which had been agreed upon with Saturn by her brother Titan.

These were the people who came forth into the fame even of deity through the ignorance—nay, madness—of the men of that age. Opis not only acquired the honor of being queen, but through man's error was reputed to be a marvelous goddess and the mother of the gods. Temples, priests, and sacrifices were accorded her through public laws. This shameful evil grew so much that during the Second Punic War, when the Romans were in danger, men who had been consuls were sent as ambassadors to Attalus, the king of Pergamum, and they asked with fervent prayers for the statue of Opis and the order of her sacrifices, as if it would be a great help. From the city of Pessinus in Asia Minor an oddly shaped stone, which the inhabitants claimed to be the mother of the gods, was taken and carefully brought to Rome. It was received with deep reverence and was finally placed in a famous temple as a great deity and a safeguard for the Republic. For many years it was honored with frequent sacrifices by the Romans and the Italians.

Prostrated by long fatigue, this old woman died, turned to dust, and was damned in hell. Certainly it was a marvelous jest of Fortune, or rather man's blindness, or better yet the deception and fraud of devils that caused her to be regarded as a goddess and honored by almost the entire world with divine veneration for such a long time.

·· (8) ··

CHAPTER IV

JUNO, GODDESS OF KINGDOMS

TO THE discredit of the primitive pagans, Juno, the daughter of Saturn and Opis, became more famous than all other women throughout the world because of the writings of poets and the error of the pagans. She was exalted to such a degree that envy and the silent teeth of time, which gnaw all things, have not been able to eat away her great deeds and prevent their renown from coming down to our age. Certainly we can speak more easily of Juno's outstanding fortune than relate any great deeds of hers which are worthy of comment.

She was born together with that Jupiter of Crete whom the deceived ancients imagined to be the god of heaven. In her childhood she was sent to Samos, and in that place she was brought up carefully until she reached a marriageable age. Finally she married her brother Jupiter. This has been attested for many centuries by her statue in the temple at Samos. The people of Samos believed that the fact that great Juno, whom they considered a goddess and queen of heaven, was brought up and married in their country redounded not a little to their honor and that of their descendants. To prevent the memory of this fact from soon perishing, they built a huge temple more marvelous than all the others in the world and consecrated it to her deity. They had her image carved out of Parian marble in a girl's wedding dress and placed it before her temple. Finally, having married this great king, whose power and fame were steadily increasing and were spreading his name far and wide, she herself gained no little glory.

Later she was made queen of heaven through the fictions of poets and the senseless generosity of the ancients. Although she had been a mortal queen, she was placed at the head of the celestial kingdom and the wealth of Olympus. They made her the guardian of marriage, protector of childbirth, and many other things which arouse our amusement rather than our belief. Thus through the persuasion of the Enemy of humankind very many temples and altars were erected to her everywhere, and games, sacrifices, and priests were assigned to her according to ancient custom. After Samos, she was honored for a long time with great reverence by the Argives of Achaea and the Carthaginian people,[1] not to speak of others. Finally, having been brought to Rome from Veii, she was placed in the Capitol in the sanctuary of Jupiter Optimus Maximus, thus joining her husband. The Romans, masters of the world, honored her under the name of Queen Juno for a long time and with many ceremonies, even after the time of Christ.

[1] The Latin text reads "the Argives of Achaea, who were a Carthaginian people."

CHAPTER V

CERES, GODDESS OF AGRICULTURE
AND QUEEN OF SICILY

A S SOME would have it, Ceres was a very ancient queen of Sicily, who had such great wisdom that after discovering how to till the soil she was the first among her people to tame oxen and accustom them to the yoke. She invented the plow and the plowshare, plowed the earth with them, and sowed seed in the furrows. When grain grew abundantly, men who had been accustomed to living on wild fruit and nuts were taught by her to husk the grain, grind it with stones, make it into leavened loaves, and turn it into food. Because of this accomplishment they thought that she was the goddess of agriculture and exalted her with divine honors, although she was a mortal. It was believed that she was the daughter of Saturn and Cybele. They also say that Proserpina was her only daughter, begotten by her brother Jupiter, and they tell us that to her mother's great distress[1] Proser-

---

[1] The text has *maxima maris turbatione*, meaning a great upheaval of the sea. This is probably a typographical error, and we should read *matris* instead of *maris*. This interpretation is in accordance with the fable of the ancients.

pina was kidnaped by Orcus, the king of the Molossians, who had searched a long time for her. This event gave rise to many stories.

Moreover, in Eleusis, a town in the province of Attica, there was another Ceres who was famous among her people for the same qualities and who, they say, was obeyed by Triptolemus. It seems very suitable to me to mention both of them and their great wisdom under one name since the ancients glorified them both with equal divinity and honors.[2]

I do not really know whether to praise or condemn their ingenuity. Who will condemn the fact that wild, wandering men were led out of the woods and into cities? Who will condemn the fact that men who were living like beasts were led to a better life? The fact that seeds were sown and brought forth grain through which the body becomes more refined and the limbs stronger, and which is nourishment more suitable for human consumption? Who will condemn the fact that the world, filled with underbrush, thorns, and uncultivated plants, was changed into a place of beauty and usefulness for men? The fact that barbarous times were changed into a civilized age? The fact that man's mind was aroused from idleness to thought? The fact that when the art of agriculture had been discovered, men who had lain idly in caves were brought to the farms and to the life of cities, so many towns were enlarged, so many new ones were built, so many states were built up and so many admirable customs were established and cherished?

According to the judgment of the majority, and as I myself think, the above-mentioned things are good in themselves. But, to turn the argument around, who will praise the fact that the scattered multitudes living in the forests, accustomed to nuts, wild fruit, the milk of animals, the grass and rivers, having no worries, satisfied by the laws of nature, sober, modest and without deceit, enemies only of beasts and birds, were attracted to delicate and unknown foods? If we do not deceive ourselves, we shall see that because of these the door was opened to vices which had been in hiding for a long time, afraid to come out into the open, and

[2] There is usually thought to be only one Ceres.

assurance was given them that they might proceed. For this reason the fields, which had been common to all, began to have boundaries. Then came the cares of cultivating these fields and work began to be shared by men. From this came the words "mine" and "yours," which are certainly inimical to public and private peace. From this came poverty and slavery, as well as quarreling, hatred, bloody wars, and burning envy which flies about everywhere. These things caused the curved sickles, which had been used for so short a time to harvest the grain, to be changed into straight sharp swords to draw blood. For this reason the seas have been sailed, the West is known to the East, and the East is known to the West. From this has come the softening of the body and the swelling of the belly, ornament in dress, more elaborate dinner tables, more splendid banquets, laziness and leisure. And concupiscence, which up to that time had been dormant, began to rouse itself—a great disaster for the world. And—what is perhaps worse—there is immediately a scarcity of food, and hunger is felt more harshly than before, if with the passing of years the fields do not render a good harvest, as sometimes happens through Heaven's will or through wars. Bitter starvation, which was never known in the forests, enters the humble homes of the poor, often not without danger to the wealthy. From this come ugly and exhausted emaciation, deadly pallor, weakness which makes one totter, and manifold causes of disease and untimely death. Having considered these things and others without number, I hardly know whether, or rather I do know that, those golden centuries, although primitive and uncivilized, were greatly to be preferred to our age of iron and to all other centuries.[8]

[8] The vision of this "age of gold" appears repeatedly in Italian literature after Boccaccio. Boccaccio seems to doubt the value of civilization because of his views on the dignity and freedom of man. Civilization, through its refining influence and the arts, has raised man to a nobler state; but it has also brought about the growth of certain institutions which have curbed man's freedom and threaten his essential dignity.

CHAPTER VI

MINERVA, ALSO KNOWN AS PALLAS

MINERVA, also known as Pallas, was famous for such great glory that foolish people have believed that she was not born of man. Some say that she was first seen and known on earth in Attica near Lake Triton, not far from the gulf of the Lesser Syrtis, at the time of King Ogyges. As time went by, they saw this woman do many things never seen before. For this reason not only the barbarous Africans but also the Greeks, who at that time surpassed everyone else in shrewdness, believed that she had been born from Jupiter's head without a mother and had descended from Heaven.

The more hidden her origin, the more faith was put in this ridiculous error, and they wanted her, more than anything else, to be adorned with perpetual virginity. To arouse greater faith in this belief, they imagined that Vulcan, the god of fire (that is, carnal lust), had struggled with her for a long time and had been defeated. They also state that she discovered the art of working in wool, which had been known to no one at all up to that time. She showed how wool should be cleaned, softened with an iron comb, placed on the distaff, and spun with the fingers, and she invented weaving. She taught how the threads should be woven and joined with the shuttle, and how the woven cloth should be strengthened by beating. The well-known and marvelous contest between her and Arachne of Colophon is cited in praise of her skill. She also discovered how to use oil, which had not been known to men up to that time. She showed the Athenians how to crush olives with the millstone and how to press them. Thus she was believed to have overcome Neptune in the matter of giving a name to Athens because it seemed very useful to know how to make oil. They also say that with her skill she was the first to invent the cart and make iron weapons. She first thought of covering one's body with armor, and she set down strategy for soldiers and taught all the rules of battle. They also state that she discovered numbers and arranged them in the manner which we still keep today. They believed that she was the first to make the flute or shepherd's pipes from the leg bones of some bird or from swamp reeds, and that she threw them down from heaven because on being played they made her throat swell and gave an ugly expression to her face.

Why add anything else? For so many marvelous inventions, antiquity, the dispenser of divinity, made her the goddess of wisdom. Moved by these reasons, the men of Athens took their name from her because that city seemed to have a natural tendency for those studies which make one wise and prudent. They took her as their patron and dedicated the Acropolis to her. They built a great temple consecrated to her, in which they represented her as a stern figure with frightening eyes because only rarely can one see the purpose of a wise man's intentions. They made her with a helmet on her head because the counsel of a wise man is hidden, and armed with a cuirass because the wise man is always prepared against every blow of Fortune. She was equipped with a very long lance, so that we might understand that the wise man pierces through the distance with his barb. She is also protected by a crystal shield with Medusa's head on it, showing with this that every hidden thing is clear to the wise man and that he is always armed with serpentine wisdom so that ignorant people seem turned to stone at the sight of him. They place an owl in her keeping to indicate that the wise man sees at night as well as during the day.

Finally the fame of this woman and reverence for her as a goddess spread so widely and the error of the ancients so favored her that temples were built and sacrifices held in her honor throughout almost the whole world. It grew so much that a sanctuary was erected to her on the Capitol next to that of Jupiter Optimus Maximus, and she was considered among the greatest gods of the Romans with Queen Juno, and equal to her. There are, however, some very serious men who assert that the things mentioned were not done by one Minerva but by many. I shall gladly agree with them so that there may be a greater number of famous women.

CHAPTER VII

VENUS, QUEEN OF CYPRUS

IT IS the opinion of some authors that Venus was a woman
of Cyprus, but many have doubts as to the identity of her
father and mother. Some claim that she was the daughter of
a man called Cyrus and of Cyria; some say she was the daughter
of Cyrus and of Dione, a woman of Cyprus. To magnify the
splendor of her beauty, I believe, others tell us that she was begotten by Jupiter and the above-mentioned Dione. No matter of
whom she was born, I certainly intend to place her among famous
women more for her excellent beauty than because I think she
deserves praise.

Well then, the beauty of her face and all her body was so splendid that often those who saw her could hardly believe it. Therefore,
some said that she was the star we call Venus. Others believed
that she was a celestial woman who had come to Earth from
Jupiter's loins. In short, since they were in the bonds of dark
ignorance, they said that this woman was an immortal goddess,
although they knew she had been born of a mortal woman. And
they asserted with all their strength that she was the mother of
that unhappy love whom they called Cupid. She herself did not
lack the skill to befuddle with gestures the minds of the fools
who looked at her. And because of these powers, she was thought
to be Jupiter's daughter and one of the most important goddesses
in spite of her lewd acts, which I shall not mention in their en-
tirety. She was honored with incense not only in Paphos, an
ancient city of the Cypriotes (who thought that after death this
unchaste woman would love the scent in which, while alive, she
had wallowed in the filth of brothels), but also by other peoples
and the Romans, who built her a temple under the name of
Mother Venus, Verticordia, and other titles.

It is not necessary to speak of her at length. She was believed
to have had two husbands, and it is not certain which was the
first. But it has pleased some to believe that she first was the wife

of Vulcan, king of Lemnos and son of Jupiter of Crete, and when he died[1] she married Adonis, the son of Myrrha and Cinyras, king of Cyprus. This seems more plausible to me than saying that Adonis was her first husband. Either because of the defects of her character, or because of the corruption of that region in which lasciviousness seems to have great power, or through the malice of a corrupt mind, after Adonis' death she succumbed to such enormous sexual desire that she seemed to tarnish all the splendor of her beauty with her continuous fornication. In the nearby regions it was already known that her first husband Vulcan had found her lying with a man at arms. It was believed that the myth of her adultery with Mars came about through this. Finally, they say that to remove some shame from her own immodest face and give herself more ample license in her lasciviousness, she thought of an abominable foulness. That is, she was the first to establish public prostitution by instituting brothels and forcing women to enter them. This accursed deed has been attested by the shameful custom of the Cypriotes, which they retained for many centuries. For a long time they used to send their girls to the shores so that they could lie with the foreigners who arrived, and be seen offering the flower of their virginity to Venus and earning the dowry for their marriage. This shameful madness then passed on to Italy, for one can read that at times the Locrians did the same.

[1] As a euhemerist, Boccaccio believed that the pagan gods were actually mortals and so subject to death.

CHAPTER VIII

ISIS, QUEEN AND GODDESS
OF EGYPT

ISIS, who was previously called Io, not only was a very famous queen of the Egyptians, but finally became their most holy and venerated goddess. Nevertheless, among the noted writers of histories there is disagreement as to the time in which she lived and as to her parents. Some say that she was the daughter of Inachus, the first king of the Argives, and that she was the sister of Phoroneus, who ruled at the time of Jacob son of Isaac. Others say that she was the daughter of Prometheus when Phorbas reigned among the Argives, which is a much later period. Some assert that she lived at the time of Cecrops, the king of Athens, and some say that she flourished at the time of Lynceus, the king of the Argives. These differences among distinguished men are certainly not without reason. That she was noble and most worthy of remembrance among the women of her time is affirmed by all. But, paying no attention to the discord of the writers, I am of a mind to follow what the majority thinks, that is, that she was the daughter of Inachus.

Ancient poets imagine that because of the beauty of her body Jupiter desired her and raped her. To hide this crime, she was transformed into a heifer and was given to Juno, who had asked for her. When her guardian Argus was killed by Mercury, Juno put a gadfly on the heifer, and she was driven at a rapid pace into Egypt, where she recovered her original form, and from the name Io she was called Isis. The above-mentioned facts are not in disagreement with the truth of history, since there are some who say that this virgin was seduced by Jupiter. Then, spurred by the sin she had committed and afraid of her father, she and some of her friends boarded a ship which had a cow as an emblem. Endowed with great talents and spurred on by desire to rule, she crossed to Egypt with favorable winds. Finding the region suitable to her desires, she stopped there. Finally, since it is not known how she acquired Egypt, it is thought almost certain that there she found a barbarous, unskilled people, almost ignorant of all human affairs, who lived more in the manner of beasts than of men. Not without hardship and singular industry she taught them to till the soil, seed it, and finally make food from grain after it had been harvested at the proper time. She also taught those wandering and half-savage men to live together, and, after giving them laws, she showed them how to live as civilized men. Even more marvelous for a woman, she called on the powers of her intellect and found letters suitable for the language of the men of that country. She then showed how to place them together to those who were ready to learn.

Not to mention others, these things seemed so marvelous to those people who were not used to them that they easily thought that she had not come from Greece, but had descended from heaven. For this reason they accorded her all divine honors while she was still alive. Since the devil deceived the ignorant, after her death her deity became so renowned and was held in such reverence, that at Rome, already mistress of the world, a huge temple was accorded to her, and it was ordered that every year solemn sacrifices should be held for her according to Egyptian custom. There is no doubt that this error spread all the way to the barbarous nations and to the West. It is certain that this famous woman married Apis, who was erroneously thought by the men of ancient times to be the son of Jupiter and Niobe, the daughter of Phoroneus. They say that after having been king of the Argives for thirty-five years he gave the kingdom of Achaea to his brother Aegialeus and went to Egypt where he ruled together with Isis. He also was reputed to be a god, and was called Osiris or Serapis. There are some who say that Isis' husband was a man called Telegonus, and that she bore him a son, Epaphus, who afterwards was king of Egypt. It was believed that he had been begotten of her by Jupiter.

CHAPTER IX

EUROPA, QUEEN OF CRETE

SOME writers believe that Europa was the daughter of Phoenix, but many more state that she was begotten by Agenor, the king of Phoenicia. She was of such marvelous beauty that Jupiter, the Cretan, fell in love with her without having seen her. This powerful man laid a trap to kidnap her. They say that while the girl was playing, she followed her father's flocks from the mountains to the shore of Phoenicia because of a panderer's words. There she was suddenly seized, put on a ship that had a white bull as an emblem, and taken to Crete. For this reason I believe that it is not good to give girls too much freedom to stroll about and listen to the words of strangers. For I have often read that those who do this have had their honor tarnished by stains of disgrace which afterwards could not be cleansed even by the splendor of perpetual chastity.

It is clear that from these events came the story in which one reads that Mercury (who symbolizes the glibness of panders) led the flocks of the Phoenicians to the shore, and that Jupiter turned himself into a bull and swam to Crete with the virgin Europa.

But the ancients do not agree as to the time when this rape occurred. Those who date it earliest say that it happened when Danaus was king in Argos. Others say that it was when Acrisius ruled. Those who place it most recently declare that it was during the reign of Pandion, the king of Athens. This seems to be more reasonable and in better agreement with the time of Europa's son Minos. Some say simply that Jupiter raped her and that afterwards she married Asterius, the king of Crete, to whom she bore three sons, Minos, Rhadamanthus, and Sarpedon, who are said by many to be sons of Jupiter. Others declare that Asterius and Jupiter are one and the same person.

While some disagree on the above points, many do agree that Europa was ennobled by her marriage to such a great god. In addition some claim that Europe, a third of the world, is named after her, to her eternal honor, because she was of singular nobility, or because the people of Phoenicia were more famous than other peoples of that time because of their many good qualities and the nobility of their ancestors, or through reverence for her divine husband or respect for her sons, or because of the special virtue of Europa herself. I concede that she was a woman of marvelous virtues, not only because part of the world is named after her, but also because of a marvelous bronze statue which Varro says was dedicated to her in Tarentum by the illustrious philosopher Pythagoras.

CHAPTER X

LIBYA, QUEEN OF LIBYA

LIBYA, according to the ancient authors, was the daughter of King Epaphus of Egypt and his wife Cassiopeia. She married Neptune, a powerful foreigner whose true name has not reached us. She bore him a son of enormous size, Busiris, who later became the tyrant of Upper Egypt. It is believed that her magnificent works have been consumed by time, but she had so much authority among her people that the entire part of Africa which she ruled has been named Libya after her, and this fact is sufficient indication that these deeds were very great.

CHAPTER XI

MARTESIA AND LAMPEDO, QUEENS
OF THE AMAZONS

THE sisters Martesia[1] and Lampedo together were queens of the Amazons, and because of their famous glory in war they called themselves the daughters of Mars. Since their story is a strange one, we must begin somewhat farther back.

They say that a faction of nobles sent Plinos and Scholopythus,[2] two young men of royal blood, together with part of their people, into exile from Scythia, that land which stretches out toward the East with the Black Sea on one side and the Rhiphaean Mountains on the other, and which is bounded by Asia Minor and the river Tanais to the rear, so that it extends far in latitude and longitude. At that time it was wild and had hardly been seen by foreigners. The princes of Scythia, Plinos and Scholopythus, are said to have been exiled by the party of the aristocrats. With a group of the opposite faction they arrived in Cappadocia near the Thermodon river, seized the fields of Themiscyra, and began to live off plunder and to molest with their thievery the people of the country, almost all of whom were treacherously killed in the course of time. This was not taken well by the wives who had been widowed. Stirred by thoughts of vengeance, they took up arms together with the few remaining males, and in the first assault they drove their enemies from the country. Then they eagerly waged war against the neighboring lands.

Finally, they thought that if they married men of other nations they would be slaves rather than wives, and they felt that they were able to wage war by themselves, although they were only women. They therefore attacked and in common accord killed all their husbands, so that those whose husbands Fortune had saved from the Scythians' massacre would not seem to have been

---

[1] Other forms of this name are Marpesia and Marpessa.
[2] Scholopythus' name should be Scolopitus.

favored more than the others by the gods. Then they turned their fury against the enemy as if they wanted to avenge their dead husbands and so exhausted them that they easily imposed peace upon them. This done, they occasionally joined their neighbors in order to beget children, but as soon as they became pregnant they returned home. Finally, they immediately killed the babies who were born boys and carefully saved the girls for the military arts. While the girls were small, they withered the right breast with fire or medicines, so that when they became older it would not grow and hinder them in using the bow. The left breast was left unharmed, so that they would be able to feed their future children. From this came the word "Amazon," which means "without breast."[3] But they did not have the same concern in raising girls as we have with ours. For, having discarded the distaff, the wool basket, and other womanly tasks, they practiced hunting, running, horse-taming, continual warlike exercises, archery, and similar skills, and they hardened the grown girls in the aptitudes and strength of a man. With these skills they occupied not only the fields of Themiscyra which had been already held by their ancestors, but they also acquired a large part of Europe by right of conquest, seized a good portion of Asia, and were feared by all men.

After their husbands had been killed, they elected Martesia and Lampedo queens to rule their forces. Under their leadership they augmented their first holdings a great deal, as has been shown. These two queens, who were certainly marvelous in leading armies, divided the provinces among themselves, so that while one remained to guard the homeland, the other went forth with part of the people to subjugate those whose lands bordered on their empire. Thus by turns they enlarged their domains and took great booty. Finally, when Lampedo had gone to lead an army against the enemy, Martesia, who was overly confident, was killed with part of her army during a sudden invasion by the neighboring barbarians. She was survived by some daughters. But I do not remember reading what happened to Lampedo.

[3] This derivation of the name, though commonly believed, is fanciful.

CHAPTER XII

THISBE, MAIDEN OF BABYLON

THISBE, a virgin of Babylon, became famous among men for the tragic end of her love, rather than for any accomplishments. Although we have not learned from our ancestors who her parents were, it was nevertheless believed that her house was in Babylon, next door to that of Pyramus, a young man of her own age. Because of their nearness, they lived in close intimacy, and hence, while they were still children, puerile love grew between them. Evil Fortune brought it about that, since they were both of great physical beauty, their childish love grew greatly in ardor as they grew older. As they approached adulthood, at times they indicated their mutual love, at least by signs.

When Thisbe was nearly grown, her parents wanted her to marry and began to keep her at home. Since the two young people could not endure this well and tried diligently to find a way to speak to each other at least occasionally, they found in a hidden part of the wall between their houses a crack which had never before been seen by anyone. They secretly went to this opening many times and spoke to each other. Once accustomed to this, and less shy because of the wall that separated them, they manifested their intentions more clearly, by often expressing their desire and all their passion with sighs and tears. At times they prayed together that they might have peace for their souls, might embrace and kiss each other, and might enjoy devotion, trust, and perpetual love. Finally, as their ardor grew, they began planning to flee, and they decided that the following night, as soon as they could escape from their parents, they would leave the house, go to a small wood near the city, and there, near a spring which was close to King Ninus' tomb, the one who escaped first would wait for the other to come later.

Thisbe, who perhaps loved more ardently, was the first to slip away from her parents, and she left her father's home alone at midnight, wearing a cloak. As the moon lighted her way, she went fearlessly to the wood. While waiting near the spring, raising her head eagerly whenever something moved, she saw a lioness approach and fled into the wood, carelessly leaving her cloak behind. After eating and drinking, the lioness found the cloak and rubbed her blood-stained mouth against it, as these animals usually do, and after tearing it with her claws, she dropped it and went away. In the meantime Pyramus, having left his house, arrived in the forest late and looking attentively in the silent night found Thisbe's cloak, torn and smeared with blood. He thought that Thisbe had been devoured by some wild animal, and he filled the place with his wails, accusing his wretched self as the cause of his beloved's cruel death. Scorning life, he took out the sword which he had brought along and pierced his breast, determined to die near the spring. Shortly afterwards, Thisbe, thinking that the lioness had drunk and left, returned cautiously to the spring so that it should not seem as if she had scorned her lover and kept him anxiously waiting a long time. When she arrived near the spring, she heard Pyramus still thrashing upon the ground, and, frightened, she almost went back. At last she saw in the moonlight that it was her Pyramus lying on the ground, and, running to embrace him, she found him already near death, lying in the blood which had oozed from the wound. Shocked at the sight, she attempted in vain to help him, at first sadly, and then with bitter tears trying to hold back his spirit for a while with kisses and embraces. But she was not able to get a word from him, and seeing that he did not feel the kisses which a short time before he had so ardently desired, and realizing that her lover was dying, she thought that he had killed himself because he had not found her. She determined to seek bitter death with the youth she loved. Encouraged equally by her love and by her grief, she drew out the sword, which was embedded in the wound up to its hilt, and with great laments called out the name of Pyramus. She begged him at least to watch his Thisbe die and wait for her soul as it departed, so that they could be together wherever they should go. Marvelous to say, Pyramus, his senses failing him, still heard the name of his beloved. Unable to deny her last wish, he opened his eyes weighted down by death and looked at the one who was calling him. Thisbe immediately fell onto the young man's breast and then on his sword, poured out her blood, and followed the soul of her lover, who was already dead.

Thus envious Fortune could not prevent the mingling of the unhappy blood of the two young lovers whom she had prevented from joining in happy embraces. Whoever feels no pity for them and does not shed at least a tear must be made of stone. They had loved each other from the time they were children, and for this they did not deserve a bloody death. Youth's love is a sin, but not a horrible transgression for those who are single, since it can result in marriage. Wicked Fortune sinned, as did perhaps their wretched parents. Certainly, the ardor of the young should be curbed slowly, lest by wishing to oppose them with sudden impediments we drive them to despair and perdition. The passion of desire is without temperance, and it is almost a pestilence and fury in youth. We should tolerate it patiently, because, the nature of things being as it is, when we are fully grown we are spontaneously inclined to bring forth children, so that the human race may not come to an end through delaying intercourse until old age.

CHAPTER XIII

HYPERMNESTRA, QUEEN OF THE ARGIVES AND PRIESTESS OF JUNO

HYPERMNESTRA, famous for her rank and birth, was the daughter of Danaus, the king of the Argives, and was the wife of Lynceus or, according to some, of Linus. In the histories of the ancients, one finds that in Egypt there once were two brothers, famous for their great empire, the children of old Belus. One of them was called Danaus and the other Aegyptus. Although they had an equal number of children, they were not equally fortunate in them, for Danaus had fifty daughters, and Aegyptus as many sons. Danaus was told by an oracle that he would die at the hands of one of his nephews, children of his brother. He was secretly in the grip of great fear, but did not know whom he should suspect, since there were so many of them.

It happened that, as the sons and daughters were growing up, Aegyptus asked that all the daughters of Danaus be given in marriage to his sons. Danaus, planning a horrible deed, gladly gave his consent. When his daughters had been betrothed to his nephews and the marriage ceremony was being arranged, Danaus informed all his daughters with the greatest care that if they had any consideration for his welfare each one should kill her husband with a knife on the wedding night, when she saw him in deep slumber, dulled by food and wine. In accordance with their father's command, the daughters secretly brought knives into their chambers and killed their husbands, who were helpless because of the day's feasting. Only Hypermnestra held back, since she had already fallen in love with her husband, whose name was Linus or Lynceus. She had fallen in love with him at first sight, as girls often do. Thus, to her great praise, she refrained from this shameful murder, pitying him, and advised him to flee, and

· · (28) · ·

through flight he was saved. In the morning, the cruel father lavished praise on his daughters for the crime they had committed. Only Hypermnestra was reprimanded and put in prison, where for some time she suffered for her pious deed.

Oh, wretched men, with what greed and eagerness we desire things which must perish! Scorning all consideration of the end, through what accursed ways we ascend to high places if the occasion arises, and with what crimes do we retain the positions we have reached! As if one could hold fickle Fortune with foul deeds! It is laughable to see with what crimes, with what accursed deeds we struggle to lengthen and perpetuate the short span of our frail and fleeting life, while seeing everyone else rushing toward death. Through these detestable aims and nefarious deeds we provoke God's wrath. Not to speak of others, let cruel Danaus be an ignominious witness to this, for in attempting to prolong his trembling years with the blood of his nephews, he deprived himself of a splendid, powerful line of descendants and incurred perpetual infamy. This wicked man thought that the few cold years of his old age should have precedence over the flowering youth of his nephews. Others would have thought these years more useful if he had treasured them honorably. But truly it seems very cruel to have attempted to lengthen his old age with the wounds of his young sons-in-law. What makes his shame greater is that to commit this crime he armed the hands not of his servants but of his daughters, so that not only did he cause the death of his nephews, but by his crime he made his daughters brutal, who through mercy could have been worthy of honor. Wanting to save his life by means of that crime, he did not think what a detestable example of audacity, deceit, and opprobrium he was bequeathing to wicked women in the future. He made his daughters treacherously break the faith of matrimony, and when a pious father should have commanded that they bring the sacred torches into their chambers, he ordered them to bring knives. We are accustomed to encourage our daughters to love their husbands, but he encouraged them to hatred and murder. What he did not dare do to all his nephews together, he did to each one singly through his own children. What he would not have dared do in daylight, he ordered done at night. What he would not have dared do in the field, he ordered done in the bridal chambers, not considering that the number of years he took away from his nephews' youth through cruelty and deceit would be equaled by the number of centuries in which his hateful deed would be remembered. And he, who could rightfully have had fifty sons-in-law, justly retained for his undoing one enemy from whose hand through God's just judgment the cruel old man could not escape, so that his evil blood, which he had saved by shedding that of his nephews, was spilled.

In the end Danaus was driven away, or fled, or was invited into Greece, where through his ingenuity and strength he took over and held the throne of the Argives. Some say that Danaus' abovementioned crime was committed there. But wherever it may have occurred, he was killed by Lynceus, who remembered his cruelty and reigned in Argos in his place. Hypermnestra was freed from prison and, under better auspices, was joined in marriage to Lynceus, who made her share in his reign. Not only was she renowned as queen, but after being made priestess of the Argive Juno she enjoyed the glory of double fame. While her sisters have remained in shameful infamy, she, because of her laudable mercy, has made her praiseworthy name famous even down to our time.

CHAPTER XIV

NIOBE, QUEEN OF THEBES

PRACTICALLY the most famous of noble women was Niobe, the sister of Pelops and daughter of Tantalus, the ancient and very famous king of Phrygia. She married Amphion, the king of Thebes, who at that time was renowned for being Jupiter's son and for his special eloquence. As his glorious reign went on, she gave birth to seven sons and as many daughters. It is certain that this, which should have been salutary to a wise person, caused her death, for she became proud. And having become proud because of the splendor of her famous children and because of the glory of her ancestors, she dared to speak even against the gods.

One day the Thebans, under the guidance of Manto, daughter of the soothsayer Tiresias, were engrossed in sacrificing to Latona, the mother of Apollo and Diana, who were respected gods according to the superstition of the ancients. Niobe, in regal pomp and surrounded by her children, appeared in their midst shouting as if spurred by a fury. She asked what madness was that of the Thebans that they prepared sacrifices to Latona and gave precedence to a foreign woman, the daughter of a Titan, who in adultery had conceived only two children, over herself, their queen, daughter of King Tantalus, who had borne her husband fourteen children whom they could see. She said that those sacrifices were due her for being more worthy. It happened that a short time later all Niobe's children died in the fair flower of youth because of a fatal plague. This happened within a short period of time and in their mother's sight. Amphion, who had been the father of fourteen children, found himself childless, and spurred on by grief, he killed himself with a knife wound inflicted by his own hand. The Thebans thought that this had happened fittingly, because of the gods, who were avenging Niobe's insult to the goddess. Widowed and saddened by all these deaths, Niobe fell into such deep and obstinate silence, that she seemed a motionless stone rather than a woman. For this reason the poets later imagined that she had been changed into a stone statue near Sipylus, where her children had been buried.

It is a hard and hateful thing to see proud men, not to speak of enduring them. But it is annoying and impossible to suffer proud women, because in general Nature has given men proud and high spirits, while it has made women humble in character and submissive, more apt for delicate things than for ruling. Therefore, it should not be surprising if God's wrath is swifter and the sentence more severe against proud women whenever it happens that they surpass the boundaries of their weakness, as foolish Niobe did, deceived by treacherous Fortune, not knowing that to have many children is not a virtue of the mother who gives them birth, but a work of Nature which moves Heaven's goodness to that purpose. Indeed, she should have been satisfied and have given thanks to God for granting her children, rather than seeking divine honors for herself as if having such numerous and marvelous children had been her own accomplishment. By acting more in pride than in wisdom, Niobe brought it about that she bemoaned her misfortune while she yet lived and made her name hateful to posterity many centuries later.

CHAPTER XV

HYPSIPYLE, QUEEN OF LEMNOS

HYPSIPYLE was a woman famous for the devotion she showed toward her father, as well as for her unfortunate exile, the death of her ward Archemorus,[1] and the aid she received from her sons, whom she found again at an opportune moment. She was the daughter of Thoas, the king of Lemnos, who reigned at the time when women were seized by madness and withdrew their untamed necks from the yoke of men. Scorning the old king's rule and taking Hypsipyle with them, they unanimously decided that the following night they would turn their knives against all the men. They did not fail to carry out their plan. While all the others were cruel, Hypsipyle made a more merciful decision, because she thought that it would be inhuman to sully herself with a father's blood and told him of the others' crime. After putting him on a ship so that he could avoid public wrath and flee to Chios, she immediately made a great pyre and pretended that she was performing the last rites for her father. Everyone believed this, and Hypsipyle was placed on her father's throne and substituted for him as queen of the wicked women.

The devotion of children toward their fathers is certainly very holy. What is more proper, more just, and more praiseworthy than to reward with humaneness and honor those from whose labor we received nourishment when we were weak and who watched over us with solicitude, brought us to maturity with continuous love, taught us manners and gave us knowledge, enriched us with honors and abilities, and made us strong in morals and in intellect? Since Hypsipyle solicitously repaid this debt to her father, it is not without reason that she is placed among noble women.

While Hypsipyle was queen, Jason, on his way to Colchis with the Argonauts, either brought by the winds or arriving deliber-

[1] The child's name was either Archemorus or (as Boccaccio calls him later in this chapter) Opheltes.

ately, landed on the shore while the women resisted in vain, and he was received by the queen in her house and into her bed. When he had left, she gave birth to two sons at one time. Since, as some would have it, she was forced by the laws of Lemnos to send them away, she ordered that they be taken to Chios to be brought up by their grandfather. By this act it became known that she had deceived the others by saving her father, and her subjects rose up against her. Boarding a ship, she saved herself with difficulty from the common fury. While seeking her father and her children, she was seized by pirates and made a slave. After enduring many hardships she was given as a gift to Lycurgus, the king of Nemea, and she undertook to care for the king's only son, a small boy named Opheltes. While she was watching over him, Adrastus, the king of Argos, passed through the country with his army. He was marching against Thebes with his soldiers and was perishing of thirst because of the heat. At his request Hypsipyle showed him the spring of Langia, leaving her ward in a meadow among the flowers. At Adrastus' request she told her past history and was recognized by Euneus and Thoas, her sons, who were already grown and in the king's army. Hypsipyle, moved to hope for better fortune, found her ward dead, killed by a blow from a serpent's tail while playing in the grass, and she moved almost the whole army with her tears. The army and her children took her away from Lycurgus, who was mad with grief, and she was preserved for a fate and death unknown to me.

CHAPTER XVI

MEDEA, QUEEN OF COLCHIS

MEDEA, the most cruel example of ancient wickedness, was the daughter of Perseis' son Aeetes, the famous king of Colchis, and Hypsea his wife.[1] She was quite beautiful and by far the best trained woman in evil-doing. No matter by what teacher she was taught, the properties of herbs were so familiar to her that no one ever knew them better. By intoning enchantments, she knew perfectly how to disturb the sky, gather the winds from their dens, cause tempests, hold back rivers, brew poisons, make artificial fires for all kinds of conflagrations, and all other things of this sort. Far worse, her soul was not in discord with her arts, for, if those failed, she thought it very easy to use steel.

Captivated by his excellence, she ardently loved Jason of Thessaly, who at that time was a youth of marvelous prowess. His uncle Pelias, who was jealous of his virtue, had sent him to Colchis under the pretext of a glorious expedition to acquire the Golden Fleece. Medea, in order to merit his love, acted so that discord broke out among the people of the country, war was made against her father, and Jason had time to fulfill his desire. What sensible man can imagine that the destruction of a wealthy king could occur in the twinkling of an eye?[2] Having committed that crime and having gained the embraces of her beloved youth, she secretly fled with him, taking along all her father's wealth. Not content with this great offense, her cruel soul turned to worse. Thinking that Aeetes would follow them when they fled, she took along her brother Sbsyrtus, or Aegialeus, who was a small child. To make her father delay on the road, she had her brother dismembered and scattered the parts of his body in the fields of the island

---

[1] The wife of Aeetes is usually called Idyia.

[2] Boccaccio was fascinated by the sudden downfall of the mighty, which he saw as an example of the destructive power of fortune. His *De casibus virorum illustrium* is devoted to this subject.

of Tomi in the river Phasis, through which he had to pass in following her, so that her wretched father would linger to gather together the body of his son, bury him and cry over him, thus giving the fugitives more time. She was not deceived in her expectation, for so it happened.

Finally, after much wandering she arrived in Thessaly with her Jason, where she made her father-in-law Aeson so happy for his son's return, as well as for his victory, his booty, and his noble marriage, that he seemed to regain his youth. Wanting Jason to acquire the kingdom, Medea spread discord with her arts between Aeson's brother Pelias and his daughters and armed those wretched girls against their father. Then with the passing of the years she became hateful to Jason, who replaced her with Glauce, the daughter of Creon, the king of Corinth. Angry and unable to bear this, Medea contrived many plots against Jason. Using her craft, she burned with swift fire Glauce, daughter of Creon, Creon, and the royal palace, and in Jason's sight she killed the two sons she had borne him. She then fled to Athens, where she married King Aegeus and bore him a son who was called Medus after her. After attempting in vain to poison Theseus, who was returning, she fled for the third time. Restored to Jason's good graces, she was turned out of Thessaly with him by Aegialeus,[8] the son of Pelias. She returned to Colchis with Jason and restored to the throne her father, who was old and in exile. I do not remember having read or heard what she did later, nor in what land and how she died.

Not to stop here, I will say that we must not give too much freedom to our eyes, because as we look we perceive beauty, become envious, and are attracted to concubines. By means of the eyes audacity is aroused, beauty is praised, squalor and poverty are unworthily condemned, and since they are not learned judges, the eyes believe only in the outward appearance of things. Often they place the shameful ahead of the sacred, the false ahead of the true, and impropriety ahead of blessing, and, by praising things which should be condemned and which seem sweet for a short

---

[8] Acastus, and not Aegialeus, was the avenger of Pelias.

time, they sometimes stain the soul shamefully. These ignorant eyes are captivated, attracted, seized, and held by beauty even if dishonorable, by lascivious motions, by youthful wantonness, and by corroding vices. And since the eyes are the gates of the spirit, through them lust sends messages to the mind, through them love sighs and lights blind fires. Through them the heart sends sighs and shows its shameful affections. If one knew them well, he would either keep them closed or turn them heavenward or fix them upon the ground. No other ways but these are safe. And if one must use them, they should be restrained lest they become wanton. Nature gave them lids not only so that they may be closed while sleeping, but also that they might resist evil. Certainly, if powerful Medea had closed her eyes or turned them elsewhere when she fixed them longingly on Jason, her father's power would have been preserved longer, as would her brother's life, and the honor of her virginity would have remained unblemished. All these things were lost because of the shamelessness of her eyes.

CHAPTER XVII

ARACHNE OF COLOPHON

RACHNE was an Asian woman of the common people, the daughter of Idmon of Colophon, a dyer of wool. Although she was not famous for her lineage, she must nevertheless be glorified for several virtues. Some ancient writers assert that she discovered the uses of woven cloth, and that she was the first to think of making nets. It is uncertain whether these were nets for catching birds or fish. Her son, who was named Closter, discovered the spindle for wool. Some think that in her time Arachne held first place in the art of weaving and that she was so skilled in this that with her fingers, thread, loom, and other tools for such occupations she did what a painter does with his brush. This skill should not be scorned in a woman. In truth, when she heard of her great fame not only in Colophon where she lived and had her loom, but everywhere else, she became so proud that she dared enter a contest with Pallas Athena, who had discovered that art. Not being able to endure defeat with resignation, she ended her life with a rope. This gave an opportunity to those who wanted to give a fictitious account of this matter, for since Arachne was connected in name and occupation with *Aranea*, spider,[1] and since it hangs on thread as she did on a rope, they said that Arachne, through the mercy of the gods, was turned into a spider and with continual care goes on with her ancient art. Others say that although she placed the rope around her neck to die, she did not succeed because her servants arrived and helped her. She then left her occupation and remained always in grief.

And now, if there is someone who thinks that he surpasses others in something, I beg him, if he please, to say whether Arachne herself thought she could move heaven and take all honor to herself, or with her prayers and virtues make God, the Creator of all things, so benign towards her that she could force Him to open the treasure of His munificence, to bestow upon her all His favor, and forget all other people. But why am I asking? She seems to have thought so. How foolish, by Hercules! Nature turns the heavens by eternal law and gives to all of us intellects suitable for different undertakings. As these become weak through idleness and sloth, so do they become great and capable of great things through study and practice. And, stimulated by that same Nature, we are all spurred on by the desire to know everything, although not with the same degree of concern and success. And if this is so, what is there to prevent many from being equally skilful in the same thing? Therefore, whoever thinks that he is the only one who can surpass in glory so great a multitude of men is a fool. I would certainly wish that Arachne were the only one to amuse us with her vanity, for those who fall prey to such madness are numberless, and as they hurry towards the precipice of their foolish presumption, they make Arachne less ludicrous.

[1] *Arachne* means "spider" in Greek.

CHAPTER XVIII

ORITHYA AND ANTIOPE, QUEENS
OF THE AMAZONS

O RITHYA was the daughter of Martesia[1] and, together
with Antiope, who is believed by some to have been her
sister, ruled the Amazons after her. Above all she was
marvelous and very praiseworthy for her perpetual virginity. She
was so powerful in deeds of arms with Antiope, who reigned
together with her, that she ornamented the kingdom of the
Amazons with many honors. Praise of her military prowess was
so great that Eurystheus, the king of Mycenae, thought it would
be very difficult to take her royal girdle in war.[2] It is said that for
this reason he asked his debtor Hercules to bring it to him as one
of his great labors. The fact that Hercules, who overcame all, was
sent against her because of her great prowess in arms is certainly
great praise for this woman.

Hercules started on his way with nine warships and occupied
the shores of the Amazons. While Orithya was away, the Amazons
who had risen in arms were easily defeated by Hercules because
there were few of them and they were careless. He seized Melanippe and Hippolyte, Antiope's sisters, but returned Melanippe
when he was given the queen's girdle. When Orithya heard that
a member of the expedition, Theseus, had taken Hippolyte away,
she dared wage war against all Greece after summoning allies.
After being abandoned by her allies because of discord, she was
defeated by the Athenians and returned to her kingdom. I do not
remember having learned what she did afterwards.

[1] See Chapter XI for Martesia's story.
[2] According to tradition, Hercules was sent to fetch Hippolyte's girdle, not
that of Antiope.

CHAPTER XIX

ERYTHRAEA OR ERIPHILA, THE SIBYL

ERYTHRAEA, or Eriphila,[1] was a very marvelous woman and one of the Sibyls. Some people believe that these Sibyls were ten in number and call them by proper names. Since they were very skilled in foretelling future events and knew the decisions of the gods, they were given this name because, in Aeolic, *Sios* means 'God' and *byle* means 'mind,' and so Sibyl means, as it were, 'divine mind' or 'bearer of God in the mind.' Of all these venerable women they say that Erythraea was the most renowned. She was born among the Babylonians some time before the Trojan war, although many think that she made her predictions at the time when Romulus was king of the Romans. According to what some say, her name was Eriphila, but she was called Erythraea because for a long time she lived in the island of Erythrae[2] and a number of her writings were found in that place.

[1] This name should be Herophile.

[2] Erythrae is not an island; it is located on a promontory in Asia Minor. Boccaccio may have been misled by the fact that there are two small islands lying very near the coast on which Erythrae is situated.

··(41)··

The power of her intellect was so great, and she was so deserving in God's eyes because of her prayers and devotion, that through her great studies, and not without a divine gift, if what we read about her is true, she gained the skill to write about the future with such clarity that it seems to be the Gospel rather than fortune-telling. When asked by the Greeks, she did in fact state in verse their hardships and the destruction of Troy so clearly that nothing was known more definitely after the event. Likewise, in a few accurate verses she summarized the empire of the Romans and its varied fortunes a long time before it began, so that it seems as if she had written a *résumé* in our time rather than having predicted the future. And what is more, I believe, she clarified that secret mystery of divine thought, the incarnation of the Son of God, which had been prophesied before by the ancients in symbols and in the obscure words of the prophets, or better by the Holy Ghost through their words, so that she seems not to have prophesied, but to have dictated (as if after His birth) a history of His life, His deeds, betrayal, capture, mockery, shameful death, the triumph of His Resurrection, Ascension, and return to the Last Judgment.

Because of these merits, I believe that she was greatly loved by God and is worthy of reverence above all other women of antiquity. There have also been those who assert that in addition to this she kept perpetual virginity. I can easily believe this, for I do not think that so clear a vision of the future could dwell in an unclean breast. It is not known when and where she died.

CHAPTER XX

MEDUSA, DAUGHTER OF PHORCYS

MEDUSA was the daughter and heir of Phorcys, a very wealthy ruler whose rich kingdom was in the Atlantic Ocean. Some believe that it consisted of the islands of the Hesperides. If we can believe the ancients, Medusa was of such marvelous beauty that she not only surpassed all others but, like something wondrous and supernatural, attracted very many men to see her. Her hair was golden and abundant, her face was of special beauty, and her body properly tall and straight. Among other things, her eyes had such great and pleasant force that if she looked kindly at someone, he remained almost motionless and beside himself. In addition, some have asserted that she was very skilled in agriculture and for that reason she acquired the name Gorgon.[1] Through this she not only preserved her wealth with marvelous shrewdness but greatly augmented it, so that those who knew her believed that she surpassed all the western kings in wealth. And so because of her great beauty, as well as her riches and sagacity, she acquired great renown even among the most remote nations.

Her fame reached Greece, where Perseus, the most excellent among the young men of Achaea, heard these reports and became desirous of seeing that beautiful woman and taking her treasure. Thus, boarding a ship whose emblem was the horse Pegasus, he arrived in the West with wonderful speed. In that region he used his skill and his arms to kidnap the queen and returned home laden with gold and booty. These deeds inspired the stories of the poets where we read that the Gorgon Medusa often changed into stone men who gazed upon her and that her hair had been changed into serpents because of Minerva's anger, since she had desecrated her temple by sleeping in it with Neptune, and that

---

[1] In Greek the word *gorgon* means 'fierce.' Boccaccio mistakenly associates it with farming, as there is a similar word meaning 'farmer.'

she then gave birth to Pegasus, and that Perseus, mounted on that winged horse, flew to her kingdom and conquered it by using the shield of Pallas.

To possess gold is an unhappy thing. If it is kept hidden it does not give any comfort to the owner, and if it is shown it gives rise to the attacks of many who covet it. Even if violent hands should be tied, the troublesome worries of the owner will not cease, so that, peace of mind gone, he loses sleep, falls prey to fear, lacks faith, becomes suspicious, and in short all the actions of wretched life are hindered. And if his wealth should happen to be lost, as a poor man he is tormented by anxiety while the miser gloats, the gentleman laughs at him, the envious poor are cheered, and the whole populace chants the story of his grief.

CHAPTER XXI

IOLE, QUEEN OF AETOLIA

IOLE, the daughter of King Eurytus of Aetolia,[1] was the most beautiful among the girls of that country. There are some who say that she was loved by Hercules, the master of the world. It is said that Eurytus promised him his daughter in marriage but later refused when his son dissuaded him. Angered by this, Hercules bitterly waged war against him and killed him. After conquering the country he took his beloved Iole to himself. She was certainly moved more by her father's death than by love for her husband. Desiring vengeance, with marvelous and constant slyness she covered her feelings towards him with false love. With caresses and a certain artful wantonness she made Hercules love her so much that she could see very well that he would not deny her anything she might ask. For this reason, before anything else she told that powerful man to put aside the club with which he had tamed the monsters and to remove the skin of the Nemean lion, which was a sign of his strength, as if she were afraid of her lover, who was so rough because of his clothes. She made him put aside the poplar wreath and his quiver and arrows. This not being sufficient for her heart, she moved more daringly against her defenseless enemy with weapons prepared in advance. First she asked him to adorn the fingers of his hands with rings, anoint his head with Cyprian unguents, comb his shaggy hair, anoint his rough beard with nard, and adorn himself with girlish garlands and the Maeonian headdress. Then she made him dress in dainty purple clothes, believing that she, a young woman armed with her deceit, had performed a greater deed by weakening with luxury such a robust man, than if she had killed him with steel or poison. Certainly, thinking that she had not sufficiently satisfied her wrath, she brought that man, who had given himself up to luxury, to such a pass that he would sit like a woman among other common women and tell the story of his labors. Taking the

[1] Eurytus was the king of Oechalia, not Aetolia.

distaff, he would spin wool, and his fingers, which had been hard enough to kill serpents when he was still a baby, now at a vigorous age, in fact in his prime, were being softened by spinning wool.

In truth, for those who wish to consider it, this is not a small example of human weakness and the trickery of women. To Hercules' eternal shame, this ingenious girl with this punishment avenged her father's death, not with arms but with deception and lasciviousness, and made herself worthy of everlasting fame. For, by vanquishing Alcides, she triumphed over all those monsters which he had conquered for Eurystheus. This pestilential passion usually creeps upon delicate girls, and very often it seizes lustful and idle young men, because Cupid scorns seriousness and is a great worshiper of wantonness. Therefore, the fact that it entered Hercules' hard breast is a far greater marvel than the deeds which he himself had performed. This must instill great fear in men who are solicitous of their well-being and must shake them out of their lethargy, when it is clear what a strong and powerful enemy threatens them. We must therefore be vigilant and arm our hearts with great strength, so that we are not overcome against our wishes. First a man must resist. He must curb his eyes so that they do not see vain things, close his ears like an asp, and tame lust with continual toil, because love seems alluring to men who are not wary, and at first sight it is pleasing. If it is well received, when it first enters it pleases a man with happy hopes, makes him adorn himself, encourages good behavior, *savoir-faire*, dances, songs, music, games, conviviality, and similar things. But after love through foolish consent has seized the entire man, conquered freedom, and chained and bound the mind and the fulfillment of desires is delayed beyond what had been hoped, it awakens sighs, forces the mind to make use of wiles without differentiating between vices and virtues as long as it achieves its desires, and it numbers among its enemies anything which is contrary to this. His breast enflamed, the unhappy man goes back and forth and with tireless striving seeks his beloved. Often on seeing her again new ardor is engendered. And since it is impossible to repent, he cries, makes entreaties sweetened with flattery, secures the services of panderers, promises gifts, makes presents, and degrades himself. At times guards are deceived, and, besieged with watchfulness, hearts are taken, and sometimes the desired embraces are won. Then the enemy of chastity and encourager of crimes casts shame and honor aside, makes ready the pig-sty, and, grunting, gives himself up to the allurements of copulation. Temperance thrown aside, warmed by Ceres and Bacchus, they invoke Venus and spend the whole night in shameful lasciviousness. Nor does this always extinguish such a fury; in fact it often grows into a greater madness. For this reason it happened that Alcides fell into that shameful obedience. Because of this men often forget their honor, consume their wealth, bring hatred upon themselves, and often endanger their lives. Among these results grief is not lacking. There are quarrels, brief periods of peace, and once more suspicion and jealousy, consumer of souls and bodies. If the lovers do not attain their desires, then love, lacking reason and using his spurs and whip, increases their worries, heightens desire, and brings almost intolerable pain, which cannot be cured by any remedy except tears, laments, and at times death. They turn to old women for remedies, consult soothsayers, try the powers of herbs and enchantments. From flattery they turn to threats, they think of force, curse their blighted love, and at times this perpetrator of evil instills so much fury that it drives poor wretches to rope and knife. How sweet, how beautiful is this love which we raise on high like God, although we should fear and flee from it. We honor it, we humbly adore it and make sacrifices of tears and sighs to it. We offer it dishonor, adultery, and incest, and on it we place the crown of our lewdness.

CHAPTER XXII

DEIANIRA, DAUGHTER OF KING OENEUS OF AETOLIA

SOME authors tell us that Deianira was the daughter of Oeneus, the king of Aetolia,[1] and that she was Meleager's sister. She was a virgin of such striking beauty that Hercules and Achelous fought to take her to wife. After she had been won by Hercules, the centaur Nessus fell in love with her. As Hercules was bringing her to his country from Calydon, he was delayed by the Evenus, a river in Calydon, which had flooded because of the previous day's torrential rain. There he was met by her admirer Nessus. Since he was on horseback,[2] Nessus offered to help Hercules by taking Deianira across. Hercules agreed, intending to swim after his wife. Nessus, his desire almost satisfied, ran away after crossing the river with his beloved. Hercules was unable to catch him on foot but reached him with an arrow poisoned with the Hydra's venom. Feeling this, Nessus knew that he was dying and immediately gave Deianira the cloak infected with his blood, telling her that if she put it on Hercules, bloody as it was, she would win him back from any other loves. Credulous Deianira took the cloak as a great gift and kept it hidden for some time. When Hercules loved Omphale or Iole, she cautiously sent it to him by his servant Lichas. When the poisoned blood mixed with his perspiration and penetrated through his pores, Hercules became so crazed that of his own will he threw himself in the fire. Thus Deianira was bereft of so great a husband, having hoped to recapture his love but having lost him instead, and also avenged Nessus' death.

[1] Oeneus was the king of Calydon in Aetolia.

[2] Boccaccio's statement that Nessus was on horseback is a rationalization of the tradition that Nessus was a centaur.

CHAPTER XXIII

JOCASTA, QUEEN OF THEBES

JOCASTA, the queen of Thebes, was more famous for her misfortunes than for her merits or reign. She had noble ancestors in the first founders of Thebes and was married as a girl to Laius, the king of the Thebans. When she was pregnant with a child of his, Laius, because of the adverse answer of an oracle, ordered that the child be abandoned to wild animals as soon as it was born. Jocasta obeyed in grief. She thought that he had been immediately devoured, but he was brought up as a son by the king of Corinth. After reaching manhood, he killed Laius in the land of the Phocians. The widow Jocasta, not recognizing her own son, took him as her husband. She bore him two sons, Eteocles and Polynices, and as many daughters, Ismene and Antigone. She seemed happy in both her reign and her children when, through the response of an oracle of the gods, she learned that the man she thought was her legitimate husband was her son. Although this was a great blow to her, her husband felt it so much more that through shame for the sin he had committed he gouged out his eyes, seeking eternal night, and abandoned his kingdom.

The sons took over the kingdom amid discord, broke their agreement, and came to war. To Jocasta's great sorrow, they often fought each other. Finally, when the two fought in single combat, they were delivered up to her dead of mutually inflicted wounds. Although she saw her brother Creon already king, the wretched mother and grandmother, seeing the man who was her husband and son blind and in prison, and Antigone and Ismene enveloped by misfortune, unable to bear her grief and already old because of her affliction, plunged steel into her despairing and struggling heart. Thus, together with her life she put an end to her sorrows. There are some, however, who say that she could not endure her grievous errors for so long a time, and that when she saw Oedipus gouge his eyes out she immediately killed herself.

·· (49) ··

CHAPTER XXIV

THE SIBYL AMALTHEA, OR DEIPHOBE

IT IS said that the virgin Amalthea, called Deiphobe by some, was the daughter of Glaucus. She is believed to have been born in Cumae, an ancient city of the Chalcidians in Campania. Since she was one of the Sibyls, it is presumed that she flourished at the time of Troy's destruction and she lived for so long a time that some believe she was still alive at the time of Tarquinius Priscus. As some of the ancients testify, she held virginity in such value that in the space of many centuries she did not allow herself to be defiled by man's touch. Although the writings of the poets state that she was loved by Phoebus and that he gave her the gifts of longevity and prognostication, I certainly believe that it was because of the merits of her virginity that she received the light of prophecy, through which she wrote about and predicted many future events, from that true Sun which lightens every man who comes into this world. It is said that on the Baian shore near Lake Avernus she had a marvelous temple, which I have seen, and I have heard that it has retained her name up to this time. This temple, although in decay because of its antiquity and half destroyed by negligence, retains its ancient majesty even in ruins, and those who behold its greatness marvel.

There are some who say that when Aeneas was a fugitive, Amalthea was his guide in the underworld, but I do not believe it. We shall speak of this later. Those who say that she lived for many centuries declare that she came to Rome and brought Tarquinius Priscus nine books, of which she burned three in his presence when he refused to give her the amount she asked for them. The next day she demanded for six the price she had asked for nine, stating that if he did not give it to her immediately she would burn three more, and this she did. The next day, for the three remaining books she received the price she had originally asked. These were preserved, and posterity later found that they contained all the exploits of the Romans. For this reason the

Romans later guarded them with great care, and as the need arose for counsel about the future, they ran to them as if to a temple. It is difficult for me to believe that Amalthea and Deiphobe were the same person, for I have read that the latter died in Sicily, where for a long time her grave was pointed out by the inhabitants.

We become famous through study and divine grace, which is not denied anyone whose actions are worthy of it. If we looked at how we languish in sloth, we would plainly see that because of time fruitlessly lost since birth we shall go to our graves without honor, even if aged. Finally, if women through genius, industry, and God's grace reach such divinity and sanctity, what must one think of men, who have greater aptitude for everything? If they reject idleness they will certainly reach that divinity. Let those who through their indolence lose so great a blessing cry and rot, and let them confess that they are stones among living men, for by their silence they will acknowledge their crime.

CHAPTER XXV

NICOSTRATA, WHO WAS CALLED CARMENTA

NICOSTRATA, who was later called Carmenta in Italy, was the daughter of Ionius, the king of Arcadia. According to some she married Pallas of Arcadia, and according to others she was his daughter-in-law. Not only was she marvelous for the brilliance of her reign, but she was very learned in Greek literature. Her intellect was so versatile that with great study she even learned the art of foretelling the future, so that she became a renowned prophetess. Since at times she was accustomed to disclose the future in verse (*carmen*) to people who questioned her, the Latins called her Carmenta, almost eliminating her previous name Nicostrata. She was the mother of Evander, the king of Arcadia, who, according to the stories of antiquity, is said to have been Mercury's son either because he was fluent and eloquent or because he was clever. According to some he was exiled from the kingdom of his forebears because he had accidentally killed his true father, or, as others would have it, because of discord which had arisen among the citizens for another reason. His mother Carmenta advised him and prophesied many great things if he would go to a country which she would show him. He boarded a ship with his mother, who had become the companion of his wanderings, and with part of his people, coming from the Peloponnesus, he arrived with a favorable wind at the mouth of the Tiber, guided by her. He stopped with his mother and his people on the Palatine hill, where later mighty Rome was built. He called it Palatine after either his father Pallas or his son, and there he built the city of Pallanteum.

Carmenta found that the inhabitants of that place were half savage, although they had earlier learned to till the soil through the industry of Saturn, who had fled to that place. Seeing that they were almost illiterate and that the little they knew was in

Greek, and considering with her god-like mind the fame which was in store for that place and region, she thought it would be unworthy for their great deeds to be told to posterity in a foreign tongue. With all the power of her intellect, she decided to give that people its own letters completely different from those of other nations. God did not turn His eyes from this enterprise. Through His grace it happened that she found new symbols suitable for the Italic language, just as a long time before Cadmus, the founder of Thebes, had done for the Greeks, and she taught how they should be put together, being satisfied with only sixteen letters. We have kept them until now because of her gift, and we call them letters; certain learned men have added a few useful ones without losing any of the original symbols. Even though the Latins were amazed by that woman's prophecies, this invention seemed so marvelous that foolish men believed she was a goddess and not a woman. For this reason during her life they paid homage to her with divine honors, and when she died they built a temple in her name on the lowest part of the Capitoline hill where she had lived. To perpetuate her memory the nearby area was called *Carmentalis* after her. When Rome became great, it did not allow this to be changed. In fact, a gate which the citizens had to build was for many centuries called *Carmentalis* in her honor.

Italy was renowned among the other regions of the world for her many blessings and was splendid with almost celestial light. Her great splendor was not gained only under her skies, for wealth and royal ornaments came from Asia Minor. The nobility came mainly from the Trojans, although the Greeks augmented it greatly. Arithmetic and the art of geometry first came from Egypt. From the above-mentioned Greeks came philosophy, eloquence, and almost all the mechanical arts. Agriculture, which formerly was known only to a few, was taught by Saturn while in exile. The unfortunate adoration of the gods came from the Etruscans and from Numa Pompilius. Public laws first came from Athens and were then enacted by the senators and the emperors. Simon Peter brought the Papacy and perfect religion from Jerusalem. Military discipline, however, was discovered by the ancient

Romans, by means of which and through strength of spirit and body and love for the republic they acquired for themselves dominion over the whole world. From what has been said, it is clear that letters were given to our ancestors by Carmenta after she had come to Italy from Arcadia. It was also believed that she first invented grammar, which, as time went by, the ancients amplified. By means of these inventions an infinite number of books have been written on all subjects: the accomplishments of men, and the great deeds of God, which are preserved perpetually for mankind, so that through their help we may know things which we cannot see. With these inventions we send our requests and receive accurately the answers of others. With them we enter into friendship with people far away and preserve it by answering one another. They describe God for us all as far as that can be done. They describe the sky, the earth, the seas, and all the animals, and through them there is nothing that one cannot understand by studying if he so desires. In short, we entrust to their faithful care whatever the mind cannot retain. Although these things are done by others in other languages, this does not in the least detract from ours.

In sum, we have lost some of these noble virtues, we have added to some of them, and some we still retain, at least in name if not in practice. Regardless of what has happened to other things through our fault or through an act of Fortune, neither the rapacity of the Germans, nor the fury of the Gauls, nor the wiles of the English, nor the ferocity of the Spaniards, nor the rough barbarity and insolence of any other nation has been able to take away from the Latin name such great, marvelous, and rightful glory, so that they have never said or dared say that the first letters were found through their own talents, and much less that they invented grammar. As we discovered these things, so did we give them of our own free will, but always distinguished by our name. So it happens that the farther abroad they are spread, the greater are the praise and the honor of the Latin name; they make clearer the evidence of our ancient honor, nobility, and intellect, and preserve a perfect

NICOSTRATA

example of our genius in spite of the barbarians' indignation.[1] Although we have to give thanks for this singular glory to God, Who gave it, nevertheless we owe Carmenta great praise and gratitude. For this reason it is proper and just that we glorify her name with eternal memory, so that no one will deem us ingrates.

[1] The theme that Rome's greatness lies in the civilizing influence of the Latin language and literature, rather than in the might of her armies, recurs often in the works of Alberti, Valla, and the other humanists of the fifteenth century. Faced with the might of France, Spain and other nations, the Italians of the Renaissance also based their claim to superiority on the greatness of their culture; it was their defense against the "barbarians."

CHAPTER XXVI

PROCRIS, WIFE OF CEPHALUS

PROCRIS was the daughter of Pandion, the king of Athens,[1] and was the wife of Cephalus, who was King Aeolus' son.[2] Because of her greed she was as much hated by honest women as she was approved of by men, for through her the faults of other women were made clear. While Cephalus and Procris lived as man and wife, they loved each other with happy and devoted affection. But to their misfortune it happened that a woman of unusual beauty, called Aura (or Aurora, according to some), fell in love with Cephalus. She tempted him a long time, but in vain, for he was very much in love with his wife Procris. Angered by this, Aura said, "You shall be sorry to have loved Procris so ardently. You will see that I shall arrange it so that if there is someone to tempt her, she will value money more than your love."

When he heard this, young Cephalus became anxious to test his wife. He pretended that he was going on a long voyage and left home. Doubling back, he returned to the city and through go-betweens tempted his wife's fidelity with gifts. Although large, these did not sway her during the first assault. But when he persevered and added jewels, her will, which was already vacillating, broke, and she promised to give him that night the embraces he desired if he would give her the gifts he had offered. Then Cephalus, stricken with grief, made himself known after learning through his stratagem how weak Procris' love was. Procris, full of shame and troubled by her conscience for her misdeed, immediately fled into the woods and began to live in solitude. The young man, impatient for her love, pardoned her of his own volition and with prayers took her back into his graces against her will. But what good was it, since the power of pardon cannot prevail against the pangs of conscience? Procris' feelings changed constantly.

[1] Procris was the daughter of Erechtheus of Athens.
[2] According to tradition, Cephalus was the son of Dion, not of Aeolus.

Torn by jealousy, she thought that because of Aurora's wiles her husband was doing to her what she had done to him for money. She began to follow him secretly while he hunted through mountains, hilltops, and hidden valleys. This went on for a while, and it happened that as Procris moved secretly in a grassy valley among the reeds of a swamp, her husband thought she was a wild animal and killed her with an arrow.

I do not know whether to say that gold is the most powerful thing on earth or that it is very foolish to seek something which one does not wish to find. This silly woman proved both these things and found for herself perpetual infamy and a death which she had not sought. Not to speak of the unbridled love of gold which moves almost all foolish persons, I shall ask those who fall prey to such stubborn jealousy to tell me what usefulness, what honor, what praise or what glory they get from it. In my opinion, this is a ridiculous infirmity of the mind, which is caused by the pusillanimity of people who are sick, because we see it only in those who deem themselves of such small value that they would easily admit that anyone is to be preferred to them.

CHAPTER XXVII

ARGIA, DAUGHTER OF KING ADRASTUS

ARGIA was a Greek woman, the noble descendant of Argos' ancient kings and daughter of King Adrastus. She was a happy sight to her contemporaries because of her marvelous beauty, and she left to posterity an untainted and noble record of conjugal love. For this reason her fame has reached our times clear and splendid. She married Polynices, the son of King Oedipus of Thebes. While Polynices was in exile, she bore him a son, Thersander. She noticed that he was tormented by bitter worries because of his brother's deceit, and she shared these worries with him. She not only begged her father, who was already old, but with tears and prayers persuaded him to take up arms against Eteocles, who was holding the kingdom of Thebes through tyranny in violation of both the law and his agreement with his brother. Not to receive harm from the augurs' fatal answer, she became generous beyond the nature of women and of her own accord gave to Eurydice,[1] wife of the seer Amphiaraus, the precious necklace which in previous times had proved unlucky for Theban women.[2] Because of this Amphiaraus, who had been in hiding, was found and went to Thebes, where he met with misfortune. For after many battles, the other princes being dead, Adrastus was left without help and was almost put to flight.

Anxious Argia heard that Polynices had been left unburied among the bodies of commoners. Casting aside royal splendor, the comfort of her chamber, and womanly weakness, she immediately set out on her way to the battlefield with a few companions. She was not frightened by the dangers of the road, bandits, beasts, birds which seek out carrion, the souls of the dead which fly about (as foolish people think), or (even more terrible) Creon's

---

[1] According to tradition, the name of Amphiaraus' wife was Eriphyle.

[2] This was the fatal necklace which Harmonia had received on her wedding day, and which brought misfortune to all those who came in possession of it. According to tradition, it was not Argia but Polynices, who had inherited it and who gave it to Eriphyle.

order that under pain of death no one should bury any of the fallen. When at midnight she went with eager but saddened spirits to the battlefield, where the corpses gave off a fetid stench, she turned over this or that body to see, with a small lamp, if she recognized the rotting face of her beloved husband, and she did not stop until she found the one she sought. It was a miracle that the half-eaten face, already covered by dust and the rust of arms, dirt and putrid blood, and which certainly no one could have recognized, did not remain unrecognized by the loving wife. The filth on the putrefied face could not prevent her kisses, nor could Creon's terrible order stop her tears and laments. For, having repeatedly sought his vital spirit by kissing his mouth, she washed the putrefied limbs with her tears, and, lamenting, called this dead man to her embraces. Then she placed his body in the burning pyre, and when it was consumed she placed the ashes in an urn, not to leave anything of her pious office undone. Her deed was disclosed by the fire, but she feared neither prison nor the cruel tyrant's knife.[8]

Many women have often lamented their husbands' illness, imprisonment, poverty, and evil fate, while the hope of a more benign fortune continued, and when fear of a more cruel one was absent. Although this seems praiseworthy, one cannot say that it is an extreme sign of love, as can be said of Argia's last rites for her husband. She went into the enemy's territory when she could have cried at home; she touched the fetid corpse which she could have had others find for her; she paid him royal honors with fire when she could have buried him in secret, which, considering the circumstances, would have been sufficient. She cried where she could have passed by in silence. She had nothing to hope for since her husband had died away from home, but she had much to fear from her enemy. She was counseled thus by true love, complete faith, the sanctity of marriage, and the chastity she had preserved inviolate. For these things Argia should be worthily praised, honored, and glorified with splendid fame.

[8] In having Argia seek her husband's body, Boccaccio follows Hyginus' account (Fab. 72). Common tradition, however, has it that Polynices was buried by his sister Antigone, who was then buried alive by Creon in her brother's tomb.

CHAPTER XXVIII

MANTO, DAUGHTER OF TIRESIAS

MANTO, daughter of Tiresias, the greatest soothsayer of Thebes, was renowned in the time of King Oedipus and his sons. Taught by her father, she had such a quick and capable mind that she learned the ancient art of foretelling the future from fire. This art was first discovered by the Chaldeans, and according to some by Nimrod. She learned it so well that in her time no one knew better the movements of flames, their colors and murmurings in which, they say, are signs of the future, through what diabolic arts I know not. Moreover, through her keen sight, she could also find these signs in the entrails of sheep, the liver of oxen, and the vitals of any other animal, and she extracted them often. It was believed that with her arts she forced malignant spirits and the gods of the underworld to speak and answer those who questioned them.

When the Greek kings who besieged Thebes had been killed in battle and Creon had taken over the rule of the city, Manto left and went to Asia Minor to flee from the new king, as some are pleased to believe. There she built the temple of the Clarian Apollo, which was later very famous for its oracle, and she gave birth to Mopsus, a glorious soothsayer in his time, although the ancients do not tell by whom she conceived him.[1] But others believed differently and stated that for a long time after the Theban war she wandered with certain companions and finally reached Italy. There she gave birth to a son called Citheonus, begotten by a certain Thyberinus.[2] Others called him Bianor. She then went with her son to Cisalpine Gaul, where near Lake Garda she found naturally fortified swampy areas and settled on land which rose above the water in the middle of the swamp, so that she could attend to her witchcraft with greater freedom and lead

---

[1] According to tradition, Mopsus' father was either Apollo or Rhacius.
[2] According to tradition, the name of her son was Ocnus, and his father was Tiberis.

the rest of her life with greater safety in the midst of this marsh. After some time she died and was buried there. Some say that Ocnus built a city near her grave and called it Mantova after his mother. Others believe that with firm determination she preserved her virginity unto death itself. It would have been a famous, beautiful, and most holy deed, and highly praiseworthy, if she had not stained it with her wicked arts, and if she had preserved it for God, to Whom virginity should be consecrated.

CHAPTER XXIX

THE WIVES OF THE MINYANS

T HE number and the names of the wives of the Minyans have been denied us, either because of the indolence of the writers in their time or because of the number of years which have elapsed. They ought not to be passed over in silence, for they deserved to be raised to great glory for their uncommon deeds. But since hateful Fortune willed it thus, I shall shout the praise of these nameless women with all the art in my power and strive mightily to immortalize them, for they have well deserved it.

The Minyans, then, were among Jason's companions, the Argonauts, who were famous young men of great nobility. Having finished the journey to Colchis and returned to Greece, the Minyans abandoned their ancient fatherland and chose to remain with the Lacedaemonians, who not only granted them citizenship in a friendly way but received them among the elders and senators who ruled that republic. Their descendants, not remembering that splendid courtesy, dared wish to subject the public liberty to shameful slavery. At that time they were very wealthy young men, not only famous for their own distinction, but splendid seven-fold through their connections with noble Lacedaemonians. Among other things, they had beautiful wives, born of very noble citizens, and certainly this is not the least of worldly honors. In addition to this, they had many followers. They did not feel grateful to their common fatherland for these blessings but attributed them to their own merits. This led them to such madness that they felt they should be given precedence over others. From this they fell prey to a desire for power, and therefore they presumptuously bent their efforts toward seizing the republic. For this reason, when their crime had been discovered, they were taken and imprisoned, and by authority of the people they were sentenced to death as enemies of the state.

They were to be put to death by the executioners on the following night, according to the ancient custom of the Lacedaemonians,
when their sad, tearful wives conceived an unheard-of plan for
the liberation of their husbands and did not delay in acting on it.
When night came, they dressed in simple clothes, with their faces
veiled and in tears, and as noblewomen they easily received permission from the guards to enter the prison to see their husbands
who were to be executed. When they reached them, they did not
waste time in tears and laments, but immediately explained their
plan to their husbands. They changed clothes with them, and
their husbands veiled their faces as women do, wept, lowered their
eyes to the ground, and feigned sorrow. Protected by the shadows
of night and by the respect owed to noblewomen, they slipped
past their guards although they were under sentence of death.
The women took the doomed men's place, and the deception
was not discovered until the executioners came to kill the condemned and found their wives instead. The faith and love of
women are mighty indeed. But let us put aside the deceiving of
the guards (which resulted in the safety of the condemned), the
feelings of the senators, and the results of the wives' action, and
let us consider a while the power of sacred, wedded love and the
daring of these women.

Some say that, since marriage is an ancient and indissoluble
bond of nature, there is no greater love than that of happy wives,
just as there is no more deadly hatred than that of discontented
ones. For this fire of love, when ignited by reason, does not burn
to drive one to madness, but warms to please, and unites hearts
with such love that they always want or reject something together.
Accustomed to such peaceful unity, love does not fail to do whatever is necessary for its preservation, does nothing lax or luke-
warm, and if Fortune is unfriendly, it will gladly endure toil and
dangers. Watching vigilantly, it makes plans for its safety and
finds remedies and deceptions if need be. This most sweet love,
already strengthened by peaceful intimacy, moved the spirit of the
wives of the Minyans with such fervor that they were able to see
what they could not have seen before. Their husbands being in

danger, they gathered the powers of their intellect and found the stratagems, prepared the tools, arranged the time and the order of things which had to be done, so that they could deceive the stern and wary guards. Curbing their emotions, they thought that no honorable thing should be left undone for the safety of a loved one. Calling forth a sense of duty from the secret recesses of their hearts, they embarked with temerity on that course to save their husbands from danger, so that the wives' pure love might free men who had been condemned by public authority, loose those who were confined in prison, and give life and safety to those who already seemed gripped by hard and mortal punishment by delivering them from the executioners' hands.

It seems very extraordinary that, having tricked the power of the law, the public decree, and the authority of the Senate, and thwarted the will of the whole city, they did not fear to imprison themselves in the power of the deceived guards in the condemned men's place so that they could accomplish what they wished. I cannot sufficiently admire such pure faith and complete love. I strongly believe that if they had loved temperately, if they had been bound to their husbands by feeble bonds (since it was really proper for them to remain idly at home), they would not have accomplished such great deeds. To cut the matter short, I dare affirm that these wives were true and tried men, while the young Minyans whom they impersonated were but women.

CHAPTER XXX

PENTHESILEA, QUEEN OF THE AMAZONS

THE virgin Penthesilea succeeded Antiope and Orithya as queen of the Amazons, but I have not read who her mother and father were. It is said that, scorning her great beauty and mastering the softness of her body, she dared to wear the armor of her predecessors, to cover her blond hair with a helmet, and wear a quiver at her side. She climbed onto chariots and mounted horses in military fashion and showed herself marvelous in power and skill above all previous queens. It is clear that she did not lack intelligence because we read that she invented the battle-axe, which had been unknown up to her time.

Some are pleased to believe that Penthesilea, hearing of the prowess of the Trojan Hector, loved him ardently without having seen him. Wishing to leave as successor to her reign a child of such noble parentage, she willingly moved with a great number of her people to the mighty enterprise of aiding Hector against the Greeks.[1] She was not frightened by the great fame of the Greek princes, for, desiring to please Hector with arms and bravery as well as beauty, she often took part in the battles where the fighting was thickest. At times she hurled down the enemy with her lance, and with her sword she opened a path among those who blocked her way. Often she pursued the fleeing ranks with her arrows and did so many and such great deeds that at times she amazed even Hector who watched her. Finally, this valiant woman was fighting alone against the most powerful enemies to show herself more than usually worthy of so great a lover, when, with many of her followers already dead, she received a mortal blow and fell wretch-

---

[1] Justin, on whom Boccaccio depends for the history of the Amazons, does not mention Penthesilea's love for Hector. He states, however, that one of her successors, Minithya, spent thirteen days with Alexander the Great, hoping to have a child by him. This probably suggested to Boccaccio the reason he attributes to Penthesilea for her journey to Troy.

edly among the Greeks whom she had hurled to the ground. Others say that she arrived in Troy after Hector's death and was killed there while fighting bitterly.

Some may be surprised by the fact that women, no matter how armed, dared to fight against men. However, surprise will cease if we think of the fact that custom had changed their nature, so that Penthesilea and women like her were much more manly in arms than those who were made men by Nature but were then changed into women or helmeted hares by idleness and love of pleasure.

CHAPTER XXXI

POLYXENA, DAUGHTER OF
KING PRIAM

THE virgin Polyxena was the daughter of Hecuba and of Priam, the king of Troy. As a young woman she was of such radiant beauty that she was able to enflame with love the harsh breast of Achilles, the son of Peleus. Through the treachery of her mother Hecuba, she led him to his violent death by bringing him alone at night into the temple of the Thymbraean Apollo. There, foully and shamefully struck by Paris' arrow, Achilles fell dead. When the power of the Trojans had collapsed and Troy had been destroyed, Polyxena was brought by Neoptolemus to his father's grave to appease his spirit. On that site, if we are to believe the writings of the ancients, she saw that harsh young man pull out his sword while the onlookers cried, and the harmless girl offered him her throat with constant spirit and fearless expression.

Everyone's heart was moved by admiration for her fortitude no less than by Neoptolemus' filial piety towards Achilles. It was certainly a great thing worthy of remembrance that neither her tender age, sex, royal softness, nor the change of fortune was able to overcome the sublime spirit of this girl, and that she was strong in the face of the enemy and the conqueror's sword, which sometimes makes noble men waver and often lose their courage. I can easily believe that Polyxena was the creation of noble Nature, a fact which she proved by her scorn of death. What a woman she would have been if hostile Fortune had not killed her so young.

CHAPTER XXXII

HECUBA, QUEEN OF THE TROJANS

HECUBA, the most famous queen of the Trojans, was a true example of misery and a great illustration of how prosperity perishes. According to some, she was the daughter of the Aonian Dymas. Others assert that she was the daughter of Cisseus, the king of Thrace, which I myself believe since the majority of opinion concurs in this. As a girl she married Priam, the illustrious king of the Trojans, and bore him nineteen children, male and female, among whom was that singular light of Trojan goodness, Hector, whose brilliance in war was so great that not only did he gain everlasting renown for himself, but also gave eternal fame and glory to his ancestors and his country.

Yet Hecuba did not become famous for a happy reign and satisfaction in her many children as much as for the fact that she became known to all the world through the blows of Fortune. With great sadness she mourned her most beloved son Hector, whose death was almost as if the strongest pillar of the kingdom had fallen, and Troilus, a young man whose daring was greater than his strength, who were both killed at Achilles' hands. And she wretchedly saw Paris killed by Pyrrhus, and Deiphobus, who was killed in a horrible manner after having his ears and nose cut off. She saw Troy burned by the fire of the Greeks, Polites cut down in his father's lap, old Priam himself disemboweled before the altars of his own house, and her daughter Cassandra, her daughter-in-law Andromache, and herself taken as slaves by the enemy. She saw Polyxena killed before the grave of Achilles, and her grandson Astyanax taken from his hiding place and dashed against a rock.

Finally, on the Thracian shore she found the tomb of her young son Polydorus, treacherously killed by Polymnestor, and there she mourned him. Some say that because of these many great sorrows she became mad and went howling like a dog through the

Thracian fields. Thus, they say, she died and was buried in Cynos-
sema, on the shore of the Hellespont. Some claim that she was
taken by the enemy into slavery along with the others. And so
that she should not lack the slightest particle of misery, after
Agamemnon's death she saw Cassandra killed at Clytaemnestra's
order.

CHAPTER XXXIII

CASSANDRA, DAUGHTER OF
KING PRIAM OF TROY

CASSANDRA was the daughter of Priam, the king of the Trojans. The ancient writers tell us that she possessed the art of prediction. It is not certain whether she gained it by study or by the gift of God — or rather the Devil's trickery. Nevertheless, it is believed by many that long before Paris' brazen abduction of Helen Cassandra had predicted very often in clear words Helen's arrival, Troy's long siege, and finally Priam's death and Ilion's destruction. It is said that since her words were not believed she was beaten as a punishment by her father and brothers. This gave rise to the story that she was loved by Apollo, who asked her to become his mistress. They say that she promised this to him if he would first give her the art of knowing the future, and that after receiving it she abjured her promise. Apollo, unable to take back what he had given her, added to his gift the proviso that no one would believe what she said. And so the result was that her words were taken as foolish.

Cassandra, married to a young nobleman called Coroebus, lost her husband in the war before he took her to the wedding bed. Finally, when everything had been destroyed, she was taken prisoner and fell by lot to Agamemnon. While he was taking her to Mycenae, she predicted to him both the snares which were being prepared for him by Clytaemnestra and his death. Her words were not believed, and after a thousand dangers at sea she arrived at Mycenae with Agamemnon. There Agamemnon was killed through his wife's treachery, and so was Cassandra at Clytaemnestra's order.

CHAPTER XXXIV

CLYTAEMNESTRA, QUEEN OF MYCENAE

CLYTAEMNESTRA was the daughter of Tyndareus, the king of Sparta, and of Leda, and was the sister of Castor, Pollux, and Helen. While she was a young girl she married Agamemnon, the king of Mycenae. Although she was well known because of her family and her husband, she became even more famous through her wicked daring. For, while Agamemnon led the Greek host at Troy, she, having already had a number of children by him, fell in love with Aegisthus, an idle and vile young man, the son of Thyestes and Pelopia, who had not taken up arms because he was a priest. According to what some have said, she gave herself up to his embraces, encouraged by Nauplius, the old father of Palamedes. The result of her misconduct was that this brave woman, with firm spirit, treachery, and fearless daring, rose against her husband, either through fear of the sin she had committed, since Agamemnon was returning, or instigated by her lover and through desire for power, or through indignation, since Agamemnon was bringing Cassandra to Mycenae.

When Agamemnon returned as a conqueror from Troy, exhausted by storms at sea, she received him in the royal palace with a false expression of joy. Some are pleased to believe that while he was dining, perhaps already drunk with wine, she had him killed by the adulterer, who was in hiding. But some other writers say that as he was reclining at the table, encumbered by the vestments earned in victory, his faithless wife, as if about to give a great feast for the Greeks, calmly persuaded him to dress in the clothes of his own country, which she had prepared for her purpose with no opening for his neck. She brazenly handed them to him, and when Agamemnon had put his arms in the sleeves and was trying to find the opening to put his head through, she handed him half-bound to her lover, recruited by her as an assassin. And so Agamemnon was killed without seeing by whom it was done. As soon as this was finished, Clytaemnestra seized power and reigned for seven years with the adulterous Aegisthus. But by that time Agamemnon's son Orestes, who had been secretly saved by his friends from his mother's fury, had become a man. He made up his mind to avenge his father's death, waited for an opportune time, and killed Clytaemnestra along with her lover.

I do not know which I condemn more, the crime or the daring. The first was a great evil which that noble man had not deserved; the second was the more abominable as it was the more unbecoming to the perfidious woman. And I must praise Orestes' virtue, which could not be held in check for long by his pity for his lewd mother, so that he undertook to avenge his father's undeserved death. He did to his unworthy mother what had unjustly been done to his father by the adulterous priest at the orders of the lustful woman, so that his father's spilled blood might be expiated by the blood of those through whose orders and deeds it had been shed, and so that the crime would turn against its perpetrators.

CHAPTER XXXV

HELEN, WIFE OF MENELAUS

HELEN was known to the entire world as much for her lustfulness as for the long war which resulted from it. According to many, she was the daughter of Tyndareus, the king of Sparta, and of Leda, a very beautiful woman, and she was the wife of Menelaus, king of Lacedaemon. As is said by all the ancient Greeks and by the Latins after them, she was of such extraordinary beauty that she can easily be placed ahead of all other women. Not to speak of others, even Homer, a man of divine talents, lacked the skill to describe her fittingly in verse according to the rules of poetry. Moreover, many famous painters and sculptors also undertook that same labor so that, if possible, they might leave the image of such select beauty to those who came after them. Among them, Zeuxis of Heraclea, the most famous painter of that time and honored above all others, was hired at great expense by the people of Croton, and he put all his talent and the power of art into the attempt to depict her with his brush, using no other models but Homer's poetry and her great universal fame. As from these two sources he had been able to imagine her face and the rest of her body, he thought he would be able to represent Helen's divine appearance from the beauty of others, to show his painting of her to the people who had commissioned it, and to leave it to posterity. From among some beautiful boys and then from among their sisters he chose five who were remarkable for their beauty. He called on all the power of his talent and gathered into one form the beauty of all of them. It was scarcely believed that he had fully accomplished with art what he desired. And I am not surprised, for who, with brush and paint in a painting or with chisel in a statue, could describe the happiness of the eyes, the calm pleasantness of her whole face, her heavenly smile, and the various expressions of her face according to what she heard and saw, since this is the prerogative of Nature alone? Therefore, he did what he could, and he left what he had painted to those who came after him as the celestial beauty of a goddess. From this imaginative people have created a myth and have written that she was the daughter of Jupiter transformed into a swan, because of the starry splendor of her eyes and their light never before seen by men, the marvelous whiteness of her face, light golden hair falling on her shoulders everywhere in charming curls, the resonant and pleasing sweetness of her voice, certain expressions of her scented and rosy face, her clear forehead and ivory throat, and the unique charm of her rising breast, so that through the infusion of deity in addition to the beauty received from her mother one could understand what the artists in spite of their talents could not express with paint and brush.

Theseus, attracted by this marvelous beauty, went from Athens to Sparta, and in the presence of others seized her, still a young virgin, while she was playing as usual in the palaestra. Although he could take nothing from her except a few kisses, he nevertheless gave her the ill fame of a lost virginity. According to some, while Theseus was away, his mother Aethra gave Helen back to her brothers, who came looking for her. According to others, Helen was returned by Proteus, the king of Egypt. Finally, when she was of marriageable age she was married to Menelaus, the king of Lacedaemon, to whom she bore their only daughter, Hermione.

As the years passed, Paris, who had been abandoned on Mount Ida because of a dream which his mother had when she was pregnant, returned to Troy. Without being recognized, he overcame Hector in wrestling and avoided death when he was recognized by his mother through certain marks. Remembering the promise of a most beautiful wife made to him by Venus on Mount Ida for his judgment among the three goddesses, or according to some spurred by his desire to seek Hesione, he had ships built near Mount Ida and, accompanied by a noble retinue, went to Greece, where he was welcomed in Menelaus' palace. There he fell in love with Helen as soon as he saw her resplendent in celestial beauty, wanton in royal elegance, and desirous of being admired. He became hopeful because of her behavior, and as at times he looked at her furtively with ardent eyes he instilled in her immodest breast a desire for his love. Fortune was favorable at first, for Menelaus had gone to Crete on some necessary business and had left him in the house. Because of this, some say that since they were both in love it happened that through a mutual agreement Paris brought to his country the fire which his mother Hecuba had seen in her sleep and thus fulfilled the prophecy. He took Helen away at night from the Laconian shore with the bulk of Menelaus' treasure, or, as some prefer to say, he took her from the island of Cytherea which is near that place, where Helen was in the temple keeping vigil for the sacrifice according to the custom of her country. He placed her in the waiting ship and after many dangers arrived in Troy with her. There she was received with great honor by Priam, who thought that he had purged the shame of Hesione, who had been kept by Telamon, rather than that he had received into his country the final destruction of his kingdom.

All Greece was aroused by Helen's wantonness; all the princes of Greece thought more of Paris' insult than of Helen's lustfulness, and after claiming her many times in vain they banded together for the destruction of Troy. Having gathered their forces, they landed on the shore between the promontories of Sigeum and Retheum in Phrygia with a thousand and more ships loaded with armed men and besieged Troy, while the Trojans resisted in vain. From the walls of the besieged city, Helen was able to see of what value her beauty was, seeing the whole shore filled with the enemy and everything destroyed with iron and fire, the people fighting and dying striking each other, and everything stained with the blood of the Trojans as well as the Greeks. Certainly she was demanded and withheld with such stubborn determination that, since she was not surrendered, the bloody siege lasted ten years, causing the death of many noble men. During the siege, Hector and Achilles having already been killed and Paris having been slain by the harsh young man Pyrrhus, Helen entered into wedlock again and married the younger Deiphobus, as if it seemed to her that she had not sufficiently sinned the first time.

Finally, as an attempt was being made to achieve with treachery what it did not seem possible to do with arms, Helen, who had been the cause of the siege, strove as best she could against the Trojans in order to help in their destruction and to return into the good graces of her first husband. As had been arranged, the Greeks fraudulently pretended to withdraw, and the frightened Trojans, tired from their previous labors, celebrated with renewed happiness. When they had been overcome by food and sleep, Helen pretended to dance and at the proper moment lit a torch, giving a signal from the citadel to the Greeks who were waiting. They returned to find the city half asleep; silently they opened the gates, entered, set fire to the city, and shamefully killed Deiphobus. Thus Helen was returned to her husband Menelaus more than twenty years after she had been brought to Troy. Other writers said that Helen had been taken away by Paris against her will and thus deserved being taken back by her husband. Menelaus, returning to Greece with her, was buffeted by tempests and adverse winds and was forced to alter his course towards Egypt, where he was received by King Polybus. Later, the storms having abated, he returned with the wife he had regained to Lacedaemon, where he was welcomed almost eight years after the destruction of Troy. But I do not remember reading how long she lived afterwards, or what she did, or under what skies she died.

CHAPTER XXXVI

CIRCE, DAUGHTER OF THE SUN

ACCORDING to the statements of the poets, Circe, who has been very famous up to our time because of her magic incantations, was the daughter of the Sun and of Oceanus' daughter, the nymph Perseis. She was also the sister of Aeëtes, the king of Colchis. In my opinion, she was called the daughter of the Sun because she had singular beauty, or because she was very skilled in the knowledge of herbs, or rather because she was very shrewd in conducting her affairs. Astrologers believe that all these are qualities which the sun gives to mortals at their birth in accordance with various considerations. I do not remember reading how she left Colchis and arrived in Italy. All the histories, however, state that she lived in Aetheum,[1] a mountain of the Volscians, and up to our time we call that mountain Circeii after her name.

There is nothing about this famous woman except in the works of the poets, and after touching briefly on their reports I shall explain the meaning of what they believe as far as my skill will allow. First of all they say that all sailors who landed on the shores at the foot of that mountain, which once was an island, whether of their own will or driven there by tempests, were changed into different kinds of animals through Circe's art, enchantments, or poisonous potions. They say that among these sailors were the companions of wandering Ulysses, but that he himself was saved by Mercury's advice. When he drew his sword and threatened the sorceress with death, she changed his companions back to their original form. He lived with her for a year, and they say that he fathered her son, Telegonus, and then, full of wisdom, left her. I believe that under these words the following meaning is hidden. There are some who say that not far from Gaeta, a city in Campania, this woman was powerful because of her force and eloquence and that she did not much care about keeping her chastity

---

[1] According to tradition, Circe lived in Aeaea, an island in the Tyrrhenian Sea near the promontory of Circeii in Latium.

untarnished as long as she got what she desired. Thus with her wiles and elegant words she not only brought many of those who reached her shore to her pleasures but induced some to piracy. And she deceitfully impelled some to cast all honor aside and enter into business and commerce. She made many men become haughty because of her matchless attraction, and so those who through this wicked woman's deeds appeared to have lost human reason seemed to have been deservedly changed into beasts through their own crimes.

If we consider human behavior, we can well understand from this example that there are many Circes everywhere and many other men are changed into beasts by their lustfulness and their vices. And Ulysses, instructed by Mercury's advice, obviously signifies the wise man who cannot be bound by the trickery of deceitful people and who by his example often loosens the bonds of those who are held.[2] It is very clear that the rest belongs to history, through which it is shown that Ulysses stayed for some time with Circe. It is also said that this same woman was the wife of Picus, the son of Saturn and the king of the Latins, and that she taught him the art of foretelling the future. Since he was in love with the nymph Pomona, Circe because of her jealousy changed him into the bird which bears his name. It was said that he had been changed into a woodpecker, or *picus*, because in his house there was one of these birds, through whose singing and movements he acquired knowledge of the future and because he ordered his life according to the movements of this woodpecker. I have not found out when, where, or how Circe died.

[2] This is an excellent example of Boccaccio's method of interpreting and rationalizing the myths of the ancients.

CHAPTER XXXVII

CAMILLA, QUEEN OF THE VOLSCIANS

CAMILLA, the queen of the Volscians, was a marvelous virgin worthy of fame. She was the daughter of Metabus, an ancient king of the Volscians, and his wife Casmilla, whose death she caused, for the mother died when the child was born. For his consolation, the father gave her the name of her mother, taking out only the letter *s*. Fortune was very harsh with this maiden from the moment she was born, for shortly after her mother's death Metabus was banished from the kingdom by a sudden rebellion of the leading citizens. He fled, unable to take along into exile anything but his little child, whom he loved above everything else. As he fled on foot, wretched and alone, carrying Camilla in his arms, he arrived at the Amasenus River, which was swollen because of the previous day's rain. Unable to cross it by swimming, since he was impeded by the young child, he was suddenly inspired by God, Who did not want this child, who was to become famous, to die in this shameful manner. He wrapped her in the bark of a cork-tree, tied her to the lance that he happened to be carrying, and promised her to Diana if she saved her. With all his strength he hurled the lance with the child to the other bank and immediately swam through the water after her. Finding her uninjured through God's grace, he sought hidden places in the forest, happy although in misery, and nourished her with the milk of animals, not without great trouble.

When she reached a stronger age, Camilla began to cover her body with the skins of animals, to hurl the spear, use a sling, carry a quiver, stretch the bow, chase and catch the fleeing deer and wild goats, and disdain all womanly work. Above all she preserved her virginity, scorned the love of young men, and altogether rejected the offers of the many who wanted her in marriage, giving herself wholly to the service of Diana, to whom her father had promised her. Strengthened by these exercises, the virgin Camilla was summoned back to her father's kingdom and constantly pursued her purpose. Finally, when Aeneas came from Troy and took Lavinia as his wife, and war broke out between him and the Rutulian Turnus with both sides gathering their forces, Camilla favored Turnus and went to his aid with a great Volscian army. Repeatedly rushing in arms against the Trojans, fighting bitterly, and alone, she killed many of them. Finally, as she pursued a priest of Cybele called Corebus,[1] whose armor she desired, an enemy knight called Arruns wounded her with an arrow in her chest beneath her breast, and she fell to the ground dying. Thus she died in the midst of arms, a great loss to the Rutulians.

I wish that the girls of our time would look at Camilla and, seeing that virgin already adult and free amusing herself by runing through fields, forests and the dens of animals with her quiver, curbing the pleasures of lascivious desires with work, refusing pleasures and amusements, abstaining from elaborate food and drink, and with constant spirit rejecting not only the embraces, but even the company of young men of her age, would learn from her example what is proper for them in their parents' home, in churches, and in theaters where most onlookers and harsh judges of behavior congregate. And I wish that from her example they would learn not to listen to shameful words, to keep silent, to veil their eyes with seriousness, be well-mannered, act with modesty, and avoid idleness, feasting, elegance, dancing, and the company of young men. Let young women also know that to desire everything pleasurable and to do everything possible is not in accord with chastity, so that, by becoming more discreet in the flower of praiseworthy virginity, they may attain with maturity to holy matrimony under the direction of their elders.

[1] According to tradition, Camilla was pursuing Chloreus at the time of her death.

CHAPTER XXXVIII

PENELOPE, WIFE OF ULYSSES

PENELOPE, the daughter of King Icarius and wife of Ulysses, who was a very austere man, was a woman of untarnished honor and inviolate chastity, and a holy and eternal example for women. The firmness of her chastity was tested by Fortune for a long time in vain. While she was a young maiden and greatly loved for her beauty, her father married her to Ulysses, and she bore him Telemachus. After this, Ulysses was sent — or rather almost taken by force — to the army at Troy, so that Penelope was left by him with his father Laertes, who was already old, his mother Anticlea, and his little son. The war continued, and Penelope certainly suffered no injury, except that she remained without a husband for ten years. When the Greek leaders were returning home after Troy had been destroyed, word came that some of them had been dashed against rocks by storms at sea or forced to land on foreign shores, some had been swallowed by the waves, and few had returned to their countries. Only for Ulysses was it uncertain what course his ships had followed. For this reason, when they had been waiting for him for a long time, but he had not been seen by anyone and had not returned home, Ulysses was presumed dead. Because of this belief, his wretched mother Anticlea hanged herself to put an end to her grief.

Although it had been with great sorrow that Penelope had endured her husband's absence, she took the suspicion of his death even more to heart. After shedding many tears and often calling in vain on Ulysses, she firmly decided to grow old in chaste and eternal widowhood with aged Laertes and the young boy Telemachus. But since she was beautiful, well-mannered, and of noble birth, some young men of Ithaca, Cephalenia, and Aetolia loved and desired her, annoying her with their entreaties. As hope for Ulysses' life and return diminished every day, Laertes finally retired to the country because of his annoyance at Penelope's suitors, who occupied Ulysses' own palace and with prayers and flattery repeatedly urged Penelope to marry one of them. But she, fearing that the sacred decision within her breast would be broken and seeing no other possibility of refusal, was inspired by divine light and thought that she could deceive them for some time at least. She asked those who wanted her and clamored for her that she be allowed to wait for her husband until she could finish weaving a cloth which she had begun according to the custom of royal women. This was easily conceded by the noblemen who sought her, and with womanly astuteness she secretly undid at night all that she seemed to be diligently weaving during the day. With this trick she fooled them for some time, while they consumed Ulysses' wealth with continual banquets in his palace.

When it seemed impossible to deceive them any longer, divine mercy brought it about that Ulysses, twenty years after he had left his home, returned to Ithaca alone and unknown, coming from a Phoenician kingdom.[1] He went to his shepherds to find out the state of his affairs. Since he had shrewdly dressed himself in poor clothes, he was received in a friendly way by his servant Sybotes,[2] who was already old. From him he learned almost completely the course of his affairs. He saw Telemachus, who was returning from a visit to Menelaus, made himself known to him in secret, and told him of his plans. Sybotes took Ulysses to his home without his being recognized. After he had seen how the suitors were wasting his property and how the chaste Penelope was refusing to marry them, he was angered and attacked the carousing suitors with the help of the swineherd Sybotes, his cowherd Philitia,[3] and his son Telemachus, after closing the gates of the royal palace. He killed Polybus' son Eurymachus, Antinous, Amphion,[4] Chrysippus of Samë,[5] Agelaus, and others who pleaded

---

[1] Boccaccio here has confused the word *Phoenician* with Phaeacia, the kingdom where Ulysses stayed near the end of his travels.

[2] In the *Odyssey* this man is named Eumaeus. He is Ulysses' swineherd. *Sybotes*, which Boccaccio understands as his name, is Greek for 'swineherd,' and Eumaeus is sometimes called sybotes in the *Odyssey*.

[3] This name should be Philoetius.

[4] This name should be Amphinomus.

[5] This name should be Ctessipus.

in vain for mercy — also his goatherd Melanthius, who was giving arms to the enemy, some male servants, and some of the household women, whom he knew to have been mistresses of the suitors. And so he freed Penelope from their siege. Finally Penelope, hardly able to recognize him, welcomed him with great joy after longing for him so many years.

But Lycophron, a very late Greek poet, says that old Nauplius, the panderer who led almost all the wives of the Greeks into adultery to avenge the death of his son Palamedes, persuaded Penelope to commit adultery with one of the suitors. Far be it from me to believe that Penelope, whom the writings of many authors have made famous for her chastity, was anything but completely chaste just because one writer states the opposite. Her virtue is the more renowned and praiseworthy in that it is found only rarely, and in that the more urgently she was assailed, the more constantly and firmly did she persevere.

CHAPTER XXXIX

LAVINIA, QUEEN OF LAURENTUM

LAVINIA, the queen of Laurentum and a descendant of Saturn of Crete, was the only daughter of King Latinus and his wife Amata and finally became the wife of Aeneas, the brave leader of the Trojans. She was more famous for the war between Aeneas and the Rutulian Turnus than for any other deed of hers. Because of her singular beauty and her father's kingdom, to which she seemed to be the heir, she was eagerly sought as a wife by Turnus, who was a very ardent young man and king of the Rutulians. Lavinia's mother Amata had given him hope of success, and she eagerly furthered her nephew's interests.[1] But Latinus, who was a skilful soothsayer, heard from an oracle that he was to give his daughter in marriage to a foreign lord, and so he delayed giving in to his wife. In fact, when Aeneas came as a wanderer from Troy and asked for his friendship, he promised him his daughter because of the oracle as well as Aeneas' noble ancestors. For this reason war broke out between Aeneas and Turnus. After many battles the Trojans triumphed through the wounds, the blood, and the death of many noble men, and Aeneas married Lavinia after her mother Amata had hanged herself in rage.

There are some, nevertheless, who have said that the war took place after the marriage. But no matter how this happened, it is agreed that Lavinia bore a son to the famous prince Aeneas. Aeneas was killed near the Numicius River before she gave birth, and Lavinia, fearing her step-son Ascanius, who had become the ruler, retired into the forest, where she gave birth to Postumus, and according to some she gave him the name of Iulus Silvius.[2] Ascanius, however, feeling more charitable toward his step-mother than she thought, built Alba for himself and voluntarily left to

[1] According to tradition, Turnus was Amata's nephew.
[2] There are many different traditions about Ascanius and Silvius. Some have it that Ascanius was Lavinia's own son and the father of Silvius.

Lavinia her father's kingdom. Lavinia, having in her soul her family's ancient nobility, lived honorably and chastely. With great assiduity she held and preserved the kingdom until she turned it over undiminished to the boy Silvius. Some have said that after she had left the forest she married someone called Melampus and that Ascanius brought up Silvius with brotherly kindliness.

CHAPTER XL

THE TYRIAN DIDO OR ELISSA, QUEEN OF CARTHAGE

D IDO, who early in her life was called Elissa, was both the founder and the queen of Carthage. I should like to speak somewhat more at length in her praise, if with my modest remarks I may, perhaps, partly remove the infamy undeservedly cast on the honor of her widowhood. To start rather far back, the peoples of Phoenicia, famous for their industry, as is well known, came from almost the farthest part of Egypt to the shores of Syria, and there they built many famous cities, of which Agenor, famous in our times as well as in his, was king. It is believed that the glorious line of Dido descends from him. Her father was King Belus of Phoenicia, who died after conquering the island of Cyprus. At his death he left Elissa, still a young girl, and her brother Pygmalion, almost an adult, in the care of the Phoenicians. They set Pygmalion on his father's throne and gave the extremely beautiful Elissa as a wife to Acerbas (or Sychaeus or Sicharbas as some call him), who was the priest of Hercules and among the Tyrians enjoyed the greatest dignity next to the king. Dido and Acerbas loved each other with great purity. More than all other men, Pygmalion had an insatiable desire for gold, and Acerbas was very wealthy. Although, knowing the king's avarice, he kept his treasures hidden, he was unable to keep the fact that he was wealthy from being known. Pygmalion, drawn by greed and hoping to take his treasure, treacherously killed his brother-in-law when he was off his guard.

When Elissa learned this, she took it so much to heart that she almost died. Having spent much time in tears, and having often called upon her beloved Acerbas in vain, she called down every frightful curse on her brother's head. She then decided to flee, either because she was warned in a dream, as some say, or because she planned it herself, lest her brother's greed bring about her death also. She cast aside womanly weakness and hardened her spirit to manly strength, and for this she later deserved being called Dido, which in Phoenician means 'heroic.' First of all, she joined forces with some princes of the cities who she knew hated Pygmalion for various reasons. She seized her brother's ships, which had been readied either to send her away or for some other reason, and had them immediately manned by friendly sailors. At night she took her husband's treasure, whose hiding place she knew, and whatever she could take from her brother, and secretly had it placed on shipboard. With deliberate shrewdness she had many packages filled with sand and tied, pretending that they were Sychaeus' treasure, and had them loaded on board with everyone watching. When they were out on the high seas, she ordered that these packages be thrown into the water, to the surprise of those who did not know of the trick. In tears she vowed that after throwing Acerbas' treasure into the sea she would also find the death which she had long desired. But she said that she felt pity for the sailors, who, she had no doubt, would be cut to pieces together with her by the avaricious and cruel king if they returned to Pygmalion. But if they wanted to flee with her, she would not fail to take care of their needs. On hearing this, the wretched sailors, although they were sorrowfully leaving their homes and the country where they had been born, readily consented to go into exile for fear of cruel death. They changed course and sailed to Cyprus under her direction. There, as a solace to youth and to bring forth children, she carried off some girls who were on the shore making their customary sacrifice to Venus. She took as companion on her voyage the priest of Jupiter and all his family, who foresaw great things from that flight. Leaving Crete behind and Sicily on her right, she headed for Africa and the Massylian's shores and finally entered the gulf which later became well known. There she found a safe harbor for her ships and decided to allow the weary sailors some rest.

The inhabitants of the vicinity came, wanting to see the foreigners, and some brought food and goods, according to their custom. They began to speak together and make friends. Since it seemed to please the inhabitants that they remain there, and since ambassadors from the people of Utica, who also had previously come from Tyre, came to persuade them to remain, Dido bought from the landowners of the vicinity only as much land on the shore as could be encircled by the hide of an ox for establishing her settlement, so that it would not seem that she was injuring anyone, and so that no one would suspect she was doing something of great importance for the future. She did this without fear, in spite of the fact that she had heard that her brother was threatening war. Now, this was a woman's slyness, for at her orders the hide of the ox was cut into very thin strips, which when joined one to the other encircled much more land than the sellers had thought. Here she built a warlike city under the auspices of a horse's head which had been found; she called it Carthage and named the fortress Byrsa, after the ox hide. She showed the treasure which she had slyly kept hidden and encouraged her companions who had fled with her to high hopes.

They built city-walls, temples, a forum, and public and private buildings. She gave the people laws and regulations for living, and, as the noble city grew rapidly, Dido became famous throughout Africa for her great beauty such as had never been seen before and for her unheard-of virtue and chastity. Because of this, and since the people of Africa are greatly inclined towards sensuality, it happened that the king of the Musicani[1] desired her and asked her in marriage from the elders of Carthage, threatening to wage war and destroy the growing city if she were not given to him. The citizens, who knew the widowed queen's sacred and inflexible intention of chastity, feared greatly that they would be destroyed in war if the king's request were denied. When she questioned them, they did not dare to tell Dido what the king desired, and so they decided to deceive the queen and make her accede to their wishes through her own decision. They told her that the king wanted to bring his savage, barbaric people to a more civilized way of life through their instruction, and for this reason he was

[1] This was Hiarbas or Jarbas, the king and priest of the Gaetulians in Northern Africa.

requesting some teachers and threatening to wage war if they were not given to him. And they said that they knew not who would be willing to undertake that task, leaving his country to go and live with so harsh a king. The queen, who did not realize the deception, turned to them and said: "O noble citizens, what laziness, what negligence is this? Do you not know that we were born for father and country? Can he be said to be a true citizen who rejects death or other hardships if circumstances require them for the public weal? Go forth quickly, then, and with a little danger to yourselves repel the great fury of war."

It seemed to the princes that with these reproaches of the queen they had obtained what they desired. They therefore revealed to her the king's true demands. When she heard them, the queen realized that with her statement she had approved the request for marriage, and she grieved to herself, not daring to oppose her people's treachery. Remaining firm in her intention, she immediately came to a decision which seemed necessary to her honor and said that she would marry if she were given some time. This was granted her. At the time when the Trojan Aeneas, who had never been seen in that country, arrived, Dido had decided to die rather than forego her chastity, and so she built a great fire in the highest part of the city, which the citizens believed was to placate the soul of Sychaeus. Having performed various ceremonies and having sacrificed many animals, Dido, dressed in mourning, climbed onto the pyre in the presence of a great number of citizens, who were watching to see what she would do. When she had finished all these things, Dido, because of her vow, took out a knife that she had under her dress, placed it against her completely chaste breast, called out to Sychaeus, and said: "My citizens, I go to my husband, as you desire." As soon as she had uttered these few words, she let herself fall onto the knife, to the great sorrow of all the onlookers. Having pierced a vital spot, she died shedding her chaste blood, as they rushed to her aid in vain.

O inviolate honor of chastity! O venerable and eternal example of constant widowhood! O Dido, I wish that widows would turn their eyes to you, and that especially those who are Christian would contemplate your strength. And if they can, let them consider with attentive mind you who shed your chaste blood, especially those who lightly go, I will not say to a second, but to a third wedding or more. And I ask, what will they say who are marked with the emblem of Christ, when they see this pagan to whom Christ was completely unknown, proceed with such firm spirit to win fame and go with such firm determination towards a death given not by others, but by her own hand, rather than consent to a second marriage and allow her sacred wish to respect widowhood to be broken? Since our women show great finesse in excusing themselves, I believe that someone will say: "I had to do this: I was abandoned; my parents and my brothers were dead; suitors pressed me with flattery; I could not resist, for I am made of flesh and not of iron." How ridiculous! On whose aid could Dido count, who was in exile and whose only brother was an enemy? Did Dido not have many suitors? Was Dido made of stone or wood more than the women of our time? Certainly not! But having at least a brave heart, by dying she escaped in the only way she could the lure which she did not think she could resist with force. But we, who say that we are so abandoned, do we not have Christ as a refuge, the holy Redeemer Who is always present to those who place their hopes in Him? Do you think that He Who saved the children from the fiery furnace, Who saved Susanna from false accusations, cannot save you from your enemies' hands if you so desire? Lower your eyes to the ground, close your ears, and hurl back the oncoming waves like a reef, be firm and let the winds howl, and you will be safe.

Perhaps another woman will rise and say: "My domains stretched far and wide, I had a beautiful house, royal furnishings, and great wealth. I wanted to be a mother so that so much wealth would not go to strangers." O insane desire! Did Dido not have a kingdom without children? Did she not have a king's wealth? Certainly! She refused to become a mother because she very wisely thought that nothing is more foolish than to ruin oneself to aggrandize another. Shall I then put a blot on my chastity in order to give birth to an owner for my fields, my splendid house, my furnishings, when as so often happens he may prove to be a wastrel? And if you have great wealth, you certainly should spend it and not throw it away. The poor of Christ are many, and when you give to them you build eternal palaces for yourself; when you give to them you make your chastity shine with another splendor. In addition we have friends who are more suitable heirs than anyone else, because they are as we choose them; but children are not as we would like them, but as Nature grants.

A third woman will come and say that she had to marry again because her parents ordered her, her relatives forced her, her neighbors encouraged her, as if we did not know that if her unbridled lust had not spurred her — in fact commanded her — she would have overcome everything with a single denial. Dido was willing to die in order not to live dishonorably, but this woman could not refuse marriage in order to live honorably.

Another will present herself, who in her own opinion is more shrewd than the others, and will say: "I was a young woman. As you know, youth is ardent; I could not remain continent. Saint Paul says that it is better to marry than to burn, and I followed his advice." How well spoken! As if I commended chastity only to children, or as if Dido had not been a young woman when she determined to remain chaste. How wicked it is that Paul's advice, uttered in such a saintly way, should often be brought forward by shameless people in defense of a foul deed. We can restore lost strength with food, but we cannot diminish superfluous strength with abstinence. That pagan woman, for the sake of vain glory, was able to master her ardor and curb it. Cannot a Christian woman master it in order to acquire eternal glory? Alas! Thinking that we can deceive God in this way, we forego transitory glory, not to speak of the eternal, and place ourselves in danger of eternal damnation.

Let those who consider Dido's dead body be ashamed then, and, thinking of the reason for her death, let them bow their heads, and let Christian women grieve at being surpassed in chastity by that woman who was a limb of Satan. Let them not think that by mourning and dressing in black they have fulfilled all their duties to the dead. Love must be kept whole until the end if they want to fulfill the duties of widowhood, and they must not think of adulterously contracting another marriage, which some do more to avoid the blemish of lewdness and to satisfy their ardor under the false name of marriage, than to obey its sacrament. And what is looking for the company of so many men and being joined to so many if not entering brothels, following the example of Valeria Messalina? But I shall speak of this at another time. For I confess that I have greatly exceeded the limits of the work I have commenced. But who is so much master of himself that he is not occasionally drawn away from his purpose by his fervor? I beg the reader's pardon and return to the point where I digressed.

Well then, Dido's countrymen, amid public wails and sadness, accorded her not only human but divine honors and exalted her as much as they could with a magnificent funeral. And they honored her not only as their common mother and queen, but as a goddess, their protector, and they revered her with altars, temples, and sacrifices as long as Carthage stood.[2]

[2] This version of Dido's story is very different from that which is familiar through Virgil and Ovid, in which Dido succumbs to love for Aeneas and kills herself in despair when he leaves her. Boccaccio defends her and champions her cause especially against Dante, who placed Dido among the souls of the lustful and stresses the fact that she had not remained true to her husband's memory (Inferno V, 61, 62).

CHAPTER XLI

NICAULA, QUEEN OF ETHIOPIA

AS FAR as I can learn, the extreme barbarousness of Ethiopia produced Nicaula, who is the more worthy of remembrance in that, being born among uncivilized people, she shone the more brightly for her good conduct. If we are to put any faith in the ancients, it is clear that when the Pharaohs declined, she became a famous queen either of their descendants or of Ethiopia and Egypt, and, according to some, also of Arabia. She had a magnificent royal palace on the island of Meroe in the Nile, and had so much wealth there that it was believed she surpassed almost everyone else.

I have read that she did not give herself up to rest or womanly softness among the delights of wealth. In fact, although her teacher is not known to us, we do know that she had so much knowledge that it seemed miraculous. The sacred Scriptures also seem to attest this, and through their authority it is shown that she, called Saba by the Scriptures, marveled when she heard of the wisdom of Solomon, who flourished in her time and whose fame had already spread throughout the world, while fools and ignorant people are accustomed not to admire but to scorn such things. And what is more, not only was she amazed, but she came to Jerusalem to hear him, leaving her marvelous kingdom, which is almost at the end of the other side of the world. She passed through Ethiopia, Egypt, the shores of the Red Sea, and the deserts of Arabia with such a splendid retinue, magnificent expenditure, and royal multitude of retainers, that Solomon himself, the wealthiest of kings, was amazed by that woman's magnificence. He received her with great honor. After asking him some very difficult questions, she listened attentively to his explanation and willingly confessed that Solomon's wisdom greatly surpassed his reputation and the capacity of the human intellect, saying that without doubt it had been acquired through a gift of God and not through study. Then she gave him magnificent presents, among which it is believed were those small trees from which balsam comes, which Solomon later had planted and cultivated not far from Lake Asaltis.[1]

Finally she exchanged presents with him and returned home with great praise. There are some who believe that this woman was Candace, the great queen of Meroe, after whom the kings of Egypt were later called Candaces for a long time, as before they had been called Pharaohs.

[1] This name should be Asphaltites (the Dead Sea).

CHAPTER XLII

PAMPHILE, DAUGHTER OF PLATES

PAMPHILE, I find, was a woman of Greece. Time has erased knowledge of where she was born,[1] but it has kindly allowed her father's name to survive, for it is recorded that she was the daughter of a man called Plates. Although she cannot be adorned with the greatest honors, she must not be cheated of her share of praise through silence, since she did some good for humanity. For no matter how easy it may appear afterwards, nothing new has been discovered by anyone without its proving the power of his intellect and bringing glory in proportion to its quality. Authors who are considered trustworthy say that she was the first to pick cotton from plants and cleanse it of residual matter with the comb. After it was combed, she put it on the distaff and showed how to make thread from it and how to weave it. Thus she established its use, which had been unknown up to her time. The invention of this art clearly shows how worthy Pamphile must have been in other respects.

---

[1] Pliny the Elder states that Pamphile was born in Cea. Apparently there was a gap in Boccaccio's copy of this author's work, which he used as a source for this chapter.

CHAPTER XLIII

RHEA ILIA, VESTAL VIRGIN

IN former times Rhea Ilia[1] stood out among the people of Italy for the great splendor of her noble lineage, for she was a descendant of the Silvii, who reigned as kings of the Albans and were descendants of Aeneas, the glorious leader of the Trojans. She was the daughter of Numitor, the king of the said Albans. While she was still a girl, it happened that Numitor's younger brother Amulius, spurred by desire for power and scorning the rights of man, overthrew Numitor by force. Brotherly love prevented his being cruel to Numitor, and he was satisfied to force him into retirement in the country. But he was cruel and harsh toward Lausus, Numitor's young son, to remove a rival for the throne. He killed him but spared his sister Ilia, who was still a girl. But to remove all hopes of her having husband and children, he made her a Vestal and forced her to take a vow of perpetual virginity. When she grew up, spurred by concupiscence, she was intimate with some man, although it is not known how. This was disclosed by her distended belly, for she became pregnant and gave birth to the twins Romulus and Remus, founders of the city of Rome. Because of this sin, although she was a royal woman, she was buried alive, and her children were exposed by ancient law and by royal command. Although her body was covered with earth, her children's noble work raised her name to the highest pinnacle of fame and caused the woman whom the tyrant attempted to destroy with sacred law to be honored by future generations.

So, when I consider this woman and see the bands and sacred vestments of nuns hiding furtive love, I cannot help laughing at the madness of some people. There are even men who, like misers, take away from their daughters their pittance of a dowry; under the pretext of devotion, they confine—or should I say condemn?—their daughters to nuns' cells, sometimes when they are still quite

[1] She is usually known as Rhea Silvia; Ilia is also used as her name, but not in combination with Rhea.

young, sometimes when almost mature. They say that they have dedicated those virgins to God so that with their prayers their own affairs will prosper more, and after death they will gain eternal life. This is ridiculous and foolish. They do not know that an idle woman serves Venus and that these nuns greatly envy public prostitutes, whose chambers they think preferable to their own cells. And when nuns see the marriages of secular women, their varied dresses and ornaments, dances and festivals, and realize that they themselves have no experience of marriage, they deem themselves widows from the beginning of their lives, lament their lot, curse and damn with their whole mind the souls of their parents, their own bands, and their cloisters. To console their saddened hearts, they have recourse only to thinking how they can destroy their prison and flee, or at least bring their lovers inside, trying to take furtively the pleasure which has been denied them, since they have been deprived of open marriage. And these are the contemplations of God, I won't say of all, but of the greater number; these are the prayers which rise up to heaven to prosper and save those who have imprisoned them. Wretched are parents and other relatives if they think that others can endure what they themselves avoid and cannot bear. Often they must bewail disgraceful adultery, shameful births, their grandchildren abandoned or unnaturally murdered, and their daughters shamefully expelled or, sometimes, escaping from the cloister. In the end it is necessary to support in disgrace women who could have been given away in marriage while still pure.

Let fools know, then, if they do not wish to measure the strength of others by their own, that girls must not be consecrated to God while ignorant, or young, or under coercion. On the contrary, they should be well brought up from childhood in the parental home, taught honesty and praiseworthy behavior, and then, when they are grown and with their entire mind know what they are doing, let them submit to the yoke of perpetual virginity of their own free will and not under duress. But I believe that there would be very few of these. It is, however, much better that their number be small and thus formed, rather than profane the sanctuary of God with a multitude of deceived women.

CHAPTER XLIV

GAIA CYRILLA, WIFE OF TARQUINIUS PRISCUS

ALTHOUGH I do not find any record of Gaia Cyrilla's[1] origin, I nevertheless believe that she was Roman or Etruscan. This is confirmed by the authority of the ancients, because she was the beloved wife of Tarquinius Priscus, the king of the Romans. Since this woman had an excellent mind, she did not allow herself to languish idly, in spite of the fact that she was the wife of a king and dwelled in a royal palace. In fact, she dedicated herself to the art of working in wool, which I believe was an honorable occupation among the Latins at that time. She was such a noble craftsman in this and so diligent that her fame has endured up to our times, and in her own she was not without public reward. For, since she was greatly loved by the Romans, who had not yet been corrupted by the delights of Asia, it was ordered by public law that when a woman first married she be asked her name on entering her husband's house, and she would immediately answer that her name was Gaia,[2] as if this were an omen of future virtue. Although this may seem a trifle to the proud spirits of modern people, I do not doubt at all that to wise men, considering the simplicity of those times, it will seem an indication of an excellent and most praiseworthy woman.

---

[1] This name should be Gaia Caecilia.

[2] Gaius and Gaia were the names given to the bride and groom at a wedding. The bride would use this formula: *Ubi tu Gaius, ego Gaia.*

CHAPTER XLV

SAPPHO, POETESS OF LESBOS

THE poetess Sappho was a girl from the city of Mytilene
in the island of Lesbos. No other fact has reached us about
her origin. But if we examine her work, we will see part
of what time has destroyed restored to her; that is, the fact that she
was born of honorable and noble parents, for no vile soul could
have desired to write poetry, nor could a plebeian one have written
it as she did.[1] Although it is not known when she flourished, she
nevertheless had so fine a talent that in the flower of youth and
beauty she was not satisfied solely with writing in prose, but,
spurred by the greater fervor of her soul and mind, with diligent
study she ascended the steep slopes of Parnassus and on that high
summit with happy daring joined the Muses, who did not nod in
disapproval. Wandering through the laurel grove, she arrived at
the cave of Apollo, bathed in the waters of Castalia, and took up
Phoebus' plectrum. As the sacred nymphs danced, this girl did not
hesitate to strike the strings of the cithara and bring forth melody.

All these things seem very difficult even for well-educated men.
Why say more? Through her eagerness she reached such heights
that her verses, which according to ancient testimony were very
famous, are still brilliant in our own day. A bronze statue was
erected and consecrated to her name, and she was included among
the famous poets. Certainly neither the crown of kings, the papal
tiara, nor the conqueror's laurel is more splendid than her glory.
But, if the story is true, she was as unhappy in love as she was
happy in her art. For she fell in love with a young man and was
the prey of this intolerable pestilence either because of his charm
and beauty or for other reasons. He refused to accede to her desires, and, lamenting his obstinate harshness, Sappho wrote mourn-
ful verses. I should have thought that they were elegiacs, since they

[1] Boccaccio's lofty concept of poetry is well known. His reverential attitude
towards poetry is expressed in all his works, especially in his life of Dante and
his *Genealogia Deorum Gentilium*.

are appropriate to such subjects, had I not read that she scorned the verse forms used by her predecessors and wrote a new kind of verse in a meter different from others. This kind of verse is still named Sapphic after her. Are the Muses to be blamed? They were able to move the stones of Ogygia when Amphion played, but they were unwilling to soften the young man's heart in spite of Sappho's songs.

CHAPTER XLVI

LUCRETIA, WIFE OF COLLATINUS

LUCRETIA, the outstanding model of Roman chastity and sacred glory of ancient virtue, was the daughter of Spurius Lucretius Tricipitinus, a very famous man among the Romans, and she was the wife of Tarquinius Collatinus, who was the son of Egerius, the brother of Tarquinius Priscus.[1] It is not certain whether she seemed more lovely than the other Roman women because of her beauty or because of her virtue. When Tarquinius Superbus was besieging the city of Ardea, Lucretia went to her husband's house near the fortress of Collatia, not far from the city of Rome. The siege lasted a long time, and it happened that the royal youths, among whom was Collatinus, were having supper one evening, and, perhaps warmed by too much wine, they began to argue about their wives' honor. As usual, each one placed his own ahead of the others. They came to the conclusion that while everyone thought they were away at war they would go on fast horses to their unsuspecting wives, and by seeing with their own eyes how they fulfilled their duties that night they

---

[1] Egerius was the nephew, not the brother of Tarquinius Priscus.

would settle their dispute more surely. In Rome they found the royal women enjoying themselves with their equals. They then turned their horses and went to Collatia, where they found Lucretia weaving with her ladies and dressed without any ornaments. For this reason, everyone agreed that she seemed more praiseworthy than the others. Collatinus kindly welcomed the other young men into his house. While they were being entertained there, Sextus, the son of Tarquinius Superbus, cast shameless eyes on the beauty and virtue of this chaste woman, and burning with evil love, decided in his own mind to have her through force if he could not enjoy her charms in any other way.

Not many days later, spurred on by his madness, Sextus secretly left the camp at night and went to Collatia. Since he was her husband's relative, Lucretia received him hospitably and welcomed him. But when he saw that the whole house was silent, thinking that everyone was asleep, Sextus entered Lucretia's bedroom with drawn sword. He made himself known to her and threatened to kill her if she cried out or did not give in to his desire. Because she refused his wishes and did not fear death, he stooped to a damnable trick. He said that he would slay one of her manservants next to her and tell everybody that he had killed them after having found them together in adultery. When she heard this, the trembling woman stood still, frightened by such a wicked disgrace. Fearing that if she died there would be no one to avenge her innocence, she unwillingly gave her body to the adulterer. Sextus satisfied his wicked desire and left like a conqueror, as he thought.

As soon as day broke, Lucretia, suffering from this wicked crime, sent for her father Tricipitinus, Collatinus' relative Brutus, who up to that day had been considered mad, and other relatives by blood, in addition to her husband. When they came to her, she told them tearfully in order what Sextus had done in the dead of night. As her relatives consoled her while she cried wretchedly, she took out a knife that she had under her dress and said: "Although I absolve myself of the sin, I do not free myself from the punishment, and in the future no woman will live dishonorably because of Lucretia's example." Having said these words, she drove the knife into her innocent breast, fell wounded and dying in the presence of her husband and her father, and soon poured out her soul together with her blood.

Hers was an unfortunate beauty. She cleansed her shame harshly, and for this reason she should be exalted with worthy praise for her chastity, which can never be sufficiently lauded. Because of her action, not only was her reputation restored, which a lewd young man had tried to destroy with the stain of sin, but Rome was made free.[2]

---

[2] Angered by this example of Tarquinian tyranny, the Romans expelled the Tarquins and established the Republic.

CHAPTER XLVII

THAMYRIS, QUEEN OF SCYTHIA

THAMYRIS[1] was a famous queen of Scythia. It is not known whose daughter she was, and to whom she was married, because the Scythians dwell in a sterile country under cold skies near the Rhiphaean and the Hyperborean Mountains, and so they are known only to themselves. She is famous for splendid nobility, for she governed a wild and rough people at the time when Cyrus ruled in Asia Minor.

Cyrus coveted the kingdom of the Scythians, perhaps so that Thamyris might be known better. He wanted to enhance his glory rather than enlarge his empire, for he had certainly heard that the Scythians were a poor and savage race, but he had also heard that they had never been conquered even by the greatest kings. So then, spurred on by his greed, he led his army against the queen of the Scythians, who was a widow. When she heard of his arrival, although he was feared throughout Asia and throughout almost the whole world because of his great deeds, she did not look for a place to hide like a fearful woman and did not seek terms of

[1] She is more commonly known as Tomyris.

peace through an ambassador. Instead she gathered her armies and became their leader in war. Although she could have opposed him with naval forces, she cleverly allowed him to cross the river Araxes with all his army and enter her country, thinking that she could overcome Cyrus' fury far better in her own land. When she was certain that he had entered her kingdom, she entrusted one-third of her army to her only son,[2] still a youngster, and ordered him to go and fight Cyrus. Hearing that the young man was coming with his army, Cyrus weighed both the characteristics of the terrain and the customs of those people, and decided to win by deceit rather than bravery. He pretended to flee, leaving his camp full of wine (which was not yet known to the Scythians), food, and other delicacies. The young man happily entered the camp together with his Scythians, almost like a conqueror, as if he had hurled back the enemy and had been invited with his men to feast and not to fight. They all began to gorge themselves with the food and drink with which they were not yet acquainted. This destroyed the soldiers' discipline, and they soon fell asleep. As they lay buried in slumber, Cyrus came and killed the young man and his army. Then, feeling almost certain of victory, he advanced farther.

Thamyris heard of the slaughter of her men, and although she grieved deeply for the death of her only son, she did not give herself up to tears like a woman. Repressing her tears with anger and desire for vengeance, with the remainder of her people she thought that she could destroy her enemy, in spite of his shrewdness, by using the same stratagem which had killed her son. She did not, however, leave a camp full of food for Cyrus' men. Knowing the country, she pretended to flee and led the eagerly pursuing enemy along a short stretch of road into bare, bitter-cold mountains. She then encircled them among mountains and desolate places, where they lacked almost all necessities. She then turned on them and destroyed almost the entire army. Cyrus himself did not escape; in fact by his bloody death he satisfied the widow's wrath. With ferocious spirit, she had Cyrus' body sought among

[2] Spargapises.

the others; and when it was found, she had the head cut off and ordered that it be placed in a leather bottle filled with the blood of her men. Almost as if giving burial to the proud king, she said: "Have your fill of the blood for which you thirsted." But finally, what more can we say? We know nothing more of this woman. She was famous in proportion to the power of Cyrus.

CHAPTER XLVIII

THE COURTESAN LEAENA

I T IS my opinion that Leaena was a Greek woman, and although she had no shame, I should like to place her among these famous women, begging the pardon of virtuous ladies and illustrious queens. For, as I have previously said, I did not promise to speak only of chaste women but of famous ones, no matter to what their fame might be due. Moreover, we are so devoted to virtue, that we cannot glorify only what we see in honored places, but must make an effort to bring out into worthy light what is hidden by shameful crimes. For virtue is valuable everywhere and is not stained by the blots of vice, just as the sun's rays are not sullied when they touch mud. Therefore, if at times we see virtue fixed in the breast of someone given to detestable practices, we must condemn those practices but not lessen the praise of that virtue, which is so much the more marvelous in that the person in question had been thought incapable of it. Therefore, one must not always despise the posthumous fame of courtesans. On the contrary, if they become worthy of remembrance because of some virtue, they should be glorified with greater and more felicitous praise, for virtue found in them shames lustful queens, while the vileness of queens excuses a prostitute's shamelessness. In addition, to show that noble spirits are not connected only with high titles and that virtue does not scorn anyone who desires it, Leaena must be included in a group of such famous women, so that she will be praised as very worthy in that respect in which she acted bravely.

The fact that Leaena gave herself to disgraceful prostitution, a hateful profession, has caused her family and her country to remain unknown. When Amyntas was king of Macedonia, the noble young men Armonius and Ariston killed the cruel tyrant Hyspar, moved either by desire to free their country from servitude to shameful tyranny or by other reasons.[1] Among the hostages seized by the man who succeeded that tyrant was Leaena, as one who had known of the deed because of her familiarity with its perpetrators. Subjected to cruel torture to make her name the conspirators, this dissolute woman nobly thought of the value of the holy and venerable name of friendship. Fearing that force would make her save herself by harming others, at first she steeled herself for a long time with marvelous constancy against answering what she was asked. Finally, as the tortures increased and her bodily strength ebbed, this valiant woman feared that her determination would weaken with her strength. She rose to even greater firmness and acted so that her ability to speak was lost together with her strength. She bit sharply down on her tongue, severed it, and spat it out. Thus with a single act, but a most noble one, she took from her tormentors all hope of learning from her what they were seeking.

Who will not admit that it was Fortune's fault that Leaena dwelled in brothels? Certainly, the person who said that women keep silent only about what they do not know did not know

---

[1] Boccaccio is slightly mistaken on each of these names. Harmodius and Aristogiton killed Hipparchus, whose elder brother Hippias was actually the tyrant. But the two brothers were closely associated in control of Athens after their father Pisistratus' death, and so they are often referred to as joint tyrants.

Leaena. Alas! Sometimes immodest wealth at home and excessive indulgence by their parents lead girls to their ruin. If their wanton tendency is not severely curbed and if they are not held back by the continuous watchfulness of their mothers, they will sometimes fall even if not tempted. And if despair for the loss of their honor and virginity is added to this fall, they will never return home under any circumstances. I believe that Leaena went astray because of this apathy and not because of an evil nature, especially when I consider her manly strength in the face of torture. Certainly, first with her silence and then by biting off her tongue, she gained no less glory than Demosthenes gained among his people with his florid eloquence.

CHAPTER XLIX

ATHALIAH, QUEEN OF JERUSALEM

ATHALIAH'S cruelty made her known among the Syrians and the Egyptians more than was good for the descendants of David. Her family, which was completely stained with the murder of servants and with many deaths, brought bad repute to her name as much as it brought the glory of royal crowns. First, she was the daughter of Ahab, the king of Israel, and of Queen Jezebel, a very wicked woman, and she was the wife of Jehoram son of Jehoshaphat, the king of Jerusalem. Finally, Jehoshaphat and his elder son Ahaziah, who had succeeded to the throne at his father's death,[1] were gotten rid of. Athaliah's husband Jehoram was crowned king of Jerusalem, contrary to public expectation, and he wanted his wife to be queen. When Ahab was dead, Athaliah's brother Jehoram, who succeeded to the throne of his father and his father's son,[2] added great glory to her splendor. As time passed, she was troubled with many misfortunes, but after her husband's death she saw her son Ahaziah on his father's throne, so that this woman had the lustre of royal honors on every side.

When Ahaziah died of an arrow wound, this fierce woman, burning with the desire to rule, thought of a memorable plan and steeled herself to put it into action. Casting aside feminine pity, not only did she fail to mourn her son, but gave reason for more tears, if she had had a woman's heart. While the earth was still wet with her son's blood, she drew sword against all the descendants of David's lineage. She persecuted them until no male member of that family was left alive. Only the little boy Jehoash,

---

[1] Boccaccio confuses Jehoram of Judah with Jehoram of Israel. Jehoshaphat did not have a son called Ahaziah, who succeeded him. Ahaziah was the son of Ahab and was the elder brother of Jehoram of Israel, not Jehoram of Judah. Jehoram of Israel succeeded Ahaziah, and Jehoram of Judah succeeded his father Jehoshaphat.

[2] Ahaziah, the son of Ahab and brother of Jehoram of Israel.

King Ahaziah's son, who was taken away without her knowledge, escaped her cruelty. For Athaliah's daughter Jehosheba,[3] who was Ahaziah's sister, secretly took away the boy and brought him to the house of her husband, the high priest Jehoiada, to be brought up in safety. And so reckless Athaliah wickedly dared to seat herself upon the royal throne over the blood of so many dead, since through her handiwork there were no claimants left, and to rule the affairs of the kingdom.

Why should we be surprised at Atreus, Dionysius, and Jugurtha, men of stern nature, if we hear that, spurred on by desire for power, they became rulers through the wounds of their own kinsmen, when we see that a woman killed all the royal line without sparing her own family in order to reach such rank? Athaliah was resplendent in the jewels of the royal crown, but, to be sure, was remarkable more for being bathed in blood than for royal dignity. Certainly, as she had willingly been cruel and merciless with her sword against the innocent lives of the family of David, just so did she feel the bitterness of others against her own family. If she had wanted, she could easily have seen her brother Jehoram, king of Israel, lying in the field of Naboth pouring out his blood to the dogs through his many wounds. In the same way her mother Jezebel, although decked in royal vestments, was thrown from a high tower and trampled by the feet of men running by, and she was so trampled by feet and wheels that she was turned into mud and no vestige of the wretched body remained. And thus she was able to see her seventeen brothers killed in one hour by order of their conqueror near Samaria and their heads fixed on sharp poles around their city of Jezreel as evidence of their distinguished deeds. And her other relatives were killed, so that there was no one who had not been slain by the enemy's sword. Finally, so that the wicked woman would not remain unpunished for the blood she had shed, after she had reigned seven years, she saw her grandchild Jehoash, whom she thought had been killed with the others, made king through the

[3] This name is Jehoshabeath in II Chronicles 22: 11, but Jehosheba in II Kings 11: 2.

help of the high priest Jehoiada, and she herself was forced from the royal throne. While the people shouted against her, she was shamefully dragged to the carriage entrance by her servants and ruffians, while she shouted and threatened in vain. Then she was killed for her deserts, so that this wicked woman went to hell over the same road she had forced her innocent victims to travel.

Thus acts divine justice, which if it delays does not forget, and moves with harsher punishment against those whom it does not see mend their accustomed ways. As long as we neglect to think of it, as long as we do not want to believe in it and do not care to reform, we bind ourselves with greater sins until when we least expect it we are swallowed by the tempest, and miserably we mourn our sins when it is of no avail. Certainly desire for the throne is unreasonable and tends toward law-breaking, and in most cases royal power is gained through cruelty. Only rarely does one gain it through Fortune, and usually it is necessary to ascend a throne through fraud or violence. If one ascends it through fraud, his thoughts must be tormented by deceit, artifices, snares, treachery, and similar things. If he gains it through violence, he must be plagued by uprisings, rebellions, whisperings, cruelty and madness. And no matter how one reaches it, he must use the power of wicked men, for without being their servant one cannot be the ruler of a kingdom. What more shall I say? When someone rises to a throne, he must perforce close his ears to laments, turn his eyes away from tears, crimes, and murders, and harden his heart into stone. Cruelty is spurred, justice destroyed, reason scorned, offenses honored, power, taken away from the Law, is given to one's whims, wickedness is invoked and simplicity is scorned, while rapine, luxury, and gluttony, which are a glorious king's first rewards, are praised. Neither divine nor human concerns are spared, the sacred and the accursed are confused, and mercy, overwhelmed by great sins, is changed into blood. Pious men are prostrated on the ground, the wicked are exalted, virgins are violated, and boys led into aberration. Virtue is damned, vice excused, and discord triumphs everywhere, banishing peace.

O marvelous road to the throne! And when the throne is gained with bloodshed and inhuman deeds, what then? If when they have gained it in any way they would at least live without doing harm! But at once, moved by suspicion, they send the elders into exile, reduce the wealthy to poverty, banish old friends, and imprison and kill as rivals brothers, children, nephews, and parents. There is no trustfulness or piety; no justice remains. They are anxiously watchful, sleep with difficulty, do not eat without fear, and entrust their lives to wicked men, having first banished the trustworthy. O what a beautiful, desirable, and praiseworthy possession power is when once acquired! It would have been better to enter a poor man's small hut, filled with peace and safety, strong and devoid of cares.[4] The more these lofty things are sought with bloodshed, the more they are retained with fear. Having banished those whom we suspect and, the crime requiring it, having entrusted ourselves to the deceitful, it often happens that through their work our end is similar to, or worse than, the beginning, and in one hour with our death we lose what was evilly put together through many unlucky days. Athaliah learned this, but too late.

[4] Boccaccio is not indulging in rhetoric. This passage reflects his genuine desire for a life of "literary leisure" and peace of mind.

CHAPTER L

CLOELIA, A ROMAN VIRGIN

EITHER the ancients did not preserve it for posterity, or time has destroyed knowledge about the parents of the marvelous Roman virgin Cloelia. But we may very well think that she was born of noble parents, for this is shown by the loftiness of her soul and by the fact that at the time of the war with Tarquinius Superbus she was handed over to Porsenna, the king of the Etruscans, together with other noble Roman women, as a hostage.

So that I may fully explain her praiseworthy courage, we must notice the fact that after Tarquinius Superbus had been overthrown as king because of the wicked crime committed by his son Sextus against Lucretia, open war broke out to prevent his returning treacherously. At the request of Tarquinius, Porsenna, the king of Clusium, entered the war. Since the Etruscans had been prevented from crossing the Sublician bridge by the bravery of Horatius Cocles in defending it, and since they were terrified by the determination, audacity, and plans of Mucius Scaevola, Porsenna came to an agreement with the Romans, and as a guaranty he took a number of hostages. Cloelia happened to be sent to him together with a number of other maidens. Since perhaps she did not think it honorable for the Republic that so many virgins be kept by a foreign king, Cloelia armed her womanly breast with a man's boldness. Evading her guards, by night she led many of the hostages to the bank of the Tiber, and there she mounted a horse, which she happened to find grazing near the river, although she had never been on one before. Unafraid of the river's depth and the swirling waters, she brought them all safely to the other shore and returned them to their families.

In the morning Porsenna learned of this and complained. In the full Senate it was ordered that the girl who had been the leader of the fugitives be returned to the king who demanded her, with the proviso that at the proper time he was to return her unharmed to her people. But the king, amazed by the girl's courage and pleased by her daring, not only allowed her to return to her people, but gave her permission to take along whatever hostages she pleased. Of all of them, Cloelia took only the children. This seemed praiseworthy rectitude on her part and pleased the Romans greatly, because she had freed those who were of an age more susceptible to harm. For this reason she was honored by the grateful citizens with an unusual honor, and an equestrian statue was accorded her. This statue was placed at the highest point of the Sacred Way, where it remained intact for a long time.

CHAPTER LI

THE GREEK WOMAN HIPPO

HIPPO was a Greek woman, as is clearly shown in the books of the ancients. I will hardly believe that she was great because of only one excellent deed, for we rise to lofty things gradually, and therefore no one becomes great suddenly. But since through the malignity of time knowledge of her family, her country, and other things done by her has perished, I thought that I would manifest the one deed of hers which has come down to us, so that it will not perish and the honor due her will not be taken away.

Well then, we are told that Hippo happened to be captured by enemy sailors. She was a beautiful woman, and, hearing those who had seized her make plans against her and against her honor, she valued the purity of chastity so highly that, since she could not safeguard it except through death, she did not wait for violence but threw herself headlong into the sea, where she lost her life but saved her honor. Who will not praise so firm a decision on the part of a woman? For at the cost of the few years with which she could perhaps have prolonged her life, she saved her chastity, and with her premature death she gained eternal honor for herself. The tempestuous sea could not keep hidden her virtuous deed, nor could the deserted shore prevent the perpetual testimony of literature from preserving it to her honor in the eyes of men. After being mockingly tossed by the waves for a while, her body was hurled onto the Erythraean shore, where the inhabitants of that country buried it like that of one who had been shipwrecked. But finally, when words spoken by her enemies disclosed her identity and the reason for her death, the Erythraeans with deep reverence built a great, long-lasting tomb on the shore where she had been buried, as a memorial to her chastity, so that we might know that virtue's splendor cannot be obscured by any adversity of Fortune.

CHAPTER LII

MEGULLIA DOTATA

MEGULLIA, who was also called Dotata by the ancient Romans, was a noble Roman woman in that primitive and, if I may say so, holy age when the worthy Romans had not yet left the nursing arms of poverty to rush forth seeking the splendors of Asia and the treasures of great kings, forsaking the poverty which once they had held in esteem. I believe that Megullia acquired the name of Dotata more through the lavishness of her ancestors than through the worthiness of any of her own deeds. For at that time it seemed such a marvelous thing to give 500,000 bronze coins as dowry to one's husband that the name of Dotata was bestowed on the woman who gave it.[1] This name lasted a long time, so that if anything extra was added to a girl's dowry, she was immediately called Megullia Dotata.

O wonderful simplicity! O praiseworthy poverty! What because of you seemed marvelous, and justly so, would seem laughable to our modern fancy. For we have exaggerated to such an extreme that you will hardly find a cobbler, carpenter, servant, sutler, or steward who will take a wife for so small a dowry. And this is not surprising, for even ordinary women have taken the crowns of queens, gold brooches, bracelets, and other ornaments, and wear them proudly, not to say shamelessly. Alas, I do not know whether to say that our souls have been improved by wealth (as we all too easily convince each other) or rather that vice, ambition, and men's insatiable desires have been cultivated by our own fault (which is what I really believe).

[1] Dotata means "richly dowered." Manuscripts of Valerius Maximus iv.4.10, which Boccaccio used as his source, disagree widely about the amount of money in Megullia's dowry.

CHAPTER LIII

VETURIA

THE noble Roman lady Veturia, when already old, by a praiseworthy deed gave her years perpetual freshness. She had a young son named Gnaeus Marcius, very brave and of ready wit and hands. Since the Volscian city of Corioli, anything. For this reason, when Rome was suffering because of lack of grain and the senators had a great quantity of it brought from Sicily, in a violent speech he forbade its distribution among the plebeians until the nobles should be restored to the prerogatives that the plebeians had shortly before taken from them before returning from the *Mons Sacer* whither they had withdrawn in revolt. The hostile plebeians, starved as they were, would certainly have attacked him if their tribune had not very opportunely appointed a day for discussing the question. Because he was angry, Coriolanus did not appear and was condemned to exile.

He fled to the Volscians, who shortly before had been the enemies of Rome, and was kindly received with honors, for bravery is valued everywhere. And he brought the Volscians to war once when besieged by the Romans, was thought to have been conquered through his prowess, he gained the name of Coriolanus and such good will among the nobles that he dared do or say more against the Romans through his deceit as well as that of Attius Tullius. Named commander by them, he led the army to the Cluilian dikes, four miles from Rome. He reduced the Romans to a point where they sent ambassadors to him, an exile, to sue for peace on just conditions. Marcius sent them back home with a harsh answer. Because of this the ambassadors were sent once again, but they were not received. The third time, the priests in their vestments and badges of office went to him as humble suppliants but returned without results. Complete despair had already entered the souls of the Romans, when many women went in tears to Coriolanus' mother Veturia and his wife Volumnia. They prevailed on Veturia to undertake the great journey to the enemy's camp together with his wife to calm her son with prayers and tears, since men and arms seemed unable to defend the Republic. Many other women went with her.

When Coriolanus heard of her arrival, he was dismayed at her coming, and, although his heart was filled with anger, he rose from his chair, left his tent, and went towards his mother to receive her. With Coriolanus' wife on one side and his children on the other, Veturia cast aside motherly love and became angry as soon as she saw her son. She had left Rome as a suppliant to go to the enemy's camp, but she now became the castigator, and gathering strength in her feeble body said to him: "Stand still, wild youth. Before I embrace you, I wish to know whether you have come to receive me as your mother or as a captive enemy. I am an enemy. Was old age, which men desire, to lead me to this, that I, wretched woman that I am, have seen you condemned to exile and then fighting against the Republic? I ask whether you know on what soil you bear arms. You do indeed, but if you do not know it, this is the land where you were conceived, where you were born, where you were raised through my labor. With what feelings then, with what thoughts, with what fury have you been able to bear arms as an enemy? When entering by force, did you not remember the honor due your mother, the sweet love for your wife, filial devotion, and natural reverence for your fatherland? Were these things not able to move your bitter breast, could they not extinguish your wrath, even if it were justified? When you first saw these walls, did you not think, 'There are my home, my father's gods and mine; there is my wife; there are my children; there to her misfortune and through my fault is my mother?' The senators came to you, and the priests too, but their entreaties were not able to move your stony breast to do what you should have done of your own will. I consider myself very wretched, for the child I bore has turned against his country and me. Where I thought that I had given birth to a son and a citizen, I see that I gave birth to a most hostile and implacable enemy. It would have been much better if I had not borne you, for by my sterility Rome could have remained unbesieged, and I, poor wretched old woman, could have died in a free country. But I can never suffer anything sadder for me and more shameful for you, nor shall I endure long, completely miserable as I am. Of these children of yours, consider that if you persevere they will either die before their time or will live in slavery for many a year."

After these words there came tears, and then his wife's and his children's prayers, mutual embraces with his children, and the laments of the women who cried and begged. And these words, tears, and prayers, made the wrath of the bitter leader vanish through reverence for his mother, and his mind was changed. Neither the majesty of the ambassadors nor reverence for priests had been able to do this. Having embraced his family and taken leave of them, Coriolanus made the army withdraw from Rome. Because of this, and in order that the glory of that woman would not be diminished by ingratitude, the Senate decreed that a temple and a stone altar be erected to Fortuna Muliebris in perpetual memory of her deed in the place where Veturia had softened her son's wrath. This temple, although very ancient, has endured up to our time almost undamaged. The Senate also decreed that at their passage men rise and give way to women, who up to that time had received little or no respect from men. This custom is still observed in our country through ancient usage. They were also permitted to wear the ancient ornament of Oriental women on their ears, dresses of royal purple, and gold brooches and bracelets.

There are some who assert that through this same decree of the Senate women were enabled to receive inheritances from anyone, something which previously had not been allowed. And some think that it is doubtful whether that reward was more hateful to men or more pleasing to women. But I think that there is no doubt at all, for because of these distinctions the husbands' wealth is depleted, and women go adorned with royal finery; men become poor, losing the inheritance of their ancestors, while women become rich gaining it; deserving women are honored, but so are ignoble ones. All this has been disadvantageous to men and useful to women. If the liberty of Rome had not been saved by her prayers, I would curse Veturia for the haughtiness which women have acquired because of these things. But I cannot praise the excessive generosity of the Senate and the harmful custom which has lasted for so many centuries. The women would have been satisfied with a lesser gift. The temple consecrated to Fortuna Muliebris seemed a very great thing. But what can I say? The world belongs to women, and men are womanish. Time, which consumes many useful things, has not been able to destroy what was detrimental to men, nor has it been able to diminish the prerogatives of women, since they have held on to them with tenacious perseverance. Let them applaud Veturia, then, and honor her name whenever they adorn themselves with precious jewels, royal vestments, and gold brooches, and whenever men stand up as they go by, and let them squander in idleness the wealth of the dead.

CHAPTER LIV

THE PAINTER THAMYRIS

IN HER time Thamyris[1] was a fine painter. Although time may have lessened her excellence, it has not yet been able to destroy her fame and her skill. It is said that in the time of the ninetieth Olympiad[2] she was the daughter of the painter Micon. But I have read that there were two Micons famous in Athens at the same time, and they were both painters. The only differentiation between them is found in the statement that she was the daughter of the Micon who was also called Minor. No matter whose daughter she may have been, she had such marvelous talent that she scorned the duties of women and practiced her father's art. When Archelaus was king of Macedonia, she acquired such great glory in painting that the Ephesians, who venerated Diana with special honors, kept for a long time a painting of that goddess done by Thamyris on a panel and guarded it as a precious thing. It lasted for a long time and gave such great testimony of her skill that it has seemed marvelous up to modern times. And she should be praised even more if we consider the spindles and baskets of other women.

[1] This name should be Timarete.

[2] Pliny the Elder, whose work was used by Boccaccio as his source for this chapter, does not mention the ninetieth Olympiad in connection with Timarete.

CHAPTER LV

ARTEMISIA, QUEEN OF CARIA

ARTEMISIA, the queen of Caria, was a woman of noble spirit and saintly love, and an eternal example of chaste widowhood for posterity. Although knowledge of her parents or native country has not come down to our day, it is sufficient to know in praise of her nobility that she was the wife of Mausolus, the powerful king of Caria. She loved him so much in life that, surviving after his death, she could not forget him. A wonderful monument to her love endured for a long time, for, if one can believe famous authors, as soon as her loving husband died she paid special honors to his corpse. After he had been cremated and his ashes had been carefully collected, she did not allow them to be placed in a golden urn to be preserved. She thought that any receptacle would be unsuitable for such a beloved husband except that breast within which the flame of her old love burned more than usually after his death. For this reason, in order that the remains of his earthly body be placed where there was perpetual memory of his past life, she gathered his ashes, mixed them in a drink, and slowly drank it. The rest of her life was devoted to mourning. After a life spent in this manner, she died happy in the belief that she was going to her husband.

During her widowhood she performed great deeds. It was an ancient custom to erect marvelous tombs to notable men. So that Mausolus' tomb would be a worthy symbol of her love, she put aside all parsimony and thought of having a most marvelous and sumptuous sepulcher built. Not satisfied with having one sculptor, and him from her own country, she ordered Scopas, Bryaxis, Timotheus, and Leochares, who at that time were reputed in Greece to be the greatest in the world, to come to her. Following their judgment, she had a magnificent sepulcher designed for Mausolus. When the marble had been prepared, she had the sepulcher built so that the fame of her beloved husband might be eternal because of this magnificent edifice, if not for other reasons.

Since it surpassed almost all other buildings in the world because
of its beauty as well as its cost, and since it has been remembered
for a long time as one of the seven wonders of the world, it would
certainly not be foolish for me to make special mention of it, so
that the fame of those masters and the magnificence of that noble
woman may shine even more brightly.

The architects, then, at the queen's request, laid the foundations
for this sepulcher, rectangular in shape, near Halicarnassus, which
was a famous city in Caria. The two sides which faced north and
south were sixty-three feet long, while the other two were not
so long; it rose to a height of one hundred and forty feet, and they
surrounded it on all sides with thirty-six marble columns. They
say that the part which faced east was sculptured by Scopas, the
one which faced north by Bryaxis, and the one which faced west
by Leochares. The fourth was left to Timotheus. In carving the
statues, friezes, and other things which were part of their work,
they expressed the power of their genius with such subtlety, since
each wanted to surpass the others, that those who watched sometimes thought that the marble faces were alive. And it seemed, not
only at that time but for many centuries later, that the artists'
hands had striven for glory. Artemisia did not see the magnificent
work completed, for death seized her before then. Nevertheless,
the artists did not abandon their work because of the queen's
death, but, thinking that it would be certain proof of their genius
for posterity, they brought to completion what they had begun.
A fifth artist was summoned, who crowned the structure with a
pyramid diminishing by twenty-four steps to its summit.[1] A sixth
sculptor called Pythius was added to the others, and he made a
marble quadriga which was placed atop the edifice. When this
marvelous structure was completed, it was called the Mausoleum
after King Mausolus, for whom it had been built. The sepulchers
of kings are called mausoleums after this one, the worthiest of all.

Well then, Artemisia's conjugal love was renowned, and even
more so was her perseverance in widowhood and her grief. No less
famous was the marvelous sepulcher, either the carved one or,

[1] The fifth artist is said to have been the architect Satyrus.

if you wish, Artemisia's breast, in which her husband's ashes rested after her drinking them.

Artemisia's virtue cannot be extolled with only this praise, for she was very worthy for her vigor, daring, and military leadership, and she adorned the majesty of her name with triumphs. Although at other times she had often taken up arms, I have read that after her husband's death, when time had soothed her grief, she took them up twice, once to defend the welfare of the country, and the second time to maintain faith with her allies at their request. After Mausolus' death, the people of Rhodes, which is not very far from Halicarnassus, angry at the fact that a woman ruled the kingdom of Caria, came in great numbers with a fleet, as if certain of occupying that state. Halicarnassus is a city which rises on the Icarian Sea in a place fortified by nature. It has two harbors, of which the one called Minor is within the city itself, has a narrow passage, and is so hidden that from the palace which rises above it one can prepare and bring into it everything needed without being seen by those outside or even by the citizens protecting the palace itself. The other harbor, which is larger, is next to the walls of the city on the open sea. Knowing that the men of Rhodes had to enter it, Artemisia ordered her people to arm themselves. She took with her into the palace Nauticus and Epipatis as helpers in accomplishing her plan, and she ordered the citizens to cheer the men of Rhodes until she gave a signal, to call to them from the walls, give them hope that they would surrender, and if possible lead them into the marketplace. Finally, when this was done, the enemy not realizing it, she suddenly sailed out of the smaller harbor into the open sea. Seeing that the signal had been given and that the men of Rhodes, called into the city, had left their fleet and were running into the forum like conquerors, with her ships and the great effort of the sailors she seized the Rhodians' fleet, which had been abandoned. In the rising clamor she ordered her countrymen to rush forth against the men of Rhodes from every side. And it happened that the soldiers of Rhodes, unable to flee, were all killed by the men of Halicarnassus. When this had been done, Artemisia raised pennants of victory on the enemy ships and turned their prows towards Rhodes. The Rhodians, seeing from their watch towers their fleet with such pennants, thought they had overcome the foe and opened the port and the gates of the city to them. Not realizing that they were the victorious enemy, they welcomed them as if they had been their own citizens, and thus their city was immediately seized by Artemisia. She ordered that the princes of the city be killed. Then, as a sign of victory, she had a monument raised in the forum. Two bronze statues were placed there; one represented victorious Artemisia, and the other the conquered city of Rhodes, and on them were recorded her deeds. After making the island her tributary, she left it and returned home.

When Xerxes, the powerful king of the Persians, attacked the Lacedaemonians, covering the earth with his soldiers and the sea with his ships, believing that he would not only seize but devour all of Greece, Artemisia went with him to the war with armed ships at his request. When Xerxes' armies had already been defeated on land, the fleet of Xerxes and Artemisia encountered the Greeks under Themistocles in a naval battle off Salamis. Xerxes watched from a safe place, while Artemisia among her captains urged on her men and fought bitterly, as if she had changed sex with Xerxes. If the latter had had as daring and brave a spirit, his fleet would not so easily have turned its prows and fled. Nevertheless, there are some who say that this was not the same Artemisia, but Artemidora, another queen of Halicarnassus. And they assert in proof of their belief that Xerxes' naval battle took place near Salamis during the seventy-fourth Olympiad, and it is known that Artemisia had the Mausoleum built during the one hundredth Olympiad. But I agree with those who believe that Artemisia and Artemidora were one and the same person, since the accounts which are given of her are certain and trustworthy and make the others unworthy of belief.[2] But let whoever reads this believe what

[2] There were two women with the name Artemisia. The older, as Boccaccio says, fought in the battle of Salamis (480 B.C.). The second built the Mausoleum (c. 353 B.C.) and subdued Rhodes. The rather naive way in which Boccaccio dismisses the conflict he found in the different versions of Artemisia's life is not his

he likes, for, whether there were two or one Artemisia, these still remain the deeds of a woman. While we admire the deeds of Artemisia, what can we think except that it was an error of Nature to give female sex to a body which had been endowed by God with a magnificent and virile spirit?

---

customary method of resolving historical questions. He usually shows greater critical insight.

CHAPTER LVI

THE VIRGIN VERGINIA

VERGINIA was a Roman virgin in name and in fact, and she should be reverently remembered. She was of marvelous beauty and was the daughter of the plebeian but honorable Aulius Verginius.[1] Although she was of excellent character, she is not so famous for her constancy as for her lover's wickedness and the act of her overly severe father, from which Roman liberty ensued. When the decemvirs were ruling in Rome for the second year, her father betrothed her to a stern young man, the former tribune Lucius Icilius. Chance delayed the wedding, for a Roman expedition, in which Verginius served, was on the Algidus fighting against the Aequians. This being the situation, it happened, to Verginia's misfortune, that the decemvir Appius Claudius, who had remained alone with Spurius Oppius to defend Rome while the others were campaigning, fell madly in love with her beauty. When the young virgin, her breast filled with sanctity, spurned his flattery and was not swayed by his expensive gifts, prayers, and threats, Appius burned with such mad fury that he turned his wavering mind to various devices, and, thinking it unsafe to use force openly, he decided to use fraud. He planned that as soon as the girl passed near the forum, his freedman Marcus Claudius, a man of great daring, would seize her as his fugitive slave and would take her to his house. If anyone opposed this, he was to have him summoned before Appius.

A few days later, as Verginia passed in the street, the servant seized her with presumptuous daring, claiming that she was his slave. The girl cried out and resisted the wicked man with all her strength, and while the ladies with whom she was walking helped her, a crowd gathered quickly. Icilius was among them. After much was said on both sides, she was brought to the government palace before the judge who lusted for her. Only with great diffi-

[1] Verginius' name was really Lucius.

culty did they obtain from the ardent Appius the concession that the sentence be delayed until the next day. Claudius went to the camp and ordered that if Verginius was sent for, his officers should not allow him to come to Rome, but his deceit was of no avail. When he was summoned, the father came immediately. Covered with dust, he entered the court with his daughter, Icilius, and other friends. There, opposing them, Marcus Claudius claimed the girl as his slave, and the lustful judge, without hearing Verginius, decreed that Verginia was a fugitive slave. When Marcus wanted to take her away and Verginius had attacked Appius in vain, he obtained permission from the furious man to speak briefly with the girl and her nurse, so that he could find out the truth of the matter and give the girl over to him more willingly. Having gone out opposite the court itself near the Cloatine shops, Verginius seized a butcher knife and said, "Dear daughter, I defend your liberty the only way I can." He then stabbed his daughter in the breast, to the great grief of those who were watching. In their presence the wretched girl fell to the ground as her blood and life left her. Thus the vile hopes of lustful Appius came to naught because of the innocent girl's death. The result of the actions of Verginius and Icilius was that the plebeians seceded in rebellion a second time, and the decemvirs were forced to give up power and return to the people the freedom which they had stolen. Not long after, through Verginius, as tribune of the plebeians, Appius Claudius was indicted. As Claudius went to answer the charges, he was arrested at Verginius' orders and bound with chains. In order to escape the shame which he had deserved, and to expiate the innocent soul of Verginia, Claudius killed himself either with a knife, a rope, or poison. But his rash follower Marcus Claudius did not expiate his crime as he should have, for he fled, and his property and that of his master were seized by the state.

There is nothing more harmful than a wicked judge. Whenever he follows the dictates of his wicked mind, the law is necessarily perverted, its power is broken, virtue is weakened, curbs on wicked deeds are loosened, and in short the common welfare goes to its ruin. If this is not sufficiently manifest, Appius' nefarious deed and its consequences make it clear. For this powerful man, by not curbing his concupiscence, with the aid of his fraudulent servant almost made a slave of a free woman, an adulteress of a virgin, and a prostitute of a woman who was engaged to be married. And because of his shameful sentence it came to pass that a father took arms against his daughter and parental love was changed to cruelty. To prevent this wicked man from fraudulently enjoying his desires, an innocent girl was killed, rebellion broke out in Rome and in the military camp, the plebeians broke with the Senate, and Rome was endangered. O what a glorious magistrate and noble administrator of the law Appius was! He did not fear to commit what it was his duty to punish in others with harsh torture. Alas, how many times are men endangered because of this plague, and how often, without any fault of ours, we are brought to death, are burdened with hideous slavery, are throttled, robbed, and killed at the bidding of cruelty. What evil is this? Contemptuous rulers, without any fear of God, dare turn into a license for crime what has been established to curb arbitrary violence. Although he should have equally continent eyes and soul, gentle speech, serious and saintly ways, and hands completely free of bribes, the ruler's eyes are lewd, and his mind too, and they follow the dictates not of the Law but of panderers. They are proud, unless a prostitute orders them to be humble or their anger is softened by gold. Not only do they receive gifts, but they demand them. They buy, sell, and steal justice, and if they cannot otherwise obtain what they covet, they will use force, burning with fury. Thus, with concupiscence and gold as excellent arbiters of the laws, we shall ask for justice in vain if one or the other does not help us.

CHAPTER LVII

IRENE, DAUGHTER OF CRATINUS

IT IS not really clear whether Irene was a Greek woman and in what period she flourished. She is, nevertheless, believed to have been a Greek. It is agreed that she was the daughter and pupil of the painter Cratinus. I believe that she is the more worthy of praise, the more she surpassed her master in art and in fame. Her name is respected by many, while her father is hardly known except through her, unless he was the man who, we read, gave us full information about the leaves and roots of all plants, describing them in proper form. This man, however, is called Cratinax by some writers.[1]

This Irene had unusual talent, and her skill was worthy of remembrance. Proof of her skill lasted for a long time in the painted figure of a girl which could be seen in the city of Eleusis, in a portrait of old Calypso, and also in the paintings of the gladiator Theodorus and of Alcisthenes, who was an excellent dancer in that age.[2] I thought that these achievements were worthy of some praise, for art is very much alien to the mind of women, and these things cannot be accomplished without a great deal of talent, which in women is usually very scarce.

[1] Boccaccio seems to be referring to Crateuas.

[2] Boccaccio found his information on Irene in Pliny the Elder, who states (*Hist. Nat.* xxxv.11.40): *Pinxere et mulieres: . . . Irene . . . puellam quae est Eleusine, Calypso senem et praestigiatorem Theodorum, Alcisthenen saltatorem.* Although Pliny attributes only the painting of the girl to Irene and attributes all the other paintings to another woman artist named Calypso, Boccaccio understood Calypso to have been one of Irene's subjects and all Calypso's pictures to have been done by Irene. He also miscopied Pliny's *praestigiatorem* ('juggler') as *praeterea et gladiator* ('and also a gladiator').

CHAPTER LVIII

LEONTIUM

IF I am correct, Leontium was a Greek woman and was famous at about the time of Alexander the Great, the king of Macedonia. If she had preserved womanly honor, her name would have been much more splendid and glorious, for she had great intellectual powers. According to the testimony of the ancients, she was such a scholar that she dared write against and criticize Theophrastus, a famous philosopher of that period, moved either by envy or womanly temerity. I have not seen this work. Because its fame has lasted throughout the centuries until our own age, we cannot say that it was a trifle or that it was a sign of poor scholarly ability, although it is a clear indication of envy. Since she was so brilliant in these splendid studies, I will not easily believe that she was of lowly plebeian origin. For only rarely does sublime genius rise from those dregs, and if it is sometimes implanted by heaven, its splendor is darkened by the shadows of lowly estate. But what true splendor can the noble blood of ancestors give where there is improper behavior? If we may believe highly esteemed authors, Leontium threw away womanly shame and was a courtesan, or rather a harlot.

Alas, what an unworthy crime it is that she could bring Philosophy, the queen of all human pursuits, among panderers, unclean adulterers, and prostitutes, and into brothels, and in these disgraceful chambers smear it with shameful stains, trample it with unchaste feet, and plunge it into filthy sewers—if indeed the splendor of Philosophy can be stained by the infamy of an unchaste heart. We must certainly bewail the fact that so brilliant a mind, given by heaven as a sacred gift, could be subjected to such filthy practices. Indeed, I do not know whether to say that she was too powerful in bringing Philosophy to so shameful a place, or that Philosophy was too remiss in letting her learned breast be subjected to lust.

CHAPTER LIX

OLYMPIAS OF MACEDONIA

OLYMPIAS, the queen of Macedonia, was famous for many honors. First, if lineage can give any glory to men, she was born of Neoptolemus, the king of the Molossians, who was of the blood of the Aeacides, which at that time was more famous than any in Greece or in the whole world. According to some writers Olympias was first called Mustulis, a name given her as a child.[1] In addition, Olympias had as brother Alexander, the king of Epirus, and at Philip's death her son Alexander ruled Macedonia. His deeds were so great that no one born before or since was known to have surpassed him. This added a great deal of glory to Olympias, if it is glorious for mothers to give birth to excellent sons. But this glory could not escape altogether without being blemished at times by marks of infamy, even though this made her more famous, for in her youth she fell prey to the allure of adultery. Hardly anything more shameful could have happened to the queen. Worse than this was the suspicion that Alexander had been born of an adulterous union. This suspicion so troubled Philip that he not only openly said at times that Alexander was not his son, but repudiated Olympias and married Cleopatra, the daughter of Alexander of Epirus.

Olympias could not conceal how bitter this was for her. For she, who up to that day had been famous for regal splendor except for that fault, made herself famous for various monstrous actions. It was believed that she urged Pausanias, a noble youth born in Orestis, to kill her husband Philip, and that Alexander knew of this. For while Pausanias was hanging on the cross the day after he had been crucified for the murder of Philip, he was found with a golden crown on his head, placed there by Olympias. A few days later, at Olympias' orders, his body was placed over the remains of King Philip, and, following the Macedonian rites, he

[1] According to Justin, this name should be Myrtales.

·· (133) ··

was honorably cremated and buried with funereal pomp. And the queen ordered that the sword with which Pausanias had killed Philip be placed in the temple of Apollo under the name of Nuscalis.[2] After having had Cleopatra's daughter dashed to pieces on a rock, she had Cleopatra herself brought into her presence, and so vexed her with insults and ignominy that she forced the poor wretch to hang herself. Finally, when her son Alexander, made great by his splendid victories, died of poison in Babylonia, and her brother Alexander was killed in the land of the Lucanians, Olympias went into Macedonia from Epirus. When Arridaeus, the king of Macedonia, and his wife Eurydice forbade her entrance, she had them killed. This was done because the elders of Macedonia preferred her. And she alone, a widowed queen, held the throne of Macedonia.

But since she raged like a beast against the blood of nobles as well as plebeians, she was besieged by Cassander in the city of Pydna. They were so beleaguered that she, together with her people, finally had no food left at all. This forced her to give herself into Cassander's hands after coming to terms with him. When she had surrendered, the friends of those whom she had treacherously killed demanded that she be executed. Cassander sent his wicked men to kill her in the prison where she was being kept. Realizing that she was to die at the hands of the men who were approaching, Olympias fearlessly got up leaning on two servants, combed her hair, and arranged her clothes so that she would not lie naked when she fell. She did not permit herself to beg for life, nor did she utter any cries or womanly laments, but walked towards the executioners and willingly offered her body to their blows, as if she scorned what even brave men are wont to fear greatly. With that act she showed that she was indeed the mother of so excellent an emperor as Alexander.

[2] Justin, whose work was used by Boccaccio as a source for this chapter, gives this name as Myrtales, Olympias' name as a young girl.

CHAPTER LX

THE VESTAL VIRGIN CLAUDIA

I BELIEVE that the vestal virgin Claudia was a worthy descendant of noble Roman blood, seeing the marvelous devotion she had for her father.[1] By decree of the Senate, her father was holding his triumph with a great deal of pomp in front of a great crowd of Romans. Suddenly, moved by private enmity, a tribune of the plebeians ran up to him as if to one who deserved ill. He moved forward, laid violent hands on the triumphant man with the insolent audacity of a tribune, and tried to pull him down from the chariot. The virgin Claudia, who was among the spectators, saw this and was distressed because of her love for her father. Unable to endure it, she forgot her sex and the dignity of the bands which she wore. She suddenly rushed violently into the crowd, which gave way before her determined expression, and with undaunted firmness she stepped between the tribune's arrogance and her father's glory. With whatever daring this was done, she pushed back the tribune and assured her father free access to the Capitol.

O sweet love, O unshaken piety! What shall we believe gave strength to the virgin's weak body? What shall we believe made her forget to act as a Vestal if not seeing her father shamefully attacked, her father whom she remembered as guardian of her childhood, as the one who had coaxed her with proper pleasures, who had fulfilled all wishes which were for her good, who had kept all harm from her and had guided her as she grew to womanhood? But enough of this. Who, I ask, will condemn a chaste virgin as shameless for having mingled in the tumults of men? Who will say that she was rash? Who can rightfully condemn her as defiant of the tribune's power, since to defend her father

[1] Appius Claudius Pulcher, consul in 143 B.C.

she performed such a beautiful and memorable deed of devotion, which even a very strong young man of violent spirit could not have done? Certainly I question, and not without reason, which of the two had a greater triumph, the father in the Capitol or the daughter in the temple of Vesta.

CHAPTER LXI

VERGINIA, WIFE OF LUCIUS VOLUPINUS

ANOTHER Verginia, different from the one mentioned above, was a famous woman among the Romans and the daughter of a certain Aulus, a man of the patrician order. In addition to her nobility, in her time she was placed ahead of the other Romans because of her chastity. It will be sufficient to relate one most praiseworthy deed of hers to know all her life and give her due fame. As is well known, at that time in the city of Rome near the round temple of Hercules in the cattle market there was a small temple piously consecrated to Patricia Pudicitia by the noblewomen. Under the consuls Quintus Fabius and Quintus Publius Decius, when Decius was consul for the fourth time, supplications were being made by order of the Senate in all other temples in order to avert omens, and the patrician women very chastely held rites, according to ancient custom, in that one temple only. And it happened that Verginia went to these ceremonies with the other women. A brief quarrel broke out among them when Verginia was haughtily cast out of the temple by order of the patrician women because she was the wife of a plebeian (although a former consul), Lucius Volupinus.[1] Finally Verginia, burning with more than simple womanly anger, said that she was honorable and a patrician, and that she should not be cast out of the temple of Patricia Pudicitia, although she had married a plebeian. After extolling her husband's deeds with marvelous praise, she left the patrician women and returned home angrily.

To her words she added a wonderful deed. For, since she had a large house in the long street where she then dwelt with her husband, she set aside as much space as she thought would be sufficient for a small temple. She erected an altar in that place and summoned the plebeian women and told them of the patri-

---

[1] Her husband's name was actually Lucius Volumnius.

cians' arrogance. Complaining of the insult she had received from them, she added: "I beg and implore you to compete with each other only in womanly chastity in the same way that you see the men of this city continuously vie in manly virtue, so that it will be believed, if one can believe anything at all, that at this altar, which in your presence I have consecrated to Plebeia Pudicitia, chastity is cultivated by women more saintly and chaste than at the other. And if we cultivate it, it will show that god-like souls are not found only in patrician breasts."

O praiseworthy and most holy words of a woman! Verginia's purpose and her praiseworthy wrath should be exalted to the stars with joyous applause. She did not conspire against men's wealth, nor to take up the trappings of lust. Rather, she conspired against the lustful and wanton eyes of young men and against their appetites, and proceeded with excellent precepts and holy principles to deserve the glory of her chastity. Beginning at that time, and for long thereafter, the temple of Plebeia Pudicitia was equal in sanctity to the altar of the patricians, since no one could offer a sacrifice in it unless she were of singular chastity and had had only one husband, and lascivious hope was removed from the lustful eyes of onlookers. I do not doubt that she gave many women the motive and desire to preserve their chastity because of their desire for glory and to avoid the shame of being excluded from the sacrifices.

CHAPTER LXII

THE PROSTITUTE FLORA

THE ancients tell us that Flora was a Roman woman to whom propitious Fortune gave fame equal to the good name she lost through her disgraceful occupation. As everyone agrees, she was very wealthy, but there is disagreement as to how she acquired this wealth. For some say that she spent all the flower of her youth and the beauty of her body in brothels among panderers and wretched young men in public prostitution, and with lust and cajolery, as such women usually do, she stripped this or that simpleton of his riches, and by gnawing and picking in every direction she came into such great wealth. Others have thought more honorably of her and tell a charming and droll story. They say that in Rome the keeper of the temple of Hercules, being idle, began to play dice with both hands, deciding that the right hand would play for Hercules and the left for himself. They say that he bet that if Hercules lost he would get himself dinner and a woman companion with the temple's money, and if Hercules won he would do the same for the god with his own money. Since Hercules won, being accustomed to overcome even monsters, they say that the keeper supplied him with dinner and the noble prostitute Flora. They add that as she slept in the temple it seemed to her that she had slept with Hercules and had been told by him that she would receive payment for her services from the man she would first see on leaving the temple in the morning. As she left the temple, she met Fanitius,[1] a very wealthy young man, who fell in love with her and took her to his house. She stayed with him a long time, and when he died she was his heir, and so she became wealthy. But there are some who say that this happened not to Flora but to Accia Laurentia,[2] who had nursed, or who later nursed, Romulus and Remus. This disagreement does not matter to me, as long as it is clear that Flora was a rich prostitute.

[1] This name should be Carutius or Tarrutius.
[2] This name should be Acca Laurentia.

To proceed with my story, when the end of her mortal life approached, since she had no children and since, I believe, she wanted to make her name memorable, Flora with womanly cunning named the Roman people heir to her wealth for the future glory of her name. But she set aside part of this wealth, stipulating that all the yearly income received from it be used for public games on her birthday. Nor was she mistaken in her expectation, for, having won the sympathy of the people through the inheritance she had left them, she easily succeeded in having annual games held in her honor. At these games in the presence of the people, among other foul things there were naked prostitutes who practiced their art in pantomime with various lewd gestures to show how Flora had acquired her wealth. I believe this was greatly enjoyed by the foolish spectators. Thanks to this disgraceful spectacle it happened that, either because an evil precedent had been established or since they were paid for from public treasury, these games were demanded every year as if they were a holy thing by the people, since they were inclined to lasciviousness, and they were called Floral after the name of the woman who had established them.

After some time, the Senate, knowing the origin of these games and being ashamed that the city which was already mistress of the world should be branded by this foul blot and that the whole city rushed to praise a prostitute, and knowing that it could not easily wipe this out, in order to hide their ignominy and disgrace added to it a detestable but droll fiction. A story was invented in honor of Flora, the glorious testatrix, and it was recited to the people who did not yet know it. The story was that once in that place there had dwelt a nymph of marvelous beauty called Chlora[8] and that she had been ardently loved by the wind Zephyrus (in Latin known as Favonius), who had finally married her. Zephyrus, whom in their foolishness they counted among the gods, as a wedding gift or dowry granted that she be a goddess with the duty of adorning trees, hills, and meadows with flowers in the spring. She was to be their mistress, and from that time on she was to be known as

[8] This name should be Chloris.

Flora instead of Chlora. Since flowers are followed by fruit, the ancients had granted Flora a sanctuary, altars, and games to propitiate her, so that she would grant these flowers in great profusion and would let them be followed by fruit.

The people were misled by this deception, and Flora, who while alive had dwelt in brothels and had prostituted herself for even the smallest fee, was thought to sit with Queen Juno and the other goddesses, as if Zephyrus had brought her to heaven on his wings. And thus Flora with her shrewdness and the gift of her fortune and ill-gotten money was changed from a prostitute into a nymph. Having married Zephyrus and having received divinity from him, she was honored by men with divine honors in the temples, so that not only was she changed from Chlora to Flora, but, having been a renowned prostitute while alive, after her death she became a goddess famous throughout the world.

CHAPTER LXIII

A YOUNG ROMAN WOMAN

THERE was a young Roman woman (if I am not mistaken she was not of low, plebeian birth) whose name, as well as all knowledge of her ancestors and her husband, has been lost through the malignity of Fortune. It may seem that this has deprived her somewhat of her deserved honor. But so that it may not seem that it is I who have taken it away from her by not giving her a place among famous women, I want to include her among them and mention the great filial devotion of this nameless woman.

This young girl's mother was of honorable parentage, but unfortunate, for she was condemned to death before the tribunal of the praetor in Rome for a reason unknown to me. The praetor handed her over to a triumvir to carry out the punishment already determined by the sentence, and the latter gave her to the city gaoler for this same purpose. But, since she was of noble rank, it was ordered that she be executed at night. The gaoler, moved to pity and feeling compassion for her nobility, did not want to hurt her with his own hands, and so he locked her up alive to die of hunger. Her daughter used to go to see her, and, after she had been carefully searched so that she could not bring in any food, the guards allowed her to enter the prison. Since the mother was already starving, the daughter nourished her with her milk, of which she had plenty since she had just given birth. This continued for many days, and the gaoler began to marvel that the condemned woman lived so long without food. Secretly watching what mother and daughter did, he saw that the daughter, taking out her breasts, offered them to her mother's lips to be sucked. Amazed at the filial devotion and the unusual way the daughter had found to feed her mother, he told the triumvir. The triumvir told the praetor, who told the public council. The result was that with general agreement the sentence which the mother had deserved was annulled as a reward for the daughter's devotion.

If the ancients bestowed a laurel crown on the man who saved a citizen in battle, with what crown shall we adorn this daughter who saved her imprisoned mother with her milk? To be sure, one would not find among leaves a garland sufficiently worthy for such a pious deed. This filial devotion was not only holy but marvelous and is to be deemed superior to that gift of Nature by which we are taught to raise our small children to a stronger age with our milk and save our parents from death. Marvelous is the power of devotion, for it not only pierces the hearts of women, who are easily moved to compassion and tears, but it sometimes pierces cruel, hardened, stony breasts. When it does this, it first softens all hardness with human kindness, and, looking for the opportunity and finding it, it acts so that they mix their tears with those of the unhappy and take sickness and danger upon themselves, at least in sympathy. And sometimes, if there are no remedies, they submit to death in their place. It produces such a great effect that we shall be less surprised if we children do some pious deed for our parents, since it seems rather that we are repaying our debt and returning with appropriate payment what we have received earlier.

CHAPTER LXIV

MARCIA, DAUGHTER OF VARRO

A LONG time ago in Rome there was a woman named
Marcia,[1] the daughter of Varro, who remained a virgin
all her life. But I do not remember learning which Varro
it was or even at what time she lived. I believe that this virginity
is worthy of being extolled with great praise especially since she,
a woman, kept it untarnished of her own free will and not because
of a superior's coercion. For I do not find that she was bound by
holy orders to Vesta, or by a vow to Diana, or restrained by other
commitments, which are the reasons which hold back and compel
very many women. But I find that with the integrity of her mind
alone she kept her body until death unblemished by any relations
with men, conquering the urge of the flesh by which even excellent men have sometimes been overcome.

Although Marcia should be greatly praised for her commendable constancy, she is to be lauded no less for the power of her
intellect and the skill of her hands. It is unknown whether she
learned from a teacher or whether she was gifted by nature, but
what is certain is that, scorning womanly occupations, she gave
herself up completely to the study of painting and sculpture so she
would not languish in idleness. She carved ivory figures and
painted with her brush with such skill and finesse that she surpassed Sopolis and Dionysius, who were the most famous painters
in her time. Clear proof of this was given by some pictures she
painted, which were more precious than those of other artists. And
what is far more marvelous, writers say not only that she painted
excellently, which is something done by many, but that her hands
were so swift in painting that no one else's were ever their equals.
Remarkable examples of her art lasted for many a year, among
others her portrait which she painted on a tablet with the aid of a

[1] This is the painter Lala of Cyzicus, who lived in Rome at the time when
M. Varro was a young man (74 B.C.). Misreading Pliny's account of this painter
(*Historia Naturalis* xxxv.11.40), Boccaccio asserts that she was Varro's daughter.

mirror, preserving the colors and features and the expression of the face so completely that none of her contemporaries doubted that it was just like her.

Now, to come to her unique moral sensitivity, we are told that she used to reproduce especially images of women, and those of men rarely if ever, whether she painted with her brush or sculptured with her chisel. I think that her chaste modesty was the cause of this, for in antiquity figures were for the greater part represented nude or half nude, and it seemed to her necessary either to make the men imperfect, or, by making them perfect, forget maidenly modesty. To avoid both these things, it seemed better to her to abstain from both.

CHAPTER LXV

SULPICIA, WIFE OF FULVIUS

AT ONE TIME, Sulpicia was a very venerable woman, and, according to the testimony of Roman matrons, she won no less praise for preserving her chastity than did Lucretia for killing herself with a knife. She was the daughter of Servius Paterculus and the wife of Fulvius Flaccus, who were both noblemen. After the decemvirs had consulted the Sibylline Books according to the ancient custom, the Senate decreed that a statue be consecrated in the city to Venus Verticordia, so that virgins and other women would not only abstain from lustfulness but would more easily turn to praiseworthy chastity, and, in accordance with the order of the decemvirs, it was requested that the most chaste among Roman women consecrate it. They decided that first one hundred women, who enjoyed greater fame for chastity among the others, be selected from the multitudes of chaste women which abounded in Rome at that time. Sulpicia was chosen among these. Then by order of the Senate, ten were selected who in the judgment of those one hundred women were most renowned, and Sulpicia was among the ten. Finally, when one among the ten was asked for, Sulpicia was chosen by unanimous consent.

Although at that time it was a wonderful thing to consecrate the statue of Venus Verticordia, it was much more wonderful to be placed first for chastity by such a great multitude. Not only was she looked upon with admiration by all who were present, almost like a heavenly goddess of chastity, but her name seemed to be destined for imperishable glory and reverence for all future time. But some one will ask, if one hundred chaste women had been selected, what chastity could have been attributed to this one woman alone to justify her being placed ahead of the others. The answer is clear. Let those who think that chastity consists only in refraining from having relations with any man except their husbands see this. If we examine it with clearer insight, chastity does not consist only in abstaining from the embraces of strange men, which many women do, even if unwillingly. But if a woman is to be considered completely chaste, it is necessary above all for her to curb her lustful and wandering eyes and confine them to the fringe of her dress. Her words must be not only respectable but brief, and she must speak only at the proper time. She must avoid idleness as a sure and deadly enemy of chastity, and she must abstain from feasting, for Venus is weak without food and wine. She must avoid singing and dancing as arrows of lasciviousness, and attend to temperance and sobriety. She must take care of her house, close her ears to shameful conversation, and avoid roaming from place to place. She must reject paint, superfluous perfumes, and ornaments. She must trample with all her strength on harmful thoughts and appetites, persist in sacred thoughts, and be vigilant. And, not to discuss the entire subject of real chastity, she must love only her husband with great affection and scorn others, unless it is to love them with brotherly love. She must not go without shame in her face and breast to her husband's embrace, even when it is for the sake of procreation. Perhaps, since all these qualities were not clearly found in the others, Sulpicia was justly given precedence over all women, for she alone possessed them.

CHAPTER LXVI

THE SICILIAN HARMONIA, DAUGHTER OF GELON

THE young Sicilian woman Harmonia was the daughter of Gelon, who was the brother of Hieron, the king of Syracuse.[1] Although she was distinguished for her royal lineage, she became much more worthy of remembrance because of her loyalty. There are some who say she died a virgin; others state that she was the wife of a certain Themistus.[2] Of these two opinions one may choose whichever pleases him more, for their disagreement does not detract in the least from her loyal fortitude.

When through a conspiracy and sudden insurrection the people of Syracuse raged against everyone of royal lineage, and after young King Hieronymus[3] had been killed together with Andranodorus and Themistus, who were both of royal blood, the mob with naked swords rebelliously assailed Demarata and Heraclea, Hieron's daughters, and Harmonia, the daughter of Gelon. And it happened that, through the shrewdness of Harmonia's nurse, a girl of Harmonia's age dressed in royal robes was gotten ready for the murderers in place of Harmonia. This girl did not oppose in any way the intentions of the person who had planned this, in fact, when she saw the multitude of hostile rebels run against her with their sharp-pointed swords, she was not frightened, nor did she run away. She did not give away her identity to the men who wounded her, and she did not accuse Harmonia, who was in hiding and in whose place she was dying. Silent and motionless, she received the mortal blows and died. She was happy in her death, and Harmonia was unhappy. The former was happy in her faithfulness; the other was sad because she had lost the one

---

[1] Harmonia was not the daughter of Gelon, brother of Hieron, but of Gelon, the son of Hieron II.

[2] Harmonia was actually married to Themistus.

[3] Hieronymus, the king of Syracuse and grandson of Hieron II.

who was faithful. Seeing from a hiding place the perseverance of the innocent girl and her bravery in death, and seeing the blood flow from that girl's wounds, Harmonia was amazed. As soon as she could go out, when the murderers had left after killing the girl, she admired with all her heart that girl's loyalty. Filled with devotion and shedding tears, she could not bear to see that innocent blood spilled without punishment and could not bear to prolong her own life saved by another's great loyalty, thinking it better to descend to the underworld in untimely death with such a faithful girl than to await old age with untrustworthy citizens.

O loyalty! O ancient faith! Although she had escaped, she showed herself in public, and, calling back the bloody swords, she confessed her nurse's stratagem, the loyalty of the girl who had died, and her own identity. And she voluntarily shed her blood as a sacrifice to the dead girl. Pierced by many wounds, she fell as close as she could to the body of the one who had died earlier. The years which her devotion took away from her were fittingly returned to her by literature. It is difficult to see which was greater, the faith of the one who died first or the devotion of the one who had survived her. The former immortalizes the virtue of the first, and the latter immortalizes the name of the second.

CHAPTER LXVII

BUSA OF CANUSIUM, A WOMAN
OF APULIA

USA, whom they call Paulina as if Busa were a family name, was an Apulian woman of Canusian origin. I believe she was born of noble blood and renowned for many other merits, as well as for that magnificent deed which is all that the ancients have handed down concerning her to posterity. They say that when Hannibal the Carthaginian was waging bitter war against the Romans, laying waste all of Italy with fire and sword and staining it with much blood, and when in a great battle near Cannae, a village in Apulia, he not only defeated his enemy but almost destroyed all the power of Italy, it happened that during the night, of the many who were fleeing the defeat and great slaughter through deserted places, dispersed and wandering, about ten thousand arrived at Canusium, a city which at that time held to its alliance with the Romans. The fugitives were weak, exhausted, needy, unarmed, naked, and covered with wounds, but Busa, who was not frightened by this disaster or by the power of the conqueror, received these men in her own house with friendship and gave them shelter. Before anything else, Busa told them to be brave, and having brought doctors, she had the wounded tended with maternal affection, gave clothes to the naked, helped all of them with admirable generosity, and paid their daily expenses from her own wealth. When these poor men had regained their strength and hope through her compassionate mercy and wanted to leave, she willingly gave them all money for the journey, nor was she niggardly in giving them anything they needed.

Certainly, that was a marvelous thing and more worthy of praise for a woman than if it had been done by a man. The ancients used to praise Alexander, the king of Macedonia and invader of the whole world, for his great generosity, among other things. They tell us that not only was he accustomed to give precious gems, large sums of money, and similar gifts, in accordance with the munificence of other princes, but also gave great principalities,

splendid kingdoms, and large empires to his friends and sometimes even to kings he had defeated. This is indeed a fine and
magnificent thing, to be told with great praise. But I think that
it should not be thought equal to Busa's liberality, for Alexander
was a man; Busa, a woman, and women have habitual, or even
innate frugality and very little generosity. He was a great king,
and she a private individual. He gave away what he had taken
by force; she, what she possessed through lawful inheritance. He
gave away what he perhaps could not easily retain; she, what she
had held for a long time and could have continued to hold if she
had so desired. He gave to friends and to men who had deserved
well of him; she, to foreigners whom she did not know. He gave
when his affairs were prospering; she, when hers were in doubt
and her friends in danger. He gave in foreign lands; she, in her
own country and among her own people. He gave to acquire
glory with his munificence; she, to aid those who were in need.
Why need I speak at length? If we consider the spirit, the sex and
the qualities of both, I do not doubt that under a just judge Busa
would be thought to have acquired far more glory by her generosity than Alexander by his munificence.

But let whoever you like have greater fame, in my opinion Busa
used her wealth very well, for Mother Nature did not bring forth
gold from the depths of the earth so that it might be transferred
from the mother's womb into a tomb, as misers do by burying it
and jealously watching over it with excessive vigilance as if it
might rise again. Indeed, she produced gold so that above anything
else it might be used for the common good. Then it may be used
for our proper glory and for the service of our friends, and, if any
is left over, to aid with liberal spirit people who are prostrated by
the wrongs of Fortune, burdened by the wrath of heaven, dis-
gracefully oppressed by poverty, or in jail through someone else's
fault, and all who are overcome by the anguish of extreme need.
I mean not to appear to help, but actually to do so, not for profit
but to give freely. These kinds of expenditures are proper. To this
we add the guide of reason, so that by helping others we shall not
bring poverty to ourselves, so that we may not be forced to steal
or even to covet the property of others.

CHAPTER LXVIII

SOPHONISBA, QUEEN OF NUMIDIA

ALTHOUGH Sophonisba was renowned because she was the queen of Numidia, she became much more glorious through the harshness of the death she took upon herself. She was the daughter of Hasdrubal, the son of Gisco and the greatest lord in Carthage at the time when Hannibal was harassing Italy. When she was in the flower of her youth and of her great beauty, her father betrothed her as a virgin to Syphax, the powerful king of Numidia. Hasdrubal's motive was not so much the desire to be related to this king as the fact that, being a shrewd man, he wished not only to detach the barbarian king from the Romans, since the war with Rome was becoming desperate, but to bring him to the side of the Carthaginians against the Romans through his daughter's allurements. Nor was he disappointed in his premeditated plan, for, as soon as the wedding had taken place, Syphax was drawn to such love for the girl, who had been coached beforehand and was helped by her beauty, that he thought nothing was dear or delightful except his Sophonisba. Thus the unhappy man burned with passion, and when it became apparent that Cornelius Scipio would cross with his army from Sicily into Africa, Sophonisba, advised by Hasdrubal, with her wiles and prayers brought Syphax to desire her so much that he not only joined the Carthaginians, abandoning the Romans to whom he had sworn friendship, but of his own free will assumed leadership of an alien war. Thus, perfidiously trampling the faith which shortly before he had sworn to Scipio, who was his guest, he forbade him by letter to enter Africa, before Scipio had begun to cross. Then Scipio, a young man of great courage, condemned the iniquity of the barbarian king, landed his army not far from Carthage, and, before anything else, defeated Syphax through King Masinissa, the ally of the Romans, and his own lieutenant Laelius.

After defeating his army, they took Syphax as a conquered prisoner to Cirta, a royal city in Numidia. When, burdened with chains, he was shown to his people, the city surrendered to Masinissa, who entered it before Laelius had arrived. Everything being in tumult because of the rapidity of events, Masinissa went to the royal palace armed as he was, and Sophonisba went to meet him. Conscious of her misfortune, Sophonisba saw him enter the atrium more distinguished in armor than the others and realized that he was the king. Retaining the spirit of her previous fortune, she knelt before him and said, "O Mighty King, it pleased the gods and your success that you be able to do whatever you please against us, who a short time ago were royal. I am a slave before you, who are my conqueror and the lord of my life. But if I am permitted to speak humbly and touch your knees and victorious hand, I humbly beg you to do whatever in your eyes seems merciful and good to me, once again placed in your power by adverse fortune, so long as I am not given up again to the hateful and arrogant power of the Romans. I beg this in the name of your royal rank, which not long ago I too held; I beg it by the royal blood and common name of Numidia, and so that you may be received with better omens than was Syphax when he left. O great Numidian! You can easily see what I, a Carthaginian, enemy of the Romans and Hasdrubal's daughter, would have to fear even if I were not Syphax's wife. If there is no other way, I pray and beg you to have me die at your hands rather than have me fall alive into the enemy's power."

Masinissa, who was also from Numidia and, like everyone else, was inclined to lust, saw the beauty of the suppliant woman's face, to which misfortune had added a certain unusual and gentle grace, and he was moved by kindness and drawn by lust. Since Laelius had not yet arrived, Masinissa, armed as he was and in the midst of the women's plaintive wailing and the tumult of soldiers running in every direction, gave her his hand and lifted her up while she was still pleading. He married her at once and celebrated the wedding amidst the clamor of the Romans. I believe that by doing this he thought he had found a way to satisfy both his own lust and Sophonisba's prayers.

The next day Laelius arrived, and at his orders Masinissa returned to the camp with his royal retinue, booty, and his new wife.

Scipio received them in a friendly manner for their great deeds, and then he gently reproached Masinissa for having married a captive of the Roman people. The king withdrew into his tent, where he grieved alone for a long time with sighs and tears, which were heard by the men nearby. He then sent for his most trusted servant, to whom he had entrusted the poison which he kept for the uncertain exigencies of fortune. Forced by Sophonisba's fate, he ordered the servant to bring it to her diluted in a cup and tell her that he would gladly have kept the pledge which he had willingly sworn to her, if it had been possible. But since his authority was being taken away by those who had the power to do so, he, not without sadness, kept his pledge that she should not fall alive into the hands of the Romans, if she desired to take advantage of it. Nevertheless, she should remember her father, her country, and the two kings whom she had married shortly before, and then take whatever decision seemed proper.

Sophonisba listened to this, and then, with unchanging expression, said, "I willingly accept this wedding gift, and if my husband can give me no other I shall be grateful for this. But tell him that I should have died better, had I not married at the point of death." There was more bitterness in her words than in the way she accepted the cup. Giving no sign of fear whatsoever, she quickly drank it all, and, without inveighing against the death she had sought, fell piteously to the ground. This would have been a great and admirable deed for an aged man, tired of life and with nothing to hope for except death, not to speak of a young queen who, in so far as knowledge of the world is concerned, was just entering upon life and beginning to know what joy it holds. And it is worthy of note that she met death so fearlessly.

CHAPTER LXIX

THEOXENA, DAUGHTER OF PRINCE HERODICUS

THEOXENA of Thessaly was a woman of noble birth who left for posterity glorious remembrance of herself for stern harshness on the one hand, and for tender devotion on the other. She was the daughter of Herodicus, a prince of Thessaly when Philip, the son of Demetrius, ruled in Macedonia. She had a sister called Archo, born of the same parents. Their father was killed through the villainy of that same Philip, and as time went by they were deprived of their husbands, who were wickedly and treacherously slain by that same man. The two sisters were left each with an only child. The two of them having been widowed, Archo married a prince of her country named Poris and bore him many children. Theoxena, however, although wooed in vain by many princes, preserved her widowhood for a longer time with more constant spirit. But when Archo was taken away by death, she felt pity for her nephews, and lest they fall into the hands of a step-mother or be brought up less carefully by their father, and in order to raise them herself as if they were her own, she married that same Poris, as at that time no law prohibited this. She began to look after them with devoted care as if she herself had borne them, so that it could be clearly seen that she had married Poris more to serve them than for her own comfort.

Things being this way, it happened that King Philip of Macedon, who was of restless temperament, again thought of waging war against the Romans, who at that time were enjoying great success throughout the world. For this reason, with great commotion in his kingdom, he emptied of their old inhabitants almost all the cities of Thessaly near the shore and ordered them to migrate, group by group, to Paeonia, an inland region which was later called Emathia. He gave the abandoned towns to the Thracians as men more suitable and trustworthy for the coming war.

Hearing the curses of those who were leaving, Philip thought that he would not be safe if he did not also annihilate all the sons of the men he had savagely killed earlier. He ordered them to be seized and kept under guard in order not to kill them all at once but in small numbers over a period of time. Theoxena happened to hear the edict of this infamous king. Remembering the death of her own husband and her sister's, she thought that her son and her nephews would be sought out and that if they fell into the king's hands they would not only become prey to the king's cruelty, but would also be subjected to the whims and scorn of the guards. To avoid this, she suddenly resolved on an atrocious deed. And she dared tell her husband, the children's father, that if nothing else could be done she would kill them with her own hands rather than suffer them to fall into Philip's power. But Poris, having condemned such a wicked crime, to console his wife and protect the children, offered to take them away, place them with some trusted friends, and then flee with her.

He did not delay. He pretended that he was going from Thessalonica to Aenea to be present at the annual sacrifices for the founder of the city. Having spent a day there in solemn ceremonies and banquets, during the third watch of the night when everyone else slept, together with his wife and children he secretly boarded the ship which had been prepared as if to return to his city, all the while intending to go to Euboea and not to Thessalonica. But things turned out very differently. He had hardly left the shores of Aenea when in the darkness of the night there rose a contrary wind, which did not take him where he desired to go, but against his wishes drew him back to the place he had left. The sailors strove in vain against it with their oars, but day broke and showed them that they were near the shore. The king's guards in the port, seeing the struggling ship and thinking that it was trying to escape, immediately sent out an armed boat to bring it back, with the stern order not to return without the ship they were being sent after. Poris saw the approaching boat and realized the immediate danger, and so he begged the sailors to row with all their strength and implored the gods to help them since they were in danger.

Theoxena saw this, and realized the danger. When she saw Poris praying she went back to the plan which she had previously conceived, as if the gods were now giving her the opportunity. She immediately dissolved poison in a cup and took out knives. She set them before her son and her nephews and said, "Only death can give us protection and safety. The cup and dagger are means of death, for we must flee the king's arrogance in whichever way you choose. Well then, my children, arouse your noble spirit, and you who are the oldest act bravely; take up the dagger, or drink from the cup if you prefer a more cruel death; take refuge in it since the fury of the stormy sea does not allow us to go toward life." The enemy was already near, and the strong-willed woman, counselor of death, urged and incited the hesitating youths. The young men, each of whom had already chosen a different death and who were still half alive and trembling, leaped from the ship at Theoxena's command. Theoxena, who for the sake of freedom had led to death those whom she had devotedly raised, with great courage embraced her husband who was still praying, taking him as her companion in death so that it would not seem that she reserved for herself the slavery she had spoken against for others. And she pulled him with her into the stormy sea, thinking it better to die free than to live and languish in foul slavery. Thus, leaving the empty ship to the enemy, she deprived Philip of the solace of his wickedness, and this stern woman acquired for herself fame worthy of remembrance.

CHAPTER LXX

BERENICE, QUEEN OF CAPPADOCIA

ERENICE of Pontus, who was also called Laodice,[1] has a place among famous women for the nobility of her family, but she is thought to deserve it much more not for the great love she had for her son, which most mothers have, but for her marvelous audacity in avenging him. Lest it seem that I neglect this, I shall speak of it briefly. She was the daughter of Mithridates,[2] the king of Pontus, who shortly before had waged war with the Romans against Aristonicus and had died a sudden death. She was the sister of Mithridates,[3] the son of that other Mithridates and enemy of the Romans in long war. She married Ariarathes, the king of Cappadocia, who was killed by Gordius through the treachery of her brother Mithridates. Two sons survived. At that time Nicomedes, the king of Bithynia, occupied Cappadocia as if the throne were vacant because of the king's death. Mithridates, coveting the kingdom, feigned pity and, saying that he would recover the throne for his nephews, took up arms against Nicomedes. When he learned that the widow Laodice had married Nicomedes, his pretended pity became real, and after hurling Nicomedes out of Cappadocia by force of arms, he restored Ariarathes' older son to his ancestors' throne. Later, repenting of his deed, Mithridates treacherously killed this Ariarathes. When the younger brother, also named Ariarathes, was recalled from Asia by his friends and became king, that same Mithridates had him treacherously murdered, according to some.[4]

Having lost both of her sons, the unhappy mother was so

[1] Berenice and Laodice were two different queens. Boccaccio used Valerius Maximus' account of Berenice, and Justin's account of Laodice, and he combined these two sources, thinking they both referred to the same person because of an error he made when reading Valerius Maximus. In order to combine these two stories, Boccaccio changed some of the facts reported by Justin.

[2] Mithridates V, who was assassinated at Sinope.

[3] Mithridates VI.

[4] According to Justin, the younger Ariarathes died a natural death.

grieved that, impelled by sorrow and forgetting that she was a woman, she furiously seized arms, harnessed the horses, climbed into the chariot, and pursued the rapidly fleeing Caeneus, who was the king's servant and the perpetrator of the wicked deed. She did not stop pursuing him until, after missing him with her lance, she struck him to the ground with a rock. She then wrathfully drove the chariot over his prostrate body. And she went among the enemy arms without fear of her brother, who was then her enemy, until she came to the house where she thought the body of her dead son was being kept. There the unhappy woman shed motherly tears over him and fulfilled her funeral obligations.

O good Lord, O invincible forces of Nature and fortitude of unconquered Love, what greater or more marvelous thing could you have done? You brought it about that a fearless woman, to whom daring, skill and strength had been granted, incited by you, passed armed and without fear through an army which was feared in all of Asia and perhaps already in Italy. She scorned the power and the hatred of a formidable king in order to kill a man for whom a conqueror's gifts and favors were reserved. Some writers, however, say that this boy died a natural death through illness, and that the one who was treacherously killed by Mithridates, as I have said, was the one who was avenged by his mother as best she could.

CHAPTER LXXI

THE WIFE OF DRIGIAGON THE GALATIAN

OUR ignorance of the name of Drigiagon's[1] wife, the queen of the Galatians, could have withheld her due honor and especially the reward of fame from her. I believe that the odious barbarousness of an unknown language kept her name from the Romans and hid it from our praise among the inland passes and caves of Asia Minor. But I shall not let this unfortunate accident prevent me from giving her, under her husband's name, as much of the renown she deserves as my humble words allow.

When Antiochus the Great, the king of Syria and Asia, was defeated by the Romans under Scipio Asiaticus, the consul Gnaeus Manlius Torquatus[2] was allotted the province of Asia. After destroying the remnants of the enemy near the shore, he went on his own authority to the remote, mountainous regions of Asia Minor, so that it would not seem that he had brought over his army in vain or that his soldiers were being kept idle. There he vigorously waged a bitter war against the Galatians, a savage and barbaric people, because they had sent help to Antiochus against the Romans and because they occasionally spread confusion throughout Asia Minor with their raids. The Galatians, despairing of victory, abandoned their cities, and with their wives, children, and other possessions they went up to mountain peaks protected by the nature of the place. There they defended themselves against the besieging enemy with arms and with what strength they had. But they were overcome by the great strength of the Roman soldiers, hurled down the mountain slopes, and killed. The survivors surrendered and acknowledged Manlius as their conqueror.

[1] This name should be Ortiagon.
[2] Gnaeus Manlius Vulso was the conqueror of the Galatians in 189 B.C. Boccaccio has confused him with the earlier Gnaeus Manlius Torquatus.

There were a great number of captives, men and women of all ages, and they were placed under the guard of a centurion. As soon as this man saw the wife of King Drigiagon, youthful and very beautiful, he desired her and, forgetting Roman honor, ravished her although she struggled against him as much as she could. She was so indignant at this that she desired vengeance no less than freedom. She cautiously kept her desire secret at that time by keeping silent. When the money promised for the ransom of the captives arrived, renewed wrath burned in her chaste breast. Having decided beforehand what she was to do, when she was freed of her chains she moved aside with her people and ordered that the gold be weighed for the centurion, who demanded it. While the centurion's attention was fixed on this task, she ordered her servants in her own tongue, which was unknown to the Romans, to kill the centurion and cut off his head. Then she returned unharmed to her people with the centurion's head in the bosom of her dress. When she came into her husband's presence, she told him of the shame inflicted upon her in prison and threw at his feet the head which she had carried, as if it were the price of her dishonor and womanly shame, which she had borne with grief as best she could.

Who then will not agree that this woman was, I should say not only Roman, but of the same breed as Lucretia, rather than a barbarian? They were still standing in sight of her prison and her chains, around her resounded the conquerors' weapons, and the cruel avenger's axe hung above her head. It was not sufficient for that woman to be given her freedom, for the indignation of her defiled body moved her chaste breast with such force that she, brave woman and glorious avenger of the wicked deed, was not afraid to be taken captive and feel the weight of chains once again, or if necessary, to enter a hateful prison and offer her neck to the axe. With her firm commands she drove her servants' swords against the head of her wretched ravisher. Where will you find a man more severe than this woman, a braver leader, or a stricter one against those who have deserved ill? Where will you hear of a more clever and daring woman, or a more watchful preserver of womanly honor? This woman saw with great clearness that it would be better to go to certain death than to return to her husband's house with uncertain honor, unable to prove without great daring and great danger that in her defiled body the mind had been chaste. In this manner, therefore, is a woman's honor saved, thus is it regained when lost, and thus is proof of a pure heart given. Therefore, let those women who have within their breast solicitude for glorious chastity see that to prove purity of heart it is not sufficient to say with tears and laments that one has been violated, without proceeding to wreak vengeance with noble deeds whenever possible.

CHAPTER LXXII

TERTIA AEMILIA, WIFE OF
SCIPIO AFRICANUS

TERTIA AEMILIA was distinguished much more for her own accomplishments than for the renown of the Aemilian family, from which she took her noble birth, or for her marriage to the valiant Scipio Africanus the elder. As a young man, Scipio had restored unharmed to Prince Luceius[1] the virgin to whom he was betrothed, although she was in the first flower of her youth and of remarkable beauty, and he had also returned the treasure offered by her family for her ransom. But when he had become old, he could not pull himself away from the allure of concupiscence. In fact, he fell in love and committed adultery with a little serving girl of his. And since it is almost impossible for these things to escape the notice of honorable love, he could not deceive Tertia, who learned everything as time went by.

Who will doubt that she was very much hurt by this? For they say that nothing more offensive or intolerable (not to mention embarrassing) can be done to a married woman than for her husband to take a strange woman into his bed, to which, they say, only a wife has a right. And I shall certainly believe this easily, for a woman is a very suspicious animal, whether it is due to the frailty of her sex or because she does not have a good opinion of herself. For, if the husband leans at all towards another woman, a wife immediately thinks that he is acting against the love due her. But, however difficult it seemed, this glorious woman endured it with such constant courage and hid her husband's fault, of which she was aware, with such silence that not only others but her husband himself did not realize she knew what he was doing. Moreover, this discreet wife thought that it would be too unbecoming if it were publicly known that the man who with notable

---

[1] This name should be Allucius.

bravery had subjugated kings and powerful nations had himself been conquered by love for a maid servant. Nor did it seem enough to that saintly woman that the secret be kept while Scipio was alive, for when he died, in order to remove this infamy from her husband's memory, in case his error should become public in some way, she removed the cause. To prevent the woman who had been the concubine of so famous a man from being shamed by any servants' insults, and so that she would not be joined in lust to someone unbecoming, which would seem to vilify her great husband's desire, she first generously set her free and then married her to a freed slave of hers.

O how this woman is to be raised to heaven with praise! On the one hand she silently and patiently endured the affront, and on the other she generously paid her late husband's debt to her rival, the concubine. The more we see that this rarely happens, the more splendid must we consider it. Another woman would have shouted, would have called a council of her relatives, neighbors, and all the women known to her. She would have filled their ears with many words and burdened them with numberless complaints, saying that she had been deserted, abandoned, scorned, and thought worthless by her husband, that she was a widow while he was still living, and that her servant, a vile and meretricious slave, was preferred to her. She would immediately have cast out the slave and sold her at auction; she would have harassed her husband publicly with tears and wails, and as long as she could defend her rights with her chatter she would not have cared that she was staining the great fame of her glorious husband.

CHAPTER LXXIII

DRIPETRUA, QUEEN OF LAODICEA

I HAVE READ that Dripetrua[1] was the queen of Laodicea
and daughter of Mithridates the Great. Although she should
be commended for that fidelity which makes us submit to
our parents, it seems to me that she was made much more memorable by Mother Nature through its unheard-of handiwork. For,
if the writings of the ancients are to be trusted, Dripetrua, born
with a twin set of teeth, was a monstrous spectacle for all the
people of Asia Minor in her time. Although so unusual a quantity
of teeth was no impediment in eating, she was not without wondrous ugliness, which, as I have already said, she mitigated by her
praiseworthy faithfulness. For when her father Mithridates was
defeated by Pompey the Great, she always followed him without
avoiding labor or danger. Thus, with such faithful service she
showed that deformities should be attributed to Nature and not
to one's parents.

[1] This name should be Drypetine.

CHAPTER LXXIV

SEMPRONIA

SEMPRONIA was the daughter of Tiberius Sempronius Gracchus, a very famous man in his time, and her mother was Cornelia, the daughter of the elder Scipio Africanus. She became the wife of Scipio Aemilianus, a very famous man who later acquired his grandfather's surname[1] because of his destruction of Carthage. She was the sister of Tiberius and Gaius Gracchus, and she was worthy of her ancestors in greatness and strength of spirit.

It is said that after her brothers had been killed because of their sedition, to her great dismay Sempronia was brought to trial before the people by a tribune of the plebeians. There she was urged by all the power of the tribunes and with the approval of the mob to let herself be kissed by Equitius, a man from Firmum in Picenum, as her nephew and the son of her brother Tiberius Gracchus, and she was pressed to accept him as a member of the Sempronian family. Certainly, although she was in a place where even princes usually tremble, and although she was spurred on the one side by the dissonant clamor of the ignorant multitude and on the other threatened by the lofty authority of the tribunes who glared harshly at her, this woman's constancy did not waver in anything. In fact, remembering that her brother Tiberius had had only three children, of whom one had died young while serving as a soldier in Sardinia, another had died in Rome shortly before his father's downfall, and the third, who had been born after his father's death, was a child being raised by his nurse, Sempronia, with constant spirit and stern face and without any fear whatsoever, to his disgrace rejected Equitius, the presumptuous stranger who was attempting with false proof to stain the honor of the noble family of the Gracchi. Nor could any threats or orders make her do what was commanded. When Equitius had been refused so bravely, and the presumptuousness of this madman had been

[1] Africanus.

frustrated and had become known to the tribunes who had made careful inquiries into this matter, the firmness of this woman's noble spirit was praised.

Perhaps there are some who will say that although Sempronia deserved it because of her ancestors, nevertheless, she should not have been included among famous women for her constancy because in all matters women are innately obstinate and unbending in their opinions. Although I do not deny this, I believe that women should be praised if they base their inflexibility on truth as Sempronia certainly did. There are also some who say that she was so headstrong that if she had had the power nothing would have been done against her wishes without being avenged. Because of this it was thought that she consented to the death of her husband Scipio, for after he had destroyed Numantia he was asked whether he thought that Tiberius Gracchus had been justly killed, and, without any respect for family ties, he approved the harsh death of the seditious man as well deserved.

CHAPTER LXXV

CLAUDIA QUINTA, A ROMAN WOMAN

CLAUDIA QUINTA was a Roman woman, but it is not known of what parents she was born. However, she acquired perpetual fame through her marvelous daring. Since she always used varied and elaborate ornaments, and since she always went about with her face too much embellished, the more serious matrons thought that she was not only dishonorable but unchaste.

When Marcus Cornelius and Publius Sempronius were consuls, that is, in the fifteenth year of the Second Punic War, it happened that the mother of the gods was being taken from Pessinus to Rome over the river Tiber. According to the answer of the oracle, Nasica, whom the whole Senate had judged to be the best man in the city, went there with all the women to receive it from the ship. When the ship was close and the sailors wanted to reach the nearer shore, the vessel on which the statue was being carried happened to run aground. As it was seen that it could not be moved even by a great number of young men, Claudia, who was among the other women, conscious of her virtue, openly knelt and humbly prayed the goddess that if she knew she was chaste she should follow her girdle. Getting up immediately, and hoping that what she had prayed for would occur, she confidently ordered her girdle to be tied to the ship and all the young men to move aside. As soon as this had been done, Claudia easily drew the ship out of the shallows and to everyone's surprise led it where she desired. Because of this miraculous success, everyone's opinion of her chastity immediately changed, to Claudia's great glory. Thus, she who had come to the shore stained by the blot of wantonness returned home adorned with the marvelous glory of chastity.

Although everything went according to Claudia's desire, I do not think that it is for a sane mind, however innocent, to dare to do similar things. For to do something supernatural in order to show that one is blameless is to tempt God more than to purge the blot of an assumed crime. We must live and act in a holy manner, and if we are not deemed good, God does not tolerate this opinion unless for our own good. Certainly, He subjects us to this ordeal in order to strengthen our patience, both so that pride will be driven away and virtue exercised, and so that we shall be happy within ourselves, knowing that the others are unworthy. It is sufficient for us, in fact it is a great thing, to live well with God as our witness. Therefore, we must not care if men do not think well of us, as long as we act well. If we do not, then we must strive with all our strength to mend our ways, so that we shall leave others with their evil thoughts, rather than act badly ourselves.

CHAPTER LXXVI

HYPSICRATEA, QUEEN OF PONTUS

ALTHOUGH her descent is not known, Hypsicratea was the wife of Mithridates the Great and a noble queen of Pontus. She was of marvelous beauty, and her love for her husband was invincible, for which she must be praised because through it she acquired perpetual glory. When Mithridates was engaged in a long, costly, and perilous war with the Romans, Hypsicratea, burning with her great love, was always his faithful and inseparable companion when crossing vast territories, going into battle, or preparing to cross the seas, in spite of the fact that he had other wives and concubines, according to barbaric custom. Not enduring her husband's absence easily, and thinking that no one but herself could serve him properly and that the ministering of servants was in great part untrustworthy, she decided to follow him, although this seemed difficult to her, so that she could attend to the needs of her dearly loved husband.

Since womanly clothes seemed incongruous in so great an enterprise, and it did not seem proper for a woman to march alongside a warlike king, Hypsicratea, in order to look like a man, first cut her golden hair, of which women are so proud, and not only did she endure covering her beautiful face with a helmet, together with her hair, but stained it with sweat, dust, and the rust of armor. She discarded her golden bracelets, jewels, and dresses of purple which flowed down to her feet, or cut them at the knee, and she covered her ivory breast with a corselet and fastened greaves to her legs. She cast off her rings and the precious ornaments of her hands, and in their place carried shield and lance and replaced her necklaces with the Parthian bow and quiver. She did everything so well that she seemed to have changed from a delicate queen to a veteran soldier. Hypsicratea, who had been used to the royal chamber, idleness, and luxury, and had seen arms only rarely, put aside these things; with manly spirit she learned to ride and, burdened with arms, followed her husband day and night over rough mountains and sloping valleys, overcoming heat and cold as if all these things were trifles. Often she was known to travel hastily, and overcome by sleep she would lie down on the bare earth instead of a royal bed, and, her body having become toughened, she would lie down fearlessly in the dens of beasts. Whether her husband was victorious or in flight, she was his constant companion, helper in his tasks and sharer in his deliberations everywhere. Why say more? With her devoted eyes she learned to witness without horror the wounding and the killing of men, and the blood which she often shed while fighting with her arrows. She forced her ears, which had been accustomed to the sound of songs, to listen without fear to the neighing of horses, the tumult of knights, and the blare of trumpets. Finally, after enduring labors which would have been hard even for a strong soldier, she followed the weary Mithridates, when he had been conquered by Pompey, through the mountains of Armenia, the hiding-places of Pontus, and the lands of many savage peoples, accompanied by only a few friends. Sometimes she comforted her despondent husband with hopes of better things, and at times with the pleasures she knew he desired, so that he received comfort in his wife's chamber in whatever wild places he had been driven into.

O breast, temple of conjugal tenderness! O inextinguishable virtue of friendship! With what sacred strength was that woman's soul fortified! No wife ever endured similar, not to mention greater, suffering for her husband. If for her merits the ancients gave her perpetual praise, those who have come after them should not be surprised. But that deserving woman did not receive from her husband a reward worthy of her great labors and splendid faithfulness. For when he had become old, he killed in anger a child born of her. Pressed by the power of the Romans, he withdrew not only within his lands, but into the royal palace itself, although he tried to plot great things and by means of many delegations tried to induce various distant nations to make war against the Romans. He was besieged by his son Pharnaces, who rebelled because of the cruelty he had shown against his children and his friends. Seeing this and finding Pharnaces inexorable, the king thought that this was his final ruin, and, together with his other wives, concubines, and daughters, he poisoned Hypsicratea, who had helped him so much during his life, so that she would not survive him. Mithridates' ungrateful deed could not lessen Hypsicratea's deserved glory. Her body, being mortal, was taken by untimely death through poison; but her name has come down to us through the testimony of venerable books and will live on forever in glorious fame without being destroyed by time.

CHAPTER LXXVII

THE ROMAN SEMPRONIA

I REMEMBER having often read that there was another Sempronia of famous intellect in addition to the one discussed above; but I have read that for the most part this second one was inclined to wickedness. She was famous among the Romans both for her family and her beauty, according to the ancients, and was fortunate in both her husband and her children. Not remembering their names, let us move to those things which are praiseworthy in this woman or because of which her name has become glorious—let them have the first place.

She was of such quick and versatile intellect that she immediately understood and carried out by imitation whatever she heard or saw others do. Having learned not only Latin but Greek, she dared, unlike a woman, to compose verses when she felt like it, and she wrote so skillfully that she made all who read them marvel, as they would have been extraordinary and praiseworthy even for a man. She also had such great and polished eloquence that she could incite a person to modesty, she could jest, induce laughter, and arouse wantonness and shamelessness if she so desired. And what is more, she was so charming when she spoke that no matter what form of speech she used, she sent it full of wit and elegance to the listener's ears. She also knew how to sing and dance elegantly, and these skills are perhaps the most commendable in a woman, so long as they are used properly.

For the rest, steeped in evil deeds, she seemed to be very different. For, spurred by too much daring, she sometimes stooped to things which are damnable even in a man. With dancing and singing, which are instruments of sensuality, she turned to wantonness. Burning with lust, she discarded all womanly honor and reputation, and to satisfy that lust she sought men more often than they sought her. You may judge the root of this evil, which we see is so powerful in many, to be whatever you please. But I shall not condemn Nature, for no matter how strong its powers may be, at the beginning they are so flexible that with a little effort they can be guided almost at will. But if you disregard this evil when it begins, it will always grow worse. I believe that often the indulgence of parents towards adolescent girls spoils their character. As often happens, they unrestrainedly move towards wantonness; little by little womanly timidity gives way, and their audacity immediately grows, increased by a certain foolish opinion which asserts that what is pleasant is right.[1] Once this has infected the honor of virginity and modesty has been cast aside, we strive in vain to save those who are going astray. Afterwards, not only do women give in to man's lust, they provoke it.

Sempronia also greatly coveted money. In the same way that she shamelessly desired to acquire money, she was very free in spending it for every wicked thing, so that she had no control of either her avarice or her prodigality. Greed for money is a fatal evil in a woman and a manifest sign of a corrupt heart. Prodigality should be detested in the same way; when it enters into a mind which by nature is opposed to it (as is that of women, who are naturally frugal) there is no hope of salvation except in poverty. They will lose their honor and their wealth, for they will not stop until they have come to extreme shame and unhappiness. Frugality is proper for women, and within the house it is up to them faithfully to save what is acquired by their husbands. Frugality is to be praised as much as greed and immoderate prodigality are to be condemned, for it is the slow accumulator of wealth, the great safeguard of the household, evidence of a righteous mind, solace of labor, and firm foundation for splendid fame with posterity.

Let us sum up all her crimes in this one wicked deed, her last, I believe. When the conspiracy of that perfidious man Catiline was flourishing, and as with wicked plans and a greater number of conspirators his power was growing for the eternal destruction

---

[1] Boccaccio is referring to the philosophy of Epicurus, who at that time was mistakenly regarded as the advocate of pleasure and indulgence of the senses. Petrarch also speaks of Epicureanism in this manner. There are some instances, however, where both Petrarch and Boccaccio state that this interpretation of Epicurus' thought may be incorrect.

of the Roman Republic, this vicious woman voluntarily joined the conspirators in order to give freer rein to her licentiousness. Desiring what would have seemed horrible even to wicked men, she kept the secret places of her house always ready for their seditious meetings. But God opposes evil, and through Cicero's solicitude the treachery of the conspirators was discovered. I believe that when Catiline withdrew to Fiesole, Sempronia perished, thwarted in her desire for the destruction of others. For these reasons, while we may praise her intellect and extol her for it, we must condemn her shameful actions. For, having stained the matronly robe with much lewdness, Sempronia brought it about that she became notorious, to her shame, whereas if she had preserved her modesty, she could have become glorious.

CHAPTER LXXVIII

THE WIVES OF THE CIMBRIANS

THE very numerous wives of the Cimbrians, who were conquered by Gaius Marius, should be praised for their sacred and constant purpose of chastity. In fact they should be extolled, for the greater their number the higher it seems they should be exalted and with loftier honors. For I have often read that a few women have succeeded in retaining their chastity, but I have never, or only rarely, heard that many banded together for this reason.

When the Romans were at the height of their power, the Teutons, the Cimbrians, and some other barbarian peoples from the North conspired against them. First they gathered together, so that no one could hope to put them to flight, and they brought with them their wives and children and all their household goods in a great train of carts. Then, to strike at all of Italy with one assault, they decided to enter that country with three armies over three different roads. Startled by the sudden outbreak of war, the Romans sent against them the consul Gaius Marius, in whom at that time they reposed all the hope of the Republic. He first moved

against the insolent leaders of the Teutons, and when they did not
retreat at all he joined battle with them. In the long struggle
fortune remained in doubt for many hours, but finally, after much
bloodshed, the Teutons turned their backs. Then Marius moved
against the Cimbrians, and as he had defeated the Teutons near
Aquae Sextiae so did he defeat the Cimbrians in two battles on the
Campi Raudii with a great slaughter of men.[1]

Seeing this, the Cimbrian women, who had remained with the
baggage, did not follow their husbands in flight but placed their
carts, of which they had a very large number, in the shape of a
stockade with the mad but brave purpose of defending their freedom and chastity as long as possible with cudgels, stones, and
swords. But when they had formed for battle and Marius' army
had arrived, the Cimbrian women realized after a short resistance
that their efforts were in vain. Because of this they asked whether
they could come to an agreement with the general. They had
firmly resolved on a way by which they could at least save their
freedom and their chastity, even if they had lost their husbands,
their ancestral homes, and all their wealth in battle. Thus they
unanimously asked not for peace in behalf of their fleeing husbands, or that they be allowed to return to their country, or that
the Romans compensate them with money for their losses, but
only that they be included among the Vestal Virgins in Rome.
Since this request seemed very honest to them and a sign of a
sincere mind, when it was not granted they obstinately persevered
in their desire, burning with fury, and they undertook their cruel
deed. First they dashed their little children to the ground. After
killing them to save them however they could from foul servitude,
that same night they hanged themselves with ropes and the reins
of the horses within the stockade they had built, so that their
chastity would not be dishonored and they would not be subjected
to the conqueror's derision, and they left the ardent soldiers no
other prey than their own dangling bodies.

When their men's strength had been overcome, other women

[1] Campi Raudii was the name given to a broad plain near Verona. Aquae
Sextiae is the modern Aix-en-Provence.

would have gone humbly to meet the victors, with their hair loosened, their arms raised and the air filled with moans and supplications. And—what would have been more shameful— some would have forgotten womanly honor and would have asked with caresses and embraces whether they might retain their goods and return to their own country, or they would have let themselves be dragged along like animals. But these Cimbrian women with resolute courage retained their pride worthy of a better fortune and did not allow the fame of their people's honor to be stained by ignominy. By obstinately avoiding slavery and shame by means of the rope, they showed that their husbands had been overcome through Fortune's fault and not by force. They acquired long life for their chastity in exchange for the few years they could have survived had they not hanged themselves. And they left posterity reason to be amazed at the fact that in one night such a great number of women decided to die, not through an agreement or public deliberation, but as if they had all been moved by the same thought.

CHAPTER LXXIX

JULIA, DAUGHTER OF
JULIUS CAESAR

JULIA was perhaps the most famous woman in the world because of both her ancestors and her husband, but much more because of her inviolable love and sudden death. She was the only daughter of Julius Caesar, born of his wife Cornelia, the daughter of Cinna, who had been consul four times. On his father's side, Julius Caesar was the descendant of Aeneas, the glorious prince of the Trojans, through many kings and other successors; on his mother's side, he was descended from Ancus Marcius, who had been king of the Romans. He was a very great man because of the glory of wars and triumphs and because of his permanent dictatorship. Julia became the wife of Pompey the Great, who at that time was a very famous man among the Romans. For a long time he harassed heaven and earth, vanquishing kings, deposing and then elevating them again, conquering nations, destroying pirates, gaining the favor of the plebeians of Rome, and placing the kings of the whole world under his protection.

Although this famous woman was quite young and Pompey was advanced in age, she loved him ardently, and because of this she met death before her time. For, while performing a sacrifice in the assembly of the aediles, Pompey held the animal which, on being wounded, jerked in all directions and spattered Pompey with a great deal of blood. Pompey therefore removed his clothes and sent them to his house in order to wear different ones. It happened, they say, that the man who was carrying them did not see anyone before meeting Julia, who was pregnant. Seeing her husband's bloody garments, without asking the reason, she assumed that Pompey had been violently killed. As if she did not want to survive her beloved, murdered husband, she was filled with ominous fear and fell to the ground, her eyes filled with darkness and her hands clenched. And she soon died, to the great sorrow not only of her husband and the Roman citizens, but of the whole world at that time.

CHAPTER LXXX

PORTIA, DAUGHTER OF
MARCUS CATO

PORTIA was the daughter of that Marcus Cato who, unable
to endure Caesar's victory, killed himself at Utica after
leading the remains of Pompey's host from Egypt to the
province of Africa through the burning deserts of Libya. Nor
did this great woman seem to have relapsed at all from her father's
fortitude and perseverance. However, I shall not speak now of her
other virtues and famous deeds.

Portia married Decius Brutus[1] while her father was still alive.[2]
She loved him so completely and chastely that among the things
which called for her womanly attention he was by far the first
and most special, and in due time she could not hide the honorable
flames of love in her chaste breast. Since this resulted in her eternal
fame, love freely offered itself to increase her glory. The troublesome disturbance of the Civil Wars had already been quieted,
since the followers of Pompey had everywhere been overcome
by Caesar, when the better part of the Senate conspired against
Caesar, whom they considered a permanent dictator greedy for
power. Among the conspirators was the said Brutus. Knowing
Portia's integrity, Brutus disclosed to her the secret of the infamous
deed. It happened that on the night which preceded the day when
Caesar was removed from Roman affairs by the conspirators, as
Brutus left her room, Portia took a barber's razor as if she wanted
to pare her nails, and, pretending that it was an accident, she
purposely cut herself. Her maids who were present, seeing the
blood spurt out and fearing that it was quite serious, began to
shout. Brutus, who had left, returned to the room and reprimanded
Portia for usurping the barber's duties. When the servants had

---

[1] This name should be Marcus Junius Brutus. Boccaccio has confused him with
another one of the conspirators against Caesar.

[2] Marcus Cato died in 46 B.C. Brutus and Portia were married in 45 B.C.

left, Portia said, "What I did was not done rashly as you think, but to see whether I would have the courage to slay myself with a sword and how I could endure death if your enterprise should not succeed as you wish."

O love of such inexhaustible power! Oh, how happy was that man with such a wife! But why continue? The conspirators proceeded with their crime, killed Caesar, and fled, but not with impunity. For everything turned out differently from what they had thought; the murderers were condemned by the rest of the Senate and fled to various places. Brutus and Cassius, rushing to their death, gathered a large host against Caesar's heirs Octavian and Antony. Octavian and Antony led their armies against them, and they fought at Philippi. The troops of Brutus and of Cassius were defeated and routed in flight; Brutus was killed. When Portia heard this, feeling that after her husband's death the future held no happiness, she decided to endure death with the same courage with which she had endured the wound from the barber's razor, and immediately she turned to her former plan. Since she had no instruments to bring about her suicide with the speed which her violent impulse required, without hesitation she took with her hands some live coals which were nearby, put them in her mouth, and swallowed them. Her entrails were burned by them, and her life was forced from her. Without doubt, the more unusual her way of death, the more fame for conjugal love did it give to the woman who died. Even the fact that her father had reopened his wound with his own hands could not take away any of the glory deserved by her fortitude.

CHAPTER LXXXI

TURIA, WIFE OF QUINTUS LUCRETIUS

T URIA was a Roman woman. If we can rely on the accuracy of her name, then she was of the Turian family, and if we believe her deeds, she was a splendid example of ancient firmness and complete fidelity. For in the unsettled times when by order of the triumvirs new lists of proscribed persons were being posted in Rome, her husband Quintus Lucretius was found to have been proscribed along with many others. The others fled swiftly from their fatherland and with difficulty found safe hiding places among the dens of beasts, in lonely mountain regions, or with the enemies of Rome. Only Lucretius, following the advice of his loving wife, hid fearlessly within the walls of Rome in his own house, near his wife in the secrecy of their conjugal chamber. Here he was protected by his wife with such skill, clever care, and faithfulness that with the exception of a servant girl no one among their friends and relatives suspected it, much less knew it.

We may believe that to cover this fact skillfully Turia often went among the people in humble garments and soiled dress, with sad face, tearful eyes, unkempt hair, not adorned with veils as usual, with painful sighs and pretending a mad senselessness. As if she were unaware of what she was doing, she wandered through the city, walked the streets and went into the temples so that it might seem that she honored the gods with prayers and vows. With a weak and trembling voice she asked her friends and the people she met in the street if they had seen her Lucretius, whether they knew if he was alive, where he had fled, with whom and with what hope. She also said that she wished above all to be his companion in flight, exile, and misfortune. And she did many other similar things which unhappy people are wont to do and which were excellent subterfuges for shielding her husband. Moreover, with allurements, cajoling, and encouragement she strengthened the spirit of the servant girl who knew the secret and made it firm as a rock.

Finally, with consolation and hope she strengthened the anxious breast of her uneasy husband and gave the despondent man some happiness. Thus while the others labored under such a curse in wild mountains, on the raging seas, and in storms, among the treachery of barbarians and the hatred of enemies, and were at times miserably imperiled by those who pursued them, only Lucretius was saved in his dutiful wife's arms. With this holy deed Turia achieved an eternal fame not unworthy of her.

CHAPTER LXXXII

HORTENSIA, DAUGHTER OF
QUINTUS HORTENSIUS

ORTENSIA, the daughter of the great orator Quintus
Hortensius, should be exalted with great praise. For not
only did she encompass in her lively breast her father's
eloquence, but also retained his force of delivery, which her situation required and which is often lacking in the most learned of
men. At the time of the triumvirs, when it seemed that because
of the needs of the state women were to be burdened with almost
intolerably heavy taxes, and when there was not a single man who
would dare to defend them against such an unjust thing, Hortensia alone with firm spirit dared to take up the women's cause
before the triumvirs. And she pleaded so effectively and with such
inexhaustible eloquence that to the great admiration of the audience it seemed that she had changed her sex and was Hortensius
come back to life.

She did not plan and execute this noble enterprise fruitlessly,
for, as she had not failed anywhere either by breaking the oration
or in the praiseworthy demonstration of her thesis, the triumvirs
did not fail to grant what she desired; in fact they freely agreed to
revoke the greater part of the taxes. They thought that although
silence in public is a praiseworthy quality in a woman, when the
occasion requires it a properly prepared speech should be praised.
Finally, because of this the remainder of the taxes, which did
not amount to much, was easily collected from the women, not
without great glory for Hortensia. What shall I say if not that
the spirit of her ancient family flourished so in this woman that
she deservedly bore the name of Hortensia?

CHAPTER LXXXIII

SULPICIA, WIFE OF CRUSCELLIO

SULPICIA, the wife of Lentulus Cruscellio, won undying fame for her almost equable goodwill. Lentulus had been proscribed by the triumvirs in the same disturbance I mentioned above. Having speedily saved himself by flight into Sicily, Lentulus dwelt there in exile and poverty. Once certain of this, Sulpicia decided to endure these sufferings together with her husband, thinking it improper to accept pleasant honors and propitious fortune with one's husband and then refuse to share adversity and exile with him if necessary. But Sulpicia did not easily succeed in going to her husband, for she was watched with great diligence by her mother Julia to prevent her from following her husband into exile. But true love eludes all sentinels. Therefore, seizing the proper moment, dressed as a slave she escaped her mother and her guards, and accompanied by two maids and the same number of male servants this noble woman left her country, abandoned her home, and followed her exiled husband, in spite of the fact that she could have divorced the unfortunate man and married again as the law allowed. Nor was this glorious woman afraid to follow her husband's trail in secret flight through raging seas and over the mountains of Italy, and look for him in unknown regions until she found him and joined him, thinking it more honorable to follow her husband, prostrated by Fortune, through the innumerable perils of life than to remain at home in comfort and peace while he struggled in exile.

Certainly, this opinion is characteristic of a noble mind and savors more of a wise man than of a woman. For women should not always be resplendent with gold and jewels; they should not always indulge in ornaments; they should not always flee the sun in summer and rain in winter; they should not always dwell within their chambers; they should not always spare themselves. But when the blows of Fortune demand it, they must endure toil, go into exile, bear poverty, and face danger bravely with their husbands. This is the admirable service of women; these are their battles and their victories. Their striking triumphs are to overcome ease and luxury, as well as domestic difficulties, by means of their virtue, steadfastness, and purity of mind. In this way they win perpetual fame and glory. Let, therefore, not only those women be ashamed who follow the shadow of happiness with all their efforts, but even more let those be ashamed who shun seasickness when it is a matter of helping their husbands, are worn out by light work, are frightened by foreign lands, and become pale on hearing the bellowing of an ox, although the idea of seafaring delights them as they praise flight with corrupt adulterers, and in their wickedness they have courage for all sorts of favorable opportunities.

CHAPTER LXXXIV

CORNIFICIA

I DO NOT remember learning whether Cornificia was a Roman woman or from another country. According to the testimony of the ancients, however, she was very worthy of being remembered. At the time when Octavian ruled, she excelled so much in the study of poetry that it seemed that she had not been nourished by Italian milk but by the waters of Castalia. She was equal in glory to her brother Cornificius, who was a much renowned poet at that time. Not satisfied with excelling in such a splendid art, inspired by the sacred Muses, she rejected the distaff and turned her hands, skilled in the use of the quill, to writing Heliconian verses. And she wrote many notable epigrams which were held in esteem at the time of that very holy man Saint Jerome, as he himself attests. But I do not know for certain whether they reached later times. She brought honor to womankind, for she scorned womanly concerns and turned her mind to the study of the great poets.

Let slothful women be ashamed, and those who wretchedly have no confidence in themselves, who, as if they were born for idleness and for the marriage bed, convince themselves that they are good only for the embraces of men, giving birth, and raising children, while they have in common with men the ability to do those things which make men famous, if only they are willing to work with perseverance. Cornificia succeeded in not wasting the talents Nature had given her. With her genius and labor she rose above her sex, and with her splendid work she acquired a perpetual fame which is not common but stands out for its excellence and rarity, which few men have equaled.

CHAPTER LXXXV

MARIAMNE, QUEEN OF JUDAEA

MARIAMNE, a Hebrew woman more fortunate in her birth than in her marriage, was born of Aristobulus,[1] the king of the Jews, and Queen Alexandra, the daughter of King Hyrcanus. She was of such great and unusual beauty that in her time they not only believed that she was fairer than all other women, but thought that she was of divine rather than human beauty. The triumvir Mark Antony concurred in this opinion. Mariamne's brother, whose name was Aristobulus, was born of the same parents and was equal to her in beauty and age. When her husband died, Mariamne's mother Alexandra wished to obtain the office of chief priest for her son Aristobulus from King Herod, who was Mariamne's husband. It is said that on the advice of her friend Dellius she sent a portrait of the two young people, done on a tablet by an excellent painter, to the triumvir Antony in Egypt, who was a very sensual man, in order to rouse his desire for them and as a result make him accede to their wishes. When he saw it, Antony first stood a while in admiration, then, it is said, stated that as for beauty they were certainly children of a god. Then he swore that he had never seen anywhere anyone more beautiful or even equal to them.

But let us return to Mariamne. Although she was notable for her unheard-of beauty, she was far more distinguished for her strength of character. When she was of marriageable age, she was wedded to Herod, the unfortunate king of the Jews, and to her great misfortune was madly loved by him for her beauty. He gloried in the fact that he alone in the whole world possessed such divine beauty and was so determined that no one else should be equal to him in this that he began to fear that Mariamne would survive him. To prevent this, when he was called to Egypt to explain to Antony the death of Mariamne's brother Aristobulus,

[1] Mariamne was not the daughter of Aristobulus, but of Alexander, the son of Aristobulus II.

whom he had killed, and after Antony's death when he had to go to the Emperor Octavian to excuse himself, if possible, for having helped the friends of Antony against him, he ordered his mother Cypros and his friends to kill Mariamne immediately if he should die at the hands of Antony, Octavian, or anyone else. What a ridiculous madness this was, that a king who was very wise in other matters should grieve at the uncertain pleasure of others and be jealous after death.

After some time, Mariamne found out about these arrangements, although they had been secret. Having already conceived a deadly hatred for Herod because of Aristobulus' undeserved death, when she saw that she was loved only for the enjoyment of her beauty, her wrath grew, and she ill endured the fact that he had unjustly condemned her to death twice. Although she had borne two children of his, Alexander and Aristobulus, who were very beautiful, she could not calm her thoughts in any way. In a fury, she determined to deny intercourse to her passionate husband. She scorned him and with proud demeanor strove to trample upon his power, as if all the spirit of her ancient royal lineage were reborn in her. She was not afraid to say often and openly that Herod was a foreigner and not a Jew, not of royal but of mean, low birth, unworthy and unfit to have a queen as a wife, and that he was cruel, proud, disloyal, and an accursed and savage beast. Although Herod endured these attacks with difficulty, he did not dare do anything cruel against her, since his love forbade it. Finally, some writers say, the situation was becoming worse, and Mariamne was accused before Herod by one of his servants, who had been bribed by Herod's mother, Cypros, and by his sister Salome, who detested Mariamne. The accusation was that she had attempted to prevail upon this servant to give Herod a love potion which she had prepared. Or others say that it was Mariamne herself, and not her mother at the time of which I have spoken, who of her own volition, after she had begun to hate Herod, sent her beautiful portrait to Antony to arouse his desire for her and hatred toward Herod. Because he believed these things, and Mariamne's malevolence made him believe them, Herod, angry and burning with anguished fury, complained to his friends in a long speech. Encouraged by them and by Mariamne's mother Alexandra, who was trying to gain his favor, he was persuaded to command that she be killed, condemning her to die as one who had sought the king's death.

Mariamne summoned her noble courage so that, scorning death, with all the beauty of her face intact, and not yielding at all in the fashion of women, she listened silently to her mother reprimanding her and with dry eyes looked at the others who were crying. She went to her death not only fearlessly, but with an eager expression as if going to a joyful triumph, and without begging for her life she met her death at the executioner's hands as if it were something for which she longed. Because of her great firmness, not only was the jealousy of the cruel king turned to misery, but Mariamne acquired more centuries of fame than the months of life Herod could have granted her had he been moved by tears and entreaties.

CHAPTER LXXXVI

CLEOPATRA, QUEEN OF EGYPT

CLEOPATRA was an Egyptian woman who became an object of gossip for the whole world. Although she was the descendant of Ptolemy, the son of Lagus and king of Macedonia, through a long line of kings, and the daughter of Ptolemy Dionysus,[1] or of King Minos as some are pleased to think, she nevertheless came to rule through crime. She gained glory for almost nothing else than her beauty, while on the other hand she became known throughout the world for her greed, cruelty and lustfulness.

To start at the beginning of her reign, some say that Dionysus, or Minos, who was a great friend of the Roman people, in the first consulship of Julius Caesar, when he was near death, decreed in a signed testament that his oldest son, who some say was named Lysanias,[2] was to marry Cleopatra, the oldest daughter, and at his death they were to rule together. This was done, for it was a common disgrace among the Egyptians, who prohibited only marrying one's mother or daughter. Then Cleopatra, burning with the desire to rule, as some say, poisoned the innocent fifteen-year-old boy who was both her brother and her husband, and ruled the kingdom alone. Then they tell us that Pompey the Great, after occupying almost all of Asia Minor, went to Egypt and substituted a boy who had survived for Cleopatra's brother and made him king of Egypt. Angered by this, Cleopatra took up arms against him. This being the situation, Pompey was defeated by Caesar in Thessaly and was killed on the Egyptian shore by the boy whom he had made king.

When Caesar arrived in Egypt after him, he found the Egyptians fighting among themselves and ordered them to appear before him to plead their case. I shall not speak of young Ptolemy.

---

[1] Ptolemy XII, commonly known as Auletes.

[2] Ptolemy XIII, commonly said to have taken the surname of Dionysus in imitation of his father.

Armed with wiles and great self-confidence, Cleopatra arrived in royal splendor. Thinking that she would obtain her kingdom if she could draw Caesar, the conqueror of the world, into lustfulness, and being very beautiful and captivating anyone she desired with her shining eyes and her eloquence, with little trouble she brought the lustful prince to her embraces. For many nights she stayed with him among the tumult of the people of Alexandria, and, as almost everyone agrees, she conceived a son, whom she later called Caesarion after his father. Finally young Ptolemy, abandoned by Caesar and urged on by his men, turned his arms against his liberator and went with his armies to the Delta against Mithridates of Pergamum, who was coming to Caesar's aid. There he was defeated by Caesar, who had arrived earlier by another road. When he attempted to flee in a boat, it sank, weighted down by the great number of men in it. Thus, things having quieted down and the people of Alexandria having surrendered, Caesar was about to move against Pharnaces, the king of Pontus, who had favored Pompey. Almost as if he owed her payment for her crime, and because she had been loyal, Caesar gave the kingdom of Egypt to Cleopatra, who desired nothing else. But first he removed her sister Arsinoë, lest she should lead new uprisings against him.

Thus Cleopatra, having already acquired her kingdom through two crimes, gave herself to her pleasures. Having become almost the prostitute of Oriental kings, and greedy for gold and jewels, she not only stripped her lovers of these things with her art, but it was also said that she emptied the temples and the sacred places of the Egyptians of their vases, statues, and other treasures. Later, when Caesar had already been killed and Brutus and Cassius overcome, and Antony was advancing toward Syria, she went to meet him and easily ensnared that lustful man with her beauty and wanton eyes. She kept him wretchedly in love with her and to remove all threats to her rule, she, who had poisoned her brother, made Antony kill her sister Arsinoë in the temple of the Ephesian Diana, where the unfortunate girl had fled for safety. Cleopatra received this from her new lover as the first reward of her adultery. The wicked woman, already knowing Antony's character, did not fear to ask him for the kingdoms of Syria and Arabia. It seemed to him that this was a serious and unseemly thing; nevertheless, to satisfy the desire of the woman he loved, he gave her a small piece of both countries. And he added also all the cities which are near the Syrian shore between Egypt and the river Eleutherus, keeping Sidon and Tyre for himself. Having obtained these things, Cleopatra followed Antony all the way to the Euphrates, when he was campaigning against the Armenians, or, according to some, against the Parthians. Returning to Egypt through Syria, she was received magnificently by Herod Antipater, who at that time was king of Judaea. She was not ashamed to send messengers to him to bring him to her embraces, so that, if he accepted, she could take as payment the kingdom he had gained shortly before through Antony. Realizing this, Herod not only refused through respect for Antony, but to free him from the shame of such a lewd woman he planned to kill her with his sword, but his friends dissuaded him. After failing in her real purpose, Cleopatra, as though she had stopped for this reason, gave Herod the revenue from Jericho, rich in balsams, a plant which she later brought to Babylon of Egypt, where it is still found down to this time. After receiving great gifts from Herod, she returned to Egypt from that country.

When Antony returned, fleeing from the Parthians, she went to meet him. Antony had treacherously seized the king of Armenia, Artavasdes son of Tigranes, together with his sons and satraps. He had taken vast treasures from him and was bringing him along shackled with silver chains. To bring covetous Cleopatra to his embraces, effeminate Antony gave her, as she approached, the captive king in all his regalia, as well as all the booty. The greedy woman, happy at the gifts, embraced the ardent man so seductively that he made her his wife with great love, after repudiating Octavia, the sister of Octavian Caesar. I shall not discuss the Arabian ointments, the perfumes of Saba, and the drunken revels. As Antony gluttonously stuffed himself continuously with delicacies, he asked what magnificent thing could be added to the daily banquets, as if he wanted to make his dinners for Cleopatra more splendid. The lewd woman answered that if he wanted she could have a dinner costing more than one hundred thousand sesterces. Antony thought that this could not be done; nevertheless, wishing to see and devour, he asked her to try it. Lucius Plautus was called to be the judge. The next day, when the food did not exceed the customary, and when Antony was already ridiculing her promises, Cleopatra ordered her servants to bring the second course. According to the instructions they had received beforehand, they brought in only a goblet of strong vinegar. Cleopatra immediately took a pearl of great value which she wore as an ornament on one of her ears, according to the custom of Oriental women, dissolved it in the vinegar, and then drank it. As she was taking an equally valuable pearl from her other ear to repeat what she had done, Lucius Plautus immediately declared that Antony had lost, and so, the queen having won, the second pearl was preserved. It was later brought to Rome and placed on the ear of Venus in the Pantheon so that for a long time those who looked at it would be reminded of Cleopatra's half supper.

As the insatiable woman's craving for kingdoms grew day by day, to grasp everything at once she asked Antony for the Roman empire. Perhaps drunk or rising from such a noble supper, Antony, who was not in full possession of his mental faculties, without properly considering his own strength or the power of the Romans, promised to give it to her, as if it were his to give. Good Lord, how great was the audacity of the woman who requested this! And the madness of the man who promised it was no less! How generous was this man who so rashly gave away to an entreating woman an empire which had just been gained after so many centuries, with such difficulty and bloodshed, through the death of so many great men and even peoples, and with so many noble deeds and battles, as if he wanted to give it away at once like the ownership of a single house! Why say more? The seeds of war between Octavian and Antony had already been sown through the repudiation of Octavia. For this reason war broke out after both sides had gathered their forces. Antony and Cleopatra proceeded to

Epirus with their fleet adorned with gold and purple sails. There they joined battle with the enemy on land, and, after being defeated, they withdrew. Reembarking in the fleet, Antony's men returned to Actium where they were to test their fortunes in a naval battle. Octavian moved against them with his son-in-law Agrippa and attacked them with a great fleet and marvelous daring. When battle had been joined, Mars kept the result in doubt for a long time. Finally, when Antony's forces seemed to be succumbing, proud Cleopatra was the first to flee on her golden ship with sixty other vessels. Antony lowered the ensign of his praetorian ship and immediately followed her.

After returning to Egypt, they sent their children away to the Red Sea and then prepared their forces in vain for the defense of the kingdom. For the conqueror Octavian followed them and destroyed their power in several victorious battles. They asked for last minute peace terms. Unable to obtain them, Antony despaired, and, according to some, entered the royal mausoleum, where he killed himself with his sword. When Alexandria had been captured, Cleopatra tried in vain with her old wiles to make young Octavian desire her, as she had done with Caesar and Antony. Angry at hearing that she was being reserved for the conqueror's triumph, and without hope of safety, Cleopatra, dressed in royal garments, followed her Antony. Lying down next to him, she opened the veins of her arms and put two asps in the openings in order to die. Some say that they cause death in sleep. In this sleep the wretched woman put an end to her greed, her concupiscence, and her life. Octavian attempted to keep her alive if possible by removing the poison from her veins.

There are some writers who say that she died earlier and in a different way. They say that while preparing for the battle of Actium Antony became suspicious of Cleopatra's loyalty, and so he made it a practice to take neither food nor drink without having it pre-tasted. Cleopatra became aware of this and devised a plan to show him that he could trust her. She poisoned the flowers with which she had previously adorned her crown, placed it on her head and then proceeded to draw Antony out and cheer him. In this merry mood she invited him to drink her garland with her. The flowers had been put into the cup, and Antony was about to drink, when Cleopatra restrained him, saying, "My beloved Antony, I am that Cleopatra whom you show you no longer trust since you have your food tasted as you used not to do. I had the opportunity and the means to poison you just now, had I been cruel enough to let you drink." When he saw the deception which she herself had disclosed to him, Antony had her imprisoned and forced her to take the potion which she had prevented him from drinking. And thus, they say, she died. The other version, however, is better attested. To this I must add that Octavian ordered that a monument which Antony had started should be finished and then had him buried in it together with Cleopatra.

CHAPTER LXXXVII

ANTONIA, DAUGHTER OF ANTONY

ANTONIA the younger left posterity an everlasting example of widowhood. It is believed that she was the daughter of the triumvir Mark Antony and Octavia, and she was called the younger because she had an older sister of the same name. She married Drusus, the brother of Tiberius Nero and stepson of Octavian Augustus, and gave birth to Livilla, Germanicus, and Claudius, who later became emperor. According to some, Drusus, while in Germany on a military expedition, died of poison through the efforts of his brother Tiberius. After his death, his wife Antonia, although very young and beautiful, thought that for an honorable woman one marriage should suffice, and she could not be persuaded by anyone to enter into a second marriage. In fact, she spent the rest of her life with her mother-in-law Livia so chastely and modestly within her husband's chamber that the fame of her widowhood surpassed that of all previous women.

Certainly it is a saintly and splendid thing for women of mature years to lead their lives without the stain of lust, following the example of the daughters of the Catos, and they should be praised along with the Cincinnati, Fabricii, Curii, Lucretii, and Sulpicii. If this is true, how shall we praise this young woman? She had great beauty and was the daughter of Mark Antony, a very dissolute man; she was not brought up in forests or in solitude, but among imperial leisure and pleasures; she was brought up with Julia, the daughter of Octavian, and Julia, the daughter of Agrippa, who were hot flames of lust and concupiscence; she was brought up among the foulness and dishonesty of her father Mark Antony and Tiberius, who later was emperor of his country, which had once been virtuous, but then was given to all types of infamy; she was brought up among a thousand examples of lust, and yet with courage and constancy she preserved her chastity, not for a short time and in the hope of a future marriage, but to keep her virtue until old age and death. Certainly my words have not been sufficient, and perhaps something is left to be considered. Since this is beyond a writer's powers, it is sufficient to have left it to pious minds to be considered and extolled by worthy consideration.

AGRIPPINA, WIFE OF GERMANICUS

AGRIPPINA was the daughter of Marcus Agrippa and of Julia, Octavian's daughter. In spite of this, Caligula, the son of the same Agrippina, being already emperor of the world and scorning the lowliness of his mother's father, stated that his mother had not been born of Agrippa but of Octavian, who ravished his own daughter Julia. He foolishly thought that he would be deemed nobler if his mother had been begotten in incest than if she had been born to a lowly father according to sacred law. Whoever her father may have been, she was married to Germanicus, an eminent young man of her own age and of great service to the state, who was the adopted son of Tiberius Caesar. She was very famous for this reason, but more so because with relentless purpose she resisted the perfidy of that most proud emperor.

When she had already borne Germanicus three sons (one of whom was the Gaius Caligula who later became emperor of Rome), and as many daughters (among whom was Agrippina, mother of the emperor Nero), her husband was poisoned through the efforts of his father Tiberius, as was later proved. Agrippina, as is the custom of women, mourned the death of that famous young man and shed many tears. By mourning him, she incurred the hatred of Tiberius, who once seized her by the arm and scolded her until she cried, saying that she was too discontent with not being empress. Later he attacked her with many accusations which he brought before the Senate and ordered her to prison, although she was innocent. But the noble woman, knowing that what the emperor was doing to her was undeserved, planned to escape the petty emperor's persecution by committing suicide. Since other means were not available, with noble courage she decided to seek death by starvation and immediately began to refuse all food.

When Tiberius was informed of this, the wicked man realized

· · (200) · ·

what the result of her fasting would be. Since neither threats nor floggings were of any avail in making her eat, Tiberius forced her to take food so that she would not escape his abuse so quickly and so surely. For as long as she received nourishment, although she wanted to die, he did not care what means were used to force food into her stomach. By these methods he thought he would not be deprived of the object of his cruelty. But the more Agrippina was provoked by indignities, the firmer did her purpose become. By persevering in what she had begun, in death she overcame the insolence of the infamous emperor, showing that although he could make many die if he so desired, yet with all the power of his empire he could not keep alive anyone who was determined to die. Although she certainly acquired great glory among her people through her death, she nevertheless left much greater opprobrium to Tiberius.

CHAPTER LXXXIX

THE ROMAN WOMAN PAULINA

T HE Roman woman Paulina acquired almost everlasting fame for a certain ridiculous *naïveté* of hers. When Tiberius was emperor of the Romans, Paulina was famous above all others for the beauty of her face and body, and after her marriage everyone thought her a glorious example of virtue. Besides her husband, she cared for nothing with special eagerness except to serve and win the favor of Anubis, an Egyptian god whom she worshipped with great veneration. Since beautiful women, especially those who take great care of their chastity, are desired everywhere by young men, a young Roman named Mundus began to court her continuously with glances, gestures, pleasantries, promises, gifts, prayers, and flattery to see if perhaps he could obtain what he so ardently desired. But all this was in vain, for this very chaste woman, devoted only to her husband, ignored all her lover's attempts. He persisted in his efforts, but seeing very clearly that the road was blocked by the woman's constancy, he turned his mind to deception.

Paulina used to visit the temple of Isis every day and worshipped Anubis with continuous sacrifices. When he learned this, the young man, counseled by love, thought of an unheard-of deception. Thinking that the priests of Anubis could be very useful to his desires, he went to them and with great gifts won them to his purpose. And it happened that the one who because of his advanced years was the most venerable among them, instigated by Mundus, gently told Paulina, when she came as usual, that Anubis had come to him at night and ordered him to tell her that he had taken great pleasure in her devotion, and that he wanted to speak to her in the temple while she slept. When Paulina heard this she thought that it had happened because of her holiness. She felt within herself great pride in those words and believed them to be as true as if she had heard them from the god Anubis with her own ears. She told all this to her husband, who, more foolish than his wife, consented to her request to spend the night in the temple. Therefore, a bed worthy of the god was spread in the sacred temple, without the knowledge of anyone except the priests and Paulina.

When the shadows had already darkened the earth, Paulina entered the temple now empty of witnesses, and after her prayers and sacrifices she got into bed to wait for the god. When she fell asleep, Mundus was brought in by the priests. Dressed in the regalia of Anubis, he approached and, desiring his beloved, embraced the woman and kissed her. When she awoke in amazement, he told her to be in good spirits for he was Anubis, whom she had honored for such a long time, and that because of her prayers and devotion he had come from heaven to lie with her so that from them would be born a similar god. But first Paulina asked her lover whether the gods could or were accustomed to have intercourse with mortals. Mundus answered immediately that they could, and that Jupiter had given the example by sliding into Danae's lap from the roof, and from their union had been born Perseus, who later was taken into heaven. Hearing this, Paulina happily consented to his request. Mundus entered naked into the bed in Anubis' place and enjoyed the desired embraces and intercourse. When night was already changing into day, he left, saying to the deceived woman that she had conceived a child.

It was already day when the priests removed the bed from the temple, and Paulina reported what had happened to her husband. That foolish man believed it and congratulated his wife on the future birth of a god. Without doubt they would both have awaited the time of labor, if the ardent young man had not carelessly disclosed his fraud. For, knowing very well that she had accepted his embraces and had eagerly had intercourse with him, he thought that if he explained to her that he had cleverly ravished her chastity, she would be more yielding and desire similar nights. Thus he could return to the coveted embraces more easily and more often. Approaching Paulina as she went to the temple, he said in a low voice, "Blessed are you, O Paulina, for you have conceived a child of me, Anubis." The result of his words, however, was quite different from what he had expected. For Paulina, in great amazement, recalling many of the things she had heard and the things which had been done, immediately realized the deception. Very upset, she returned to her husband and informed him of the trickery of Mundus and the priests as she saw it. The result of this was that the husband complained to Tiberius, who obtained proof of the deception and punished the priests with torture and Mundus with exile. Paulina, duped, became the common talk of the Romans and became better known and more famous for her *naïveté* and Mundus' trick than for her devotion to Anubis and the chastity she had preserved so religiously.

CHAPTER XC

AGRIPPINA, MOTHER OF NERO

AGRIPPINA, mother of the emperor Nero, was no less outstanding for her birth, lineage, power, and her son's and her own monstrosity than for her famous deeds. She was named Julia Agrippina and was the daughter of Caesar Germanicus, an excellent young man of praiseworthy character, and of the already mentioned Agrippina. She was the sister of the emperor Caligula, and she married Gnaeus Domitius, a very loathsome and cruel man of the Ahenobarbus family. She bore him a son, Nero, born feet first, who was known to the whole world as a monster. When Nero was still a child, Domitius died of dropsy. Since Agrippina was extremely beautiful, her brother Caligula, being a very vile man, basely ravished her. When he became emperor, he deprived her of almost all her wealth and exiled her to an island, either because he did not approve of her misconduct with Lepidus and the fact that she hoped to rule some day, or because he was spurred on by some one of her enemies. However, he was finally killed by his soldiers, and Claudius, who succeeded him as emperor, called her back.

After some time, when she heard that Valeria Messalina had been killed for various just reasons, she immediately hoped to obtain the rule of the world for herself and her son. With her great beauty, and through the aid of Pallas, she made the unmarried emperor greatly desire to marry her, although he was the brother of her father Germanicus, against Lollia Paulina, who was favored by the freedman Callistus, and against Aelia Paetina, favored by Narcissus. Respectability seemed an obstacle to her desire, since she was Claudius' niece through his brother. But it happened that an oration of Vitellius, who had been bribed and had asked the Senate to issue a decree allowing uncles to marry their nieces, forced Claudius to heed the Senate's prayers that he do what he wanted to do. And so, since Claudius was willing and the Senate requested it, Agrippina married him. She was finally

called Augusta and went to the Capitol by carriage, something
which previously only priests had been allowed to do. And she
began to punish cruelly the people who had opposed her.

Finally, being very shrewd, she seized the opportunity and,
although Claudius had children of his own of both sexes, persuaded him to adopt as his own son his stepson Nero, which was
something that no one recalled ever being done before in Claudius'
family. And she induced him to promise Nero in marriage his
daughter Octavia, who had been born of Messalina and was married to Lucius Silanus, a noble young man.[1] Claudius was persuaded by Memmius Pollio, who at that time was consul, and
urged by the freedman Pallas, who was Agrippina's protector
since he had committed adultery with her. Having obtained these
things and thinking that the beast had fallen into the snare, she
planned to murder Claudius, moved not so much by disgust for
Claudius' continuous gluttony as by her fear that his son Britannicus, for whom Narcissus pleaded very much, would come to
man's estate before his father's death, for she thought that this
would obstruct her plans. Claudius loved mushrooms and used
to say that they were the food of the gods because they grew on
their own without seed. Seeing this, Agrippina carefully cooked
some, poisoned them, and, some authors say, set them before him
while he was intoxicated. Others say that while Claudius was
eating in the temple with the priests, Agrippina sent the mushrooms to him by means of Paralotus Sarpadon,[2] his taster, whom
she had bribed. But when it seemed that Claudius, after vomiting
and defecating, would recover, his doctor, Xenophon, to keep him
vomiting tendered him poisoned feathers, so that what Claudius'
wife wanted to happen came to pass. Finally, after being carried
to his room, he died without anyone except Agrippina knowing
it. She did not disclose his death until with the aid of friends
Nero, who was already a young man, had been made emperor,
while Britannicus, being younger, was ignored. Nero was so

[1] Octavia was betrothed to Lucius Junius Silanus Torquatus, but never married
him.
[2] This name should be Halotus.

pleased that he raised his mother above everyone else in private and public affairs as one who had deserved well of him. It seemed that he had taken the title for himself and the power for his mother. Thus Agrippina, ruling the Roman empire, was famous throughout the world.

Then her great splendor was stained by a shameful blot, for she raged furiously, causing the death of many and sending many into exile. It was also believed that with her consent Nero loved Agrippina with an illicit love beyond that which it is natural to have for a mother. For he had taken among his concubines a prostitute who resembled his mother, and every time he rode in the carriage with Agrippina, their relations were apparent from the stains on his clothes. Some say that she brought her son to commit this crime, wishing to recover the power which she seemed to have lost. For she had spoken against Nero a number of times for various reasons, and they confirm this by the fact that Nero usually avoided her company or speaking alone with her. Since she had made her uncle marry her, had killed him with mushrooms and had made her inept young son emperor by violence and fraud, she was brought to a detestable although deserved death. For, because she annoyed her son in many ways, he hated her and deprived her of all honors and imperial majesty. Angry and spurred by a woman's fury, she threatened to make him lose his empire in the same way that she had gained it for him. Nero was frightened by this, and, knowing how shrewd she was and that she had the aid of many friends because of the memory of his father Germanicus, he tried three times to poison her. But she cautiously escaped harm with antidotes.

Finally, when she had avoided all the other traps he had set to kill her, Nero realized that he had to act with more cautious deceit. At Nero's request, Anicetus, who was the prefect of the fleet near Misenum and at one time had been Nero's tutor when he was a child, told him that a frail ship could be built, and that by boarding it in ignorance of the trick Agrippina would be in danger. Nero liked this idea and, as if repenting his past hatred, received his mother on her return from Antium with pretended filial affection. He embraced her and took her home. Then, the ship having been prepared for her death, she boarded it to go to supper, accompanied by the freedman Crepereius Gallus and the freedwoman Acerronia. As they sailed through the night, a signal was given to those who shared the secret, and the roof, weighted with a great deal of lead, fell and killed Crepereius. Then as the sailors attempted to capsize the ship in the calm sea, Acerronia shouted for help and was killed with the oars and the poles. Agrippina, wounded in the shoulder and finally thrown into the sea, was aided by people on the shore and taken to her villa on the Lucrine Lake. At her orders, the freedman Egerinus informed Nero that Agrippina had been saved. Nero ordered that he be thrown in prison as if he had come to murder him treacherously.

Anicetus, the tetrarch Herculeius, and a navy captain[3] were sent to kill Agrippina. When the house had been surrounded by Anicetus, and a servant who was Agrippina's only companion had fled, the henchmen entered. First Herculeius gave her a blow on the head with a club. Then Agrippina, seeing the centurion prepare to kill her with his sword, offered her belly and shouted to them to strike her in the womb. And thus she was killed. That same night she was cremated and buried ignominiously. Finally along the road near Misenum near Julius Caesar's villa a small memorial was erected to her. Others say that Nero saw her corpse after her death, and that he criticized some parts of her body and praised others, and then she was buried.

[3] This captain was named Volusius Proculus. He appears in the next chapter.

CHAPTER XCI

THE FREEDWOMAN EPICHARIS

EPICHARIS is believed to have been a foreigner rather than a Roman. She was not famous for any nobility of birth; she was even a freedwoman, daughter of a freedman. More shameful was the fact that she had never taken delight in good morals. Nevertheless, toward the end of her life she showed that she had a brave spirit and manly fortitude.

As Nero's insolence and lasciviousness increased among the Romans and all the Italic tribes, it happened that with Lucius Piso[1] as leader some senators and other citizens conspired against him. As they tried to complete their arrangements in various meetings, this fact and the names of the conspirators were learned by the above-mentioned Epicharis, I do not know how. But as she felt that this matter was being delayed too long, she went to Campania as if she were on a pleasure trip. When she happened to be in Puteoli,[2] not to let time go by uselessly, she went to Volusius Proculus, chiliarch and commander of the Roman fleet and murderer of Agrippina, thinking that she would strengthen the conspiracy greatly if she could bring him over to their side. She explained to him at length Nero's infamy, haughtiness, foolish ways, insolence, and ingratitude toward him, for, although he had deserved well of Nero, he had never been promoted in any proper way for a deed as great as Agrippina's death. She informed him of the conspiracy and with all her strength tried to add him to the conspirators as an ally.

The result was very different from what Epicharis had expected. For Volusius wanted to see whether he could obtain the emperor's favor with his fealty. As soon as he was granted an audience by the emperor he reported everything that Epicharis had said, al-

---

[1] The leader of the conspiracy was C. Calpurnius Piso.
[2] According to Tacitus, this happened at Misenum.

though she had not done what he thought, for shrewdly she had not told him the names of the conspirators while he was still undecided. Moreover, when they summoned her, they could not make her reveal anything they asked her. Finally, while she was being held in custody, the conspiracy was accidentally revealed by the conspirators themselves, and Epicharis was called back for questioning, as if she were less able to endure torture, and thus they could more easily obtain from her what they wanted. After torturing her for a long time, her tormentors willingly persisted even more in their cruelty so that they should not seem to be conquered by a woman, but with great courage she did not reveal any secrets. Finally, having been remanded to the next day, Epicharis, unable to walk, feared that if they called her a third time she could not hold out. She tore off her breast-band, tied it to the sedan chair in which she was being carried, and made a noose which she put around her neck. Letting all the weight of her body fall, she inflicted a violent death upon herself lest she do harm to the conspirators. Thus the widely-known old proverb that women keep silent only about what they do not know was proven false. And so she left Nero in ignorance and fear.

Although this seems a very great thing for a woman, it will be even more marvelous if we consider the weakness of the great men in that conspiracy. After being revealed through someone other than Epicharis, there was no one among them of such hardy youth as to endure for his own sake what Epicharis had endured for the sake of others. They could not even bear to hear the description of the tortures without immediately confessing what they knew of the conspiracy. Thus they spared neither themselves nor their friends, while that glorious woman had spared everyone but herself. I should think that Nature sometimes errs when she gives souls to mortals. That is, she gives to a woman one that she thought she had given to a man. But since God Himself is the giver of such things, it is wrong to believe that He might doze while doing His work. Therefore, we must believe that all souls are perfect, but our actions show whether we keep them so. And so I think men should be ashamed to be surpassed by a woman who was lewd but also very constant in the endurance of difficulties. For if we are stronger because of our sex, why is it not proper that we be stronger in bravery? If this is not done, we rightly seem to have exchanged characters with them and become effeminate.

CHAPTER XCII

POMPEIA PAULINA, WIFE OF
LUCIUS ANNAEUS SENECA

POMPEIA PAULINA was the glorious wife of Lucius
Annaeus Seneca, Nero's tutor. I do not remember reading
whether she was a Roman woman or a foreigner. Nevertheless, when I consider the nobility of her spirit, I prefer to
believe that she was Roman rather than a foreigner. Although we
do not know her exact origin, we do not lack a very clear example
of her devoted love for her husband, as attested by famous men.

The most worthy men of that age believed that Seneca, as
an old and very famous man, more through Nero's cruelty than
his own guilt, was marked with the disgrace of the Pisonian conspiracy, if doing something against a tyrant can be called disgrace.
With that pretext Nero found a way to be cruel to Seneca because
of his old or, rather, innate hatred of virtue. Some have thought
that at the instigation of Poppaea and Tigellinus, the emperor's
only source of cruel advice, a centurion ordered Seneca to commit
suicide. When Paulina saw him preparing to die, she paid no
attention to the allurements and the consolation with which he
encouraged her to go on living and, moved by her very chaste love,
prepared herself with great courage to die together with her husband and in the same way, so that one death would undo the bonds
of those two who had been joined together in an honorable life.
Fearlessly she stepped into the warm water and opened her veins
so that she might die at the same moment as her husband. But
against her will she was saved from death by slaves at the order
of the emperor, who did not have any particular hatred for her,
in order to subdue somewhat the infamy of his innate cruelty. The
flow of blood, however, could not be stopped quickly enough to
prevent that excellent woman from showing by her continuous
pallor that she had lost a good part of her vital spirits together
with her husband. Finally, when she had preserved her husband's

memory with praiseworthy widowhood for a few years, unable to conclude her life with her husband in another way, she at least ended it as Seneca's wife.

What if not the sweetness of love, the marvelous token of devotion, and the venerable sacrament of marriage could have persuaded that excellent woman to prefer dying with her aged husband, if she could do so honorably, rather than save her life in order to marry again, not without ignominy, as most women do? And to the great shame of womanly chastity, it is the custom nowadays for women to marry, I will not say a second or third time, for that is almost universal, but a sixth, seventh, or eighth time if given the opportunity. It is so customary for them to go to the beds of new husbands that they seem to have adopted the ways of prostitutes, whose custom it is often to change the men with whom they lie and spend the night. And they take their oft-repeated marriage vows with the same expression as if they kept them in sacred honesty. It is not sufficiently certain whether one should say that they have left the chambers of their dead husbands or those of a brothel. But there is no doubt whether one is to suspect that such a woman is more shameless for entering a new bedroom or her new husband more foolish in taking her there. Alas, how wretched we are! To what depths have our morals fallen! The ancients, whose spirit was prone to saintliness, were accustomed to think it shameful to marry a second time, not to speak of a seventh, and they thought that such women should not righteously mingle with honest women. But the women of our day are quite different. For they conceal their lust and think they are more beautiful and esteemed because, having overcome the fortunes of widowhood with their frequent marriages, they have pleased so many husbands.

CHAPTER XCIII

SABINA POPPAEA, WIFE OF NERO

SABINA POPPAEA was a noble Roman woman, the daughter of T. Ollius, a man not of the highest nobility, although she did not take her name from him but from her maternal grandfather, Poppaeus Sabinus, a famous man who had held a distinguished consulship and had been honored with a triumph. If she had been of good moral character, she would not have lacked the other womanly virtues. For she had unusual beauty and resembled her mother, who in her time exceeded all other Roman women in beauty. Moreover, her speech was gentle and resonant with praiseworthy sweetness, and she had a noble and versatile intellect, if only she had used it for honest purposes.

It was her custom to show modesty assiduously in public, while in private she practiced lasciviousness, the universal vice of women. She seldom went out in public, but was not without cunning. For since she shrewdly realized that many people, and especially the most distinguished, took pleasure in seeing her features, she always went out with her face veiled, not to hide what she desired to be coveted, but rather not to satiate the eyes of the men who looked at her by showing herself too freely and to leave in them the desire to see what she hid with her veils. Not to examine all her behavior, I will say that she never spared her reputation and her desires inclined wherever utility seemed greater, making no distinction between husbands and adulterers. Although marked with this infamy, she enjoyed very good fortune. For, having abundant wealth to maintain the splendor of her lineage, she first married the Roman knight Rufrius Crispinus. After bearing him a son, she was wooed by Otho, who was powerful and influential in Nero's entourage for his youth and sensuality. She joined him in adultery and then became his wife for a brief period. Perhaps because he was less cautious in the ardor of love, or because he already could not endure the ways of his lustful wife and for that reason attempted to bring her to Nero's pleasure, or because Poppaea's destiny exacted this, Otho on rising from the emperor's banquets was usually heard to say that he was going to the woman to whom the gods had given nobility, elegance of manner, and divine beauty, and in whom dwelt the desires of all mortals and the delights and joys of fortunate men. Nero's lust was easily aroused by these remarks, and without much delay a way was found by go-betweens to bring her willing and ardent to the emperor's embraces.

It was not long before Nero was so enmeshed by the artful wiles of this woman that he thought the things Otho had repeatedly asserted were completely true. Knowing this, Poppaea very cleverly concealed what she wanted, and, seizing the right moment, would say with many false tears that she could not give all her love as she desired, for she was bound to Otho by the bonds of marriage and the emperor was bound by his love for his concubine, the slave Acte. From this it followed that Otho, under pretence of being honored, was removed and sent to the province of Lusitania as prefect, and Acte was completely rejected. Then Poppaea began to assail the emperor's mother Agrippina, saying at times that Nero did not enjoy power, and even liberty was denied him, and that he was just a little boy governed by his nurse's authority. For this reason, and since no one opposed it because of the almost universal hatred of Agrippina's haughtiness, his wretched mother was violently killed at Nero's order, and many rivals were removed with the aid of Tigellinus, the prefect of the army. Finally, when she saw that the emperor was ardently in love with her and that all obstacles to her desires had been removed, she began to spread her nets to marry Nero. Since she had already borne him a daughter when Memmius Regulus and Verginius Rufus were consuls, and since Nero had welcomed her with great pleasure and had given her the name of Poppaea Augusta, she began to insist brazenly, saying that she had never given herself to anyone for two nights without marriage following immediately. And she said that she was not of humble birth and deserved to be the emperor's wife because of the beauty of her body and her fertility. Thus did she bring the ardent emperor to desire her in marriage. His innocent wife Octavia, who was the daughter of the emperor Claudius, was first exiled to the island of Pandateria, and then when she was twenty she was killed by order of Nero, instigated by Poppaea, whom he then married.

Poppaea did not long enjoy the greatness which she had sought and acquired with her wiles. She was pregnant once again when Nero in anger kicked her and she died. Nero refused to have her body cremated according to Roman custom but ordered her to be buried publicly with a great funeral in the manner of foreign kings. And he ordered that her body be embalmed and placed in the sepulcher of the Julii. He praised her before the assembled people in a long and elaborate oration, especially for her marvelous beauty. He attributed to her some gifts of Fortune or Nature with which she had been endowed in place of great virtues. In speaking of Poppaea's fortunes I had much to say against the excessive softness, the flattery, wantonness, and tears which are a woman's certain and deadly poison for the souls of men who trust them. But I decided to omit these matters lest I seemed to be writing a satire rather than history.

TRIARIA, WIFE OF LUCIUS VITELLIUS

THE WOMAN Triaria was not known for any nobility of lineage, except for the fact that she was the wife of Lucius Vitellius, the brother of Aulus Vitellius, who was the emperor of Rome. Either because of her ardent love for her husband or because Nature had instilled cruelty into her soul, she was so fierce, unlike the usual nature of women, that she seems worthy of being mentioned.

The emperor Vitellius and Vespasian were at odds over the empire. It happened that some soldiers under a certain Julianus, their captain, and many sailors from the Roman fleet under the prefect Apollinaris, which was not far from Actium, entered the Volscian city Tarracina and held it for Vespasian, but carelessly and lazily. And it happened that through a servant's information Lucius Vitellius entered the city at night. He fought fiercely against the disturbed, drowsy enemy and the citizens who were seizing arms. That night Triaria followed her husband and entered the city, and, desiring his victory, she mingled with Vitellius' soldiers. Armed with a sword, she rushed here and there against those poor wretches in the darkness of the night, in the midst of blood-curdling cries, flashing weapons, blood, and the death rattles of the dying, missing none of the atrocities of war. So much so, that it was said that she acted too cruelly and haughtily against the enemy.

Great is the power of conjugal love in violent breasts. They fear nothing so long as their husband's glory may be magnified. They do not remember pity or womanly shame and pay no heed to the appropriateness of the time. For her husband's honor Triaria was able to endure easily everything which would frighten not only women, who for the most part are accustomed to flee to their husbands' bosom at the slightest noise of a mouse even in daylight, but also strong and warlike young men. And if this woman bore arms with such violence at night, who will believe that she was famous only for this deed, since virtues and vices do not dwell singly within the breast of mortals? I certainly believe that Triaria was more renowned for other qualities, although memory of them has been lost.

CHAPTER XCV

PROBA, WIFE OF ADELPHUS

PROBA, whose name was a fitting one,[1] was a woman worthy of being remembered for her knowledge of literature. Since her nobility of birth and nationality are unknown, some like to assume that she was Roman. I believe this as a likely conjecture. Some other famous men assert that she was born in the city of Othrys, that she was a Christian and the wife of a certain Adelphus. Whoever her teacher may have been, it can easily be seen that she excelled in the liberal arts. Among other studies she became so well informed and familiar with Virgil's poems through continuous devotion to them that she seemed to have them always present and in her mind, as is shown by all the works she wrote.

Perhaps some time when she was reading these works with more careful attentiveness, the idea came to her that with them one could write the history of the Old and New Testaments in calm, graceful verses full of vigor. It is certainly astonishing that such a lofty plan came into a woman's mind, but more marvelous is the fact that she fulfilled it. Carrying out her pious thought, she searched here and there through the *Bucolics*, the *Georgics*, and the *Aeneid*, sometimes taking entire lines from one place or another, and at times, parts of lines. She collected them for her purpose with such great skill, aptly placing the entire lines, joining the fragments, observing the metrical rules, and preserving the dignity of the verses, that no one except an expert could detect the connections. Starting with the beginning of the world, she wrote all the stories which are read in the Old and New Testaments, up to the coming of the Holy Ghost, and so well was it done that a man unacquainted with this work would easily think that Virgil had been a prophet as well as an apostle. No less commendable in this woman is the fact that she knew the sacred Scriptures entirely, or at least sufficiently; and we know with

[1] Proba means 'excellent' or 'honorable.'

sorrow how rarely this is true of even the men of our times. This distinguished woman wanted the book which she had composed to be called *Cento,* and I have seen it several times.

The more we think this work worthy of being remembered forever, the less can we believe that the great intellect of this woman could have been satisfied with this work only. In fact, I think that if she lived to an old age she must have written other praiseworthy works, which, unfortunately for us, have not survived because of the laziness of scribes. Some are pleased to think that among them there was a Homeric *cento.* It was composed with verses taken from Homer with the same skill and from the same material which she had selected from Virgil. If this is so, she should be praised all the more for knowing Greek literature as well as Latin. But I ask if anything more praiseworthy has been heard than that a woman scanned the verses of Virgil and Homer and, taking those suitable for her work, put them together so marvelously. And let learned men consider how, in spite of their being distinguished in the profession of sacred letters, it would be difficult and arduous to select parts here and there from Holy Scripture, which is very long, and put them together in a series to give the life of Christ in prose or verse, as she did with the verses of poets who were not believers. If we consider the ways of women, the distaff, the needle, and weaving would have been sufficient for her had she wanted to lead a sluggish life like the majority of women. But, being zealous in her sacred studies, she removed from her intellect the rust of sloth and achieved eternal fame. Would that she were looked upon with good disposition by those women who yield to pleasure and idleness, think it wonderful to stay in their rooms wasting irrevocable time in vain stories, and often spend their time from morning to night and stay awake through the night in harmful or useless gossip or remain idle in their frivolity. And let them realize how much difference there is between seeking glory with praiseworthy works and having one's name buried together with one's corpse, leaving this life as if he had never lived.

CHAPTER XCVI

FAUSTINA AUGUSTA

FAUSTINA AUGUSTA, who later was included among the gods, acquired more glory in life and death through her husband's kindness than through her own deeds. She was the daughter of Antoninus Pius Augustus and his wife Faustina, and she was the wife of Marcus Aurelius Antoninus, who had previously been adopted as a son by Antoninus Pius. When her father died, she ruled together with her husband and by decree of the Senate was called Augusta, which at that time was not a small honor for a woman. Although emperors had previously been called Augustus, I do not find any empress before this one who was granted the name Augusta by decree of the Senate. She was of such exquisite beauty that something divine seemed to have been infused into her mortal body. Lest her beauty be destroyed by old age or death, her portrait as a young woman and in maturer years was engraved on gold, silver, and copper coins and is still extant today. Although in these the expression of the face, the movement of the eyes, the vivid complexion, and the cheerfulness of the face are lacking, nevertheless the features show great beauty.

Her world-wide fame was equalled by the infamy of her shamelessness. It was believed that in addition to her husband she was not satisfied with one lover but enjoyed the embraces of many. Disrepute has made known the names of some of them. Among her lovers were Vectilus,[1] Orfitus, and then Moderatus, but the one who was preferred to all the others was called Terculus,[2] whom, it is said, Marcus Aurelius found dining with her. To these they add Lucius Verus, in spite of the fact that he was her son-in-law, the husband of her daughter Lucilla. Most shameful of all, it is said that she loved a certain gladiator so much that because of her desire for him she became dangerously ill. Wishing to be cured, she told Marcus Aurelius of her lust. To quench this ardor, he followed

[1] This name should be Tutilius.   [2] This name should be Tertullus.

the doctor's advice and had the gladiator killed and his sick wife's body completely anointed with his warm blood. This cured her passion as well as her sickness. Prudent men, however, believed this remedy to be merely a fiction, since Commodus Antoninus, who was conceived at that time, lent weight through his wicked deeds (by reason of which he was thought to be the son of the gladiator rather than of Marcus Aurelius) to the belief that he was the fruit not of the blood-anointment but rather of his mother's lying with the gladiator. When these things became known to Faustina's shame, Marcus Aurelius was urged by his friends to kill her, or at least disown her, which seemed more humane. But Aurelius, who was a gentle man, refused to follow their advice, although he was greatly distressed by his wife's adultery. He preferred to bear with her rather than incur more shame. To the friends who advised him he answered only that on divorcing her he would have to give back her dowry, wanting them to understand by this that he ruled because of Faustina. But enough of this, for we must remember that very often even the most honest make mistakes in their work.

To return from darkness to light—when Antoninus was taking care of Rome's interests among Oriental kings, Faustina fell ill and died in the village of Halala on the skirts of Mount Taurus. At Marcus Aurelius' request the Senate raised her to a place among the gods, and afterwards she was known as the goddess Faustina. This had never before happened to a Roman woman. Having previously called her Mother of the Camp,[8] Aurelius had a marvelous temple built to her in the place where she had died, and he had a number of remarkable statues placed in it to her glory. He established an order of priestesses in the temple and ordered that they be known as Faustinians. Thus for a certain time Faustina was treated as a famous goddess, so that the glory which lasciviousness had taken from her might be restored by her divinity.

[8] After his victory over the Quadi in 174. This title was used by Faustina on her coins issued before her deification. Some which were issued later also bear that title.

SOAEMIAS, WOMAN OF EMESA

SOAEMIAS[1] was a Greek woman of the city of Emesa. The date of her birth is not known, although it is clear that her mother was Varia,[2] a woman from Emesa and the concubine of the emperor Severus, husband of Julia. At one time she was a dishonorable woman, but afterwards she gained much fame through her son's greatness and the preference of the Senate. Not to speak of her earlier shameful deeds, she was the mother of Varius Elagabalus, who at first was the priest of Phoebus and then emperor of Rome. She said that he was born of the emperor Antoninus Caracalla, whose concubine she had been for some time. Her notoriety was so great for having given her body to so many, that when Elagabalus was a child he was called Varius by his companions not after his grandmother Varia, as some thought, but because he seemed to have been born from the copulation of the various men with whom his mother continuously had intercourse.

Elagabalus was very handsome, and he was well known because of his priesthood. Because of his mother's claim, the soldiers in the provinces thought he was Caracalla's son. For these reasons, and because of the money which his grandmother had shrewdly accumulated at the court of the empress Julia, when the soldiers complained of their emperor Macrinus, it was agreed that Elagabalus should become emperor if he attempted to overthrow Macrinus. And it would not have been difficult, for at that time the name and family of the Antonines were so influential among the Roman armies that they asked nothing more than that one of them be their emperor. Thus he was chosen emperor not long after they had conspired against Macrinus. Not far from Antioch, Elagabalus

---

[1] Boccaccio uses the name *Semiamira*; some writers have used *Symiamira* and *Symiasera*. No satisfactory explanation has been given for these rather peculiar forms. They may have been derived from *Simea*, the name of a Syrian goddess.

[2] Julia Maesa. Boccaccio follows Julius Capitolinus in giving her the name Varia.

was hailed as emperor and named Antoninus. When Macrinus heard this in Antioch, he was surprised at the audacity of the woman Varia, for he correctly thought that this was her handiwork. When he set about besieging Elagabalus, Julianus, who had been sent for this purpose, was killed, and his soldiers went over to Elagabalus' side. And when Macrinus himself came to attack Elagabalus, he was defeated and put to flight. Shortly thereafter he was killed together with his son Diadumenus in a town in Bithynia. Thus Elagabalus seemed to have avenged the death of his father Caracalla and obtained undisputed possession of the empire through his grandmother's aid.

As he journeyed to Rome, he was awaited with great desire and welcomed by the entire Senate. Because of her son's sudden rise, Soaemias was raised almost to the stars and was called Augusta. From brothels she reached in glory the halls of the Roman emperor and was even more famous for this reason. For although Elagabalus was wicked, knowing that he was emperor because of his grandmother, and so because of her daughter, who was his mother, he paid her such honor, almost as a reward, that he did almost nothing without her consent. The same day he entered Rome he convened the Senate and ordered that his mother be summoned. When a consul requested this of her, she consented. A seat was prepared for her among the other senators, and she gave her views on what was to be done, like the others. There is no record that any other woman ever achieved this. Oh, what a shameful spectacle to see a prostitute, who had just left the brothel, seated among most worthy men, and to hear a woman accustomed to the company of panderers expressing her views where they were treating of kings! O ancient liberty, O ancient sanctity, O righteous indignation of our forefathers by which unworthy men were judged unfit by the censors and expelled from so famous a body, where are you? Do you see this infamous common woman soiling the place of the Curii, the Fabricii, the Scipios, and the Catos? But why do I complain of a woman senator, when numerous enemies of the state, foreign young men speaking unknown languages, rule the whole world? Why say more? Never afterwards did Elagabalus enter the Senate without being accompanied by his revered mother. Moreover, blind Fortune made her so esteemed by the populace that they gave her precedence over all the Sibyls.

If what has been said is shameful, what follows is ridiculous. For this woman was held in such esteem by her dastardly son that he instituted a place on the Quirinal which he called the Little Senate. Women had previously been accustomed to meet there on holy days.[8] Having appointed some women and having established that they meet in this place, Elagabalus ordered that in the same manner as the Senate they should deliberate and pass laws on the behavior and state of women. And he appointed Soaemias president of this separate Senate. It has been ascertained that many decrees emanated from this Senate, although they were ridiculous. To be sure, in that assembly it was decreed how women should dress and what ornaments were proper for each person, to whom each matron should give precedence, for whom they should rise, and whom to kiss. In addition, they decreed who should ride in a chariot, mule-drawn cart, sedan chair, or on horseback, and similar things. Although these matters seemed foolish, as they were, and more like a joke than the truth (especially since they were weighted down with womanly silliness and the inept judgment of the rabble), they were considered great at that time.

But, since nothing violent can endure, this woman easily perished and vanished with the wind. For since Soaemias behaved more like a prostitute than a lady in the royal palace, and since her son gave himself to obscene and frequent lewdness, it came about that Elagabalus was killed by his men for his deserts, and Soaemias, abandoning her shadow-like splendor, was killed with him and thrown into a sewer. From there she was carried away into the Tiber together with her son's body so that her death might seem as foul as her life. Regrettably, we who are alive do not think of this.

[8] This was the *conventus matronalis*, an organization established in the early republican period.

ZENOBIA, QUEEN OF PALMYRA

ZENOBIA was the queen of Palmyra. She was so virtuous, according to the testimony of ancient documents, that she must precede all other foreign women in fame. First of all, she was noble in lineage, for they say she was a descendant of the Ptolemies, the rulers of Egypt, although there is no record of her parents. They tell us that from childhood she scorned all womanly exercises, and when she had grown up somewhat and become strong she dwelt for the most part in forests and woods and, girding on the quiver, pursued and slew goats and stags with her arrows. Then, when she had become stronger, she dared come to grips with bears and pursued or lay in wait for leopards and lions, killing or capturing them. Without fear she wandered through steep mountain passes looking for the dens of beasts and slept in the open at night, enduring rain, heat, and cold with admirable fortitude. She used to scorn the love and companionship of men and greatly valued virginity. Having thus overcome feminine softness, she was so strong that by her strength she surpassed the young men of her age in wrestling and all other contests. Finally, having arrived at a marriageable age, they say that on the advice of her friends she married Odaenathus, a young man hardened in similar exercises and the noblest of Palmyra's princes.

Zenobia had a beautiful body, although she was somewhat dark in color, as are all the inhabitants of that region because of the heat of the sun. She also had beautiful dark eyes and white teeth. At the time when Valerian Augustus had been captured by Sapor, the king of the Persians, and condemned to shameful servitude, and his son Gallienus was languishing in his effeminacy, Odaenathus was determined to conquer the Eastern Empire. When she realized this, Zenobia, who had not forgotten her former sturdiness, decided to hide her beauty beneath armor and serve under her husband. Assuming the imperial title and purple together with Odaenathus and her stepson Herodes, she gathered an army and moved bravely against Sapor, who had already occupied much of Mesopotamia. She spared herself no toil, at times acting as an officer and at others as an ordinary soldier, and she not only bravely conquered that harsh man, who was experienced in wars and weapons, but it was believed that through her deeds Mesopotamia fell into her power. After capturing Sapor's camp and his concubines in addition to a great deal of booty, she drove him back and pursued him up to Ctesiphon. Shortly thereafter, she attended very ably to crushing Quietus, the son of Macrianus, who had entered the Eastern Empire in his father's name.

When together with her husband she already held subdued all the Eastern Empire which belonged to the Romans, Odaenathus was condemned and killed together with his son Herodes by his cousin Maeonius. Some authors say Maeonius acted through envy. Others believe that Zenobia had consented to Herodes' death because she had often condemned his softness and so that her sons Herennianus and Timolaus, whom she had borne to Odaenathus, might succeed to the kingdom. While Maeonius ruled, she remained quiet for a while. But soon Maeonius was murdered by his soldiers, leaving the throne vacant, and this woman of noble spirit immediately took over the rule she had desired. Since her children were still young, she assumed the imperial diadem and purple and ruled the empire in her sons' name better than women are expected to. She was no weak ruler, for neither the emperor Gallienus, nor Claudius after him dared try anything against her. Nor did the Egyptians, the Arabs, the Saracens, or the Armenians. In fact, fearing her power, they were glad to be able to defend their borders, for she was so thorough in military affairs and kept such strict discipline that her troops respected her as much as they feared her. She never spoke to her soldiers without wearing her helmet, and she very seldom used a chariot while on expeditions. She more often rode on horseback and sometimes would walk for three or four miles with the soldiers ahead of the flags. Nor did she scorn drinking with her captains at times, although she was a sober woman. She drank in this way with the Persian and Armenian princes to surpass them in wit and affability.

Nevertheless, she was so virtuous that not only did she keep away from other men but I have read that she never gave herself to her husband Odaenathus, while he was alive, except to conceive children. She was so careful of this that after lying with her husband once she would abstain long enough before the next time to see whether she had conceived, and if she had she would not let him touch her again until she had given birth. But if she found that she had not conceived, she would give herself to her husband at his request. How praiseworthy was this decision in a woman! It is clear that she thought sexual desire is given to men by Nature for no other reason than to preserve the species through continuous procreation, and beyond this it is a superfluous vice. However, women having similar moral scruples are very rarely found. Moreover, she never, or very rarely, let men enter her quarters unless they were eunuchs of sound morals and advanced age in order not to be distracted from her duties. She lived like a queen with great expenditures, maintaining the pomp of a sovereign. As is the Persian custom, she wanted to be adored. She gave banquets like those of the Roman emperors, using the jeweled golden vessels which she had heard had once been used by Cleopatra. Although she was very careful of her treasures, no one was more magnificent or generous than Zenobia when she thought it proper. She spent most of her time hunting and bearing arms; nevertheless, she did not fail to learn Egyptian letters, and she also learned Greek under the philosopher Longinus. With this training, she read with great care and committed to memory all the Latin, Greek, and barbarian histories. This was not all, for some believed that she made summaries of them. In addition to her own language, she knew Egyptian and Syrian, and her children were ordered to speak Latin.

Why speak further? She was so great that when the emperors Gallienus, Aurelius,[1] and Claudius had been defeated, Aurelian, a man of perfect virtue who had succeeded to the empire, moved against her to purge the shame of Rome and gain great glory.

[1] This name should be Aureolus.

When the war with the Marcomanni had ended and matters in Rome had been settled, Aurelian undertook his expedition against Zenobia with great care. Having been very successful in attacking the barbarian nations, he finally arrived very close to the city of Emesa with his legions. There Zenobia, who was not frightened at all, took her position together with Zeba,[2] whom she had taken as an ally in the war, and there a long and bitter general struggle took place between Zenobia and Aurelian. Finally, when Roman valor seemed triumphant, Zenobia was forced into flight with her men and withdrew to Palmyra, where she was immediately besieged by the conqueror. For some time she refused to hear of any terms for surrender and defended herself with great skill, but she came to a point where she lacked necessary supplies. The people of Palmyra were unable to withstand the power of Aurelian, and when the Persians, Armenians, and Saracens who were coming to Zenobia's assistance were intercepted, the city was stormed by the Romans. Zenobia left the city on camels with her children and fled towards Persia. She was pursued and captured by Aurelian's soldiers and taken to him with her children.

Aurelian was very proud of this conquest of a great leader and bitter enemy of Rome. He reserved her for his triumph and took her to Rome with her children. There Aurelian's triumph was celebrated and it was marvelous because of Zenobia's presence. Among other great things worthy of remembrance, he brought the precious chariot of gold and gems which Zenobia had had built hoping to come to Rome, not as a prisoner, but as a triumphant conqueror arriving to take possession of the Roman Empire. With gold chains around her neck and fettered hand and foot with shackles of gold, Zenobia went before the chariot with her children. She wore her crown and royal robes and was loaded with pearls and precious stones, so that in spite of her great strength she often stopped, exhausted by the weight. When the triumph, marvelous for its treasures and Aurelian's prowess, was over, they say that Zenobia grew old with her children, wear-

[2] Septimius Zabdas, also called Zaba or Saba.

ing private attire among the Roman matrons. The Senate granted her an estate near Tivoli, which for a long time afterwards was known as Zenobia, after her name. It was not far from the palace of the deified Hadrian, which is in the place called Concha by its inhabitants.

CHAPTER XCIX

POPE JOAN

ALTHOUGH John would seem from the name to be a man, in reality she was a woman whose unheard-of audacity made her known to the whole world and to posterity. Some say she was from Magontiacum, but her real name is hardly known. There are, however, some who say it was Giliberta. On the assertion of some this much is known: she was loved by a young student when she was a maiden. They say that she loved him so much that she cast aside maidenly fear and shame and fled to him in secret from her father's house. Changing her name and dressing as a young man, she followed her lover. While she studied with him in England, she was taken for a cleric by everyone and pursued the study of letters and of love.

When her lover died, Joan, knowing that she had a good mind and attracted by the charms of learning, retained a man's dress and refused to attach herself to anyone else or acknowledge that she was a woman. She persisted diligently in her studies and made such progress in liberal and sacred letters that she was deemed to excel all others. Thus, endowed with admirable knowledge, she left England and went to Rome when she was already mature in years. There for a number of years she lectured on the trivium and had excellent students. Since in addition to her scholarly knowledge she was very virtuous and saintly, everyone believed her to be a man. She was so widely known that when Pope Leo V[1] died, she was elected to succeed him as Pope by the unanimous vote of the cardinals. She was called John, and if she had been a man she would have been the eighth of that name. This woman was not afraid to mount the Fisherman's throne, to deal with all the sacred mysteries and proffer them to others, something which the Christian religion does not allow to any woman, and she held the highest ecclesiastic office for a number of years.

A woman, then, was the Vicar of Christ on earth. God from on high was merciful to His people and did not allow a woman to hold so lofty a place, govern so many people, and deceive them with such a wicked fraud, and He abandoned that unduly audacious woman to herself. Spurred by the devil, who had led her into this wickedness and made her persist in it, Joan, who in private life had been remarkably virtuous, now that she had risen to the lofty pontificate fell prey to the ardor of lust. And she, who for a long time had been able to hide her sex, did not lack the wiles necessary to quench her desire. And so, finding someone who would secretly mount on Saint Peter's successor and assuage her lecherous itching, the Pope happened to become pregnant. Oh, what a shameful crime! How great is God's patience! But what followed? This woman, who had been able to bewitch men's eyes for a long time, lacked the astuteness to hide the shameful fact that she was about to give birth to a child. For, being closer to the time of birth than she thought, as she went from the Janiculum to the Lateran in sacred procession around the city, between the Colosseum and the church of Pope Clement she publicly gave birth without the presence of any midwife. This made clear how she had deceived all men except her lover. And so she

[1] Pope Joan, although purely legendary, was traditionally thought to have succeeded Leo IV.

was thrown into a horrid dungeon by the cardinals, where this wretched woman died in the midst of her laments.

Down to our time, to condemn her dishonesty and perpetuate her infamy, when the Pope goes on a procession with the clergy and the people, at the halfway point, when they reach the place where Joan gave birth, the Pope turns away and takes different streets because of his hatred for that place. Having thus bypassed that shameful site, they return to their road and finish their procession.

IRENE, EMPRESS OF CONSTANTINOPLE

IRENE was a very noble Athenian woman, remarkable for her great beauty. Having called her to Constantinople from her home, the Emperor Constantine[1] gave her in marriage to his son Leo, also called Leo Chazarus. After Constantine's death, she became empress of the Romans and bore her husband a son named Constantine. Finally, when Leo had departed from this earth, she ruled nobly over the empire for ten years with her very young son.

When he grew up, however, her son asserted that he alone had inherited the throne and, according to some, removed Irene from his court for eight years. That woman, because of her great spirit and thirst for power, quarreled with her son who trusted in his own strength, seized him with womanly cunning, deposed him, and had him imprisoned. She thus ascended alone the throne from which the whole world had once received its laws. Famous beyond other mortals, she ruled as empress for five years with great glory. But it happened that, through the aid of Constantine's friends and the Armenians, Irene was deposed, and Constantine, freed from prison, once again took possession of his father's throne. More merciful towards his mother than she had been to him and trusting in his friends' strength, Constantine did not imprison her. He was satisfied to send her away from him to live in great luxury in the palace of Eleutherium, which she herself had had built, and he sent all her friends into exile. But when he undertook an unsuccessful war against the Bulgarians, and for this reason the nobles attempted to remove him and put a certain Nicephorus on the throne in his place, in savage wrath Constantine turned to evil cruelty and had the tongues of the brothers Nicephorus and Christophorus torn out.[2] Then he had his men gouge out the eyes

---

[1] Constantine V, surnamed Copronymus, Emperor of the East 741-775.

[2] This conspiracy was formed by Constantine's four uncles, who were supported by the Armenian guard. Constantine disarmed the Armenians, whose

of Alexis, the leader of the Armenians, and forced his own wife Maria to take the veil. He then married the chamber maid Theodota, whom he immediately crowned.[3]

Because of these atrocities, Irene, who had kept her noble spirit although she had been compelled to lay down her power, shrewdly began hoping to seize it again by giving a great deal of money to the patricians. With the treasure which, while she ruled, she had hidden in the palace where she later lived in banishment, she secretly won the princes of the empire over to her. Having brought them to her way of thinking with lavish gifts, she arranged that the men who had deposed her from the throne seize her son Constantine and blind him. Thus this brave woman recovered the empire which had once been taken from her. After an illness, Constantine died. When she had ruled five more years, Irene was besieged in the Eleutherian Palace by Nicephorus, who had rebelled. Nicephorus had received the crown of the empire from Acarisius, the Patriarch of Constantinople,[4] and had been helped by the patricians Leo and Triphilus and by the treasurer Sycopeus, all of whom had recently been enriched by Irene.[5] Nicephorus went to Irene and tried to flatter her with humility. But she realized the truth, and of all the empire she asked only the palace where she dwelt and said that if this were promised her she would give up all her treasure. After promising this, the wicked man broke his word and sent her into exile to Lesbos. There, already old, she ended her famous life.

Other writers, however, seem to give a different version of her end. They say that when mother and son were in disagreement and in turn deprived each other of the empire, the Romans rebelled against them and gave the empire to Charlemagne, who at that

---

leader Alexis had his eyes put out. One of the uncles was blinded; the other three had their tongues cut off and were forced to become ecclesiastics in order to incapacitate them for reigning.

[3] Theodota was a lady of Irene's court.

[4] This name should be Tarasius.

[5] The patricians who proclaimed Nicephorus emperor were: Nicetas, the commander of the guard, his two brothers, Sisinnius and Leo Clocas, the quaestor Theoctistus, Leo of Sinope, Gregorius, and Petrus, all of whom were eunuchs.

time was the king of the Franks. He tried to unite the empire, which was divided, by marrying Irene, and she consented. When the patrician Eutitius[6] realized this, he immediately crowned Nicephorus. By besieging Irene, he forced her to abandon her throne and enter a convent, where she lived to an advanced age.

[6] This name should be Aetius. This second version of Irene's last years is untrue.

THE FLORENTINE MAIDEN ENGELDRUDA

ENGELDRUDA was a descendant of the Ravennati family, which at one time was very famous among those of our city.[1] I have decided to place her among famous women, not undeservedly, because of her great bravery in defending her integrity before the Roman emperor. When she was attending a festival with many Florentine women in the temple which had once been dedicated to Mars, but which was later consecrated to the true God under the name of Saint John the Baptist, the Roman emperor Otho IV, who had just come to Florence to embellish the festival and render it greater with his presence, happened to enter the temple accompanied by many gentlemen. Seated in the highest place, he inspected the ornaments of the temple, the citizens, and the women seated in a circle, and his eyes happened to fix upon Engeldruda. Having first admired for a while and then praised her beauty, her plainness of dress, her dignity and girlish seriousness, he addressed Illitio,[2] a citizen venerable in age and nobility who happened to be standing next to him on duty, and asked, "Who is that girl seated facing us, who in our opinion surpasses all the others in dignity and in the beauty of her face?"

Illitio, laughing, answered with humorous sophistication, "Your Majesty, whoever she may be, she will kiss you if you desire it and I so command her." Hearing these words, the girl immediately became indignant and bore ill the fact that her father had such a poor opinion of her constancy and so little concern for her chaste virginity. She could not long endure the insult. The emperor had not yet answered, when she rose blushing, looked at her father and then, lowering her eyes to the ground, said in a steady but humble voice, "Be silent, father, and do not speak, for I swear

[1] Gualdrada, daughter of Bellincione Berti dei Rovignani.
[2] This name should be Bellincione.

that without violence no one except the man to whom you will give me in legitimate and sacred marriage will receive what you offer so freely."

Oh, good God! What is well and elegantly said is never allowed to slip from the soul of a great man. The emperor remained surprised for a while. Then in spite of German barbarity and the fact that he did not know the girl, he realized the saintly and chaste purpose of her breast. After praising at length her outspoken indignation, the emperor sent for a certain young nobleman named Guido. So that the girl would not lack for long someone whom she could honestly kiss if she so desired, before leaving he gave Engeldruda, who was of marriageable age, to Guido as his wife, in the presence of her father, who thanked him. And he gave her a noble dowry, thinking that the good and just things she had said were not merely something in the girl's mind, but were based on great veneration of virtue and uttered in just and rightful indignation, and that therefore she was worthy of the emperor's gift.

Thus, because of her virtue and chastity, this girl who had entered the temple as a virgin returned married to her father's home, to the great joy of her father and her family. In the process of time, she gave birth to many children and on dying she left her husband's house famous and adorned by her noble progeny. Her family has survived in great numbers to this day. It does not please me to have said these things to the shame of the girls of our time who are so fickle and of such loose morals that with their eyes and gestures they seem to rush to the embraces of anyone who gazes upon them.

CONSTANCE, EMPRESS OF THE ROMANS AND QUEEN OF SICILY

CONSTANCE, the Roman empress, was famous throughout the world. But since this honor held in common with many other women seems to have diminished in the admiration of those who look upon it, one must find another reason for renown for those who wish to stand out in our age. This reason is not lacking for Constance, for she is famous because of her only son, if for nothing else.

She was the daughter of William, an excellent king of Sicily.[1] According to many, at her birth a certain Joachim, a Calabrian abbot endowed with a prophetic spirit, told William that his daughter would cause the destruction of the Kingdom of Sicily. Amazed and frightened by this prophecy, William believed it and anxiously began to think how this could be caused by a woman. He saw that it could happen only through her husband or through a child and, grieving for his kingdom, decided to prevent this if he could. To remove all hope of marriage and children, he placed the young girl in a nuns' cloister and made her promise God eternal virginity. This plan was not to be scorned, if it had succeeded. But why do we powerless fools pit our strength against God, Who justly corrects the wicked deeds of men? Certainly we let ourselves be deceived by a single trifling impulse.

When her saintly father and her brother died, there was no legitimate heir to the kingdom except Constance, whose youth had already been spent and who was now an old woman. After William's death, Tancred assumed the crown of the kingdom, and after him his son William, who was still a child.[2] Because of

[1] Constance was the daughter of Roger I, not of William. She was the sister of William I and the aunt of William II.
[2] Before his death in 1189, William II ordered that his aunt Constance be recognized as his lawful heir and gave her in marriage to Henry VI. However,

the frequent changes, or because of the unworthy succession of kings, it happened that wars broke out everywhere on account of the many factions, and the kingdom seemed on the way to destruction by fire and sword. For this reason, some who grieved at the misfortune had the idea of giving Constance in marriage to some great prince, so that through his efforts and power the deadly strife might be quelled. This was done. With the Pope's approval, they obtained Constance's consent, but not without great effort and deceit, for she held firmly to the purpose of her vows, and her age seemed to be an obstacle. While she was still objecting, however, matters had proceeded to a point where it was not easy to retreat, and she was given in marriage to Henry, the emperor of Rome and son of Frederick I.[8]

Thus this wrinkled old woman abandoned the sacred cloister, discarded her monastic veil and, dressed in regal vestments, was married and took her place as empress. This woman, who had promised God eternal virginity, entered the royal chamber and the marriage bed and lost it unwillingly. The result of this was that at the age of fifty-five this old woman conceived, to the surprise of all who heard of it. Since no one believed the truth of her pregnancy and the majority believed that it was a fraud, when the time of birth approached, to avoid suspicion the King prudently ordered that all the women in Sicily be summoned, so that all who wanted could be present at the birth. They came even from far away and pitched their tents in the meadows outside the city of Palermo and in the city itself, according to some. In their presence, the aged empress gave birth to Frederick, who later became a monstrous man and the pestilence not only of Sicily but of all Italy, so that he proved correct the prophecy of the Calabrian abbot.

Who then will not believe that Constance's pregnancy was a

---

in 1190 the Sicilian nobles proclaimed Tancred King of Sicily, and war broke out between the two rivals.

[8] The legend which states that Constance was an old woman at the birth of her son, and that she had previously been a nun and married with the Pope's permission was very popular and appears in the works of a number of writers. Dante places Constance among those who had not been true to their vows (Paradiso III, 109-120).

marvelous thing? For except for this one, no pregnancy of such an old woman has been heard of in our times, or rather since Aeneas' arrival in Italy, except for that of Elizabeth, the wife of Zacharias, of whom through God's wondrous deed John was born, and afterwards no woman's son was born equal to him.

THE WIDOW CAMIOLA

THE widow Camiola, famous for her beauty, good conduct, high-mindedness, probity, and praiseworthy virtue, was born in Siena, the daughter of Lawrence of Torringo,[1] who was a man of high rank. She spent her noble and praiseworthy life with her parents and with her only husband, while he was alive, near Messina, a very old city in Sicily, at the time when Frederick III reigned in that island.[2] When her family died, she became heiress to almost royal wealth and remained virtuous.

The above-mentioned Frederick died, and his son Peter[3] succeeded him. It happened that at the King's order a great fleet was being prepared in Messina under the command of Count John of Chiaramonte, a man of great prowess, to bring aid to the inhabitants of Lipari, who were under siege and in dire straits because of hunger. I believe that in this fleet there were not only mercenaries but many nobles, from the shore as well as from inland, who had volunteered their help in order to acquire glory. Godfrey of Squillace, a valiant man who at that time was fleet commander for Robert, the king of Jerusalem and Sicily, had besieged that city. He had so weakened the defenders of the city with siege, war machines, and frequent attacks that it was hoped they would soon surrender. But when he learned from some scouting vessels that the enemy fleet was much larger than his own, he gathered all his ships and went to wait in safety for further developments. The enemy, however, without any opposition immediately occu-

---

[1] Also Turingo, or Turringa.

[2] Frederick, father of Peter II, is usually known by the title of Second, although he was the third Frederick to rule in Sicily. The other Frederick II was the son of Henry VI and Constance. A number of critics have pointed out Boccaccio's "error." However, it seems clear that Boccaccio is using the logical title of Third, rather than Second, in order to distinguish this king from Henry's son, of whom he had spoken in a previous chapter.

[3] Peter II.

pied the places which had been abandoned and brought their
aid to the inhabitants of the city.

Elated by his success, John challenged Godfrey to a battle, and
that spirited man did not refuse. At night he fortified his vessels
with wooden plates and towers, drew up the line of ships, and
arranged other matters. When dawn came, Godfrey encouraged
his men to fight with a fiery oration. Then they raised anchor
and, when he gave the signal, turned their prows towards the
Sicilians. John, who did not believe that Godfrey would attack or
even wait for the mighty Sicilian fleet, had prepared his ships
not for battle but to pursue the fleeing enemy. When he saw the
eager preparations of the approaching enemy, John almost lost
his courage, became frightened, and was sorry that he had made
the challenge, which he had thought would be refused. He lost
his confidence, and his ardor cooled, but in order not to seem
completely cowed, John immediately changed his formation to
a line of combat in the time which was given him and gave the
signal for battle. The enemy was already near. They raised a huge
war cry and locked prows with the Sicilian ships, which were
moving slowly. In the first assault they hurled grappling hooks,
shots, and arrows. While the Sicilians hesitated, almost stunned
by the sudden change of plan, Godfrey's men, ready and rushing at the enemy, attacked the ships and began to fight with
their swords and with their hands and covered everything with
blood. Among the Sicilians, who were already losing confidence,
those who could turned their prows and fled. Victory seemed to be
Godfrey's, with many Sicilian ships sunk and many captured.
A few fled to safety, being swifter because of the prowess of their
rowers. Few men died in that battle, but many were wounded.
John, the leader, was captured together with almost all the nobles
who had voluntarily joined the fleet, as well as many soldiers and
sailors. Many military and naval flags and the great royal standard,
which flew from the commander's ship, were also taken. The city
surrendered, and after long wanderings, buffeted by storms, the
prisoners were taken to Naples in chains and were imprisoned.

Among them there was a handsome, powerful young man

called Roland, who was the son of King Frederick and his concubine. Attempts were made to ransom the other prisoners, and when this had been done they left, while only Roland, unwanted, remained sadly in prison. For King Peter, who had the obligation to take care of his brother's affairs, hated him as well as all the others who had taken part in the naval engagement, for it had not been handled well and they had gone beyond his orders. Thus, while Roland remained in prison, languishing in shackles almost without hope of freedom, Camiola happened to remember him. Seeing that he was neglected by his brothers, she pitied his misfortune and determined that she would free him, if it could be done honestly. As there was no other way to free him and preserve her virtue than to marry him, she secretly sent someone to ask him if he wanted to be freed from his chains on that condition. He readily agreed. Thus, with his consent and with all the solemnity of law, he married her by proxy with the pledging of a ring. Without delay Camiola sent a ransom of two thousand ounces of silver, and Roland returned free to Messina.

As if not a word had been spoken of marriage, he did not go to his wife's house. At first, Camiola was surprised; then, realizing his ingratitude, she became angry. Not to seem impelled by wrath rather than reason, she first had him courteously asked to consummate the marriage. When he denied that he had anything to do with her regarding marriage, she had him summoned before the ecclesiastical judge and with legal documents and the testimony of honorable men proved that he was her husband. Ashamed, he confessed. When Camiola's kindness toward him became known, Roland, reprimanded by his brothers and spurred by his friends, was persuaded to consent to the woman's claim and requested the marriage ceremony. But in the presence of many this noble woman spoke to the petitioner in approximately these words: "I have reason to thank God, Roland, for, before taking away my chastity under the pretense of marriage, you showed your iniquity and wickedness, and with the help of Him whose holy name you have tried to mock with your wicked perjury I struck down your lies as you deserved. And for me that is enough of you and your marriage.

I believe that while still in prison you thought I had forgotten my position, madly wished a husband of royal lineage, and burned with womanly concupiscence for your manly beauty. When you had regained your freedom because of my money, you thought that you could deny these things, scorn and suppress them, and then, when you had regained your former high station, marry a nobler woman. You strove to do this with all your might. But He who sees lowly things from on high and does not abandon those who place their hopes in Him, appreciated my sincerity and brought it about that with little effort on my part I have upset your frauds, uncovered your ingratitude, and made clear your perfidy. I did not do this through hatred of your wickedness, but so that from now on your brothers can see what can be entrusted to you, and others can see what your friends may hope from you and what your enemies may have to fear. I have lost my money; you, your reputation. I have lost my hope; you, the favor of the King and of your friends. The women of Sicily admire my generosity and glorify me with their praise; you have become ridiculous and disgraced in the eyes of your friends, as well as those who do not know you. I was, however, deceived for some time. I foolishly thought that with gold I was delivering from bondage a royal and illustrious young man, whereas I now see that I have freed a lying camp-follower, a faithless rake, and a monstrous beast.

"Nor do I want you to think so much of yourself as to believe that you alone induced me to do this. I was moved by the memory of your father's old kindness to mine, if King Frederick of sacred memory was your father, for I find it hard to believe that such a disgraceful son could be born of so famous a prince. You thought it improper for a widow not of royal blood to have a young, robust, handsome husband of royal lineage, and I confess this freely. But I should like you to answer me, if you can do so justly. When I believed that I had made you mine with my services, and when I paid a great deal of money for your freedom, where was your royal splendor then, where was your great strength, where was your beauty? They were covered by the darkness of the cell in which you were held. All these things, the squalor of your rusty chains, the paleness from lack of sunlight, and the stench of your gloomy prison, because of which you were weakly and fetidly rotting away abandoned by everyone, had suppressed these qualities of yours which you now proudly magnify. Then you were wont to say that not only was I worthy of a royal youth but of a celestial god. Oh, how happily and how quickly you turned your mind elsewhere, O wretched man, as soon as you saw the sky of your country, which was more than you could hope for, forgetting, once you were your own master, that I am Camiola, the only one who remembered you, the only one who felt pity for your misfortune, the only one who spent her money for your safety. I am Camiola, and with my money I took you out of the hands of your ancestors' deadly enemies and delivered you from shackles, from prison, and from extreme wretchedness. When you were already in despair, I raised you up toward hope; I brought you back to your country, to the royal palace, to your former life; I changed you from a weak, ugly prisoner into a robust, royal, and handsome young man.

"But why do I remind you of these things which you must remember and cannot deny? You thanked me for these great services by daring to deny that you are my husband, by scorning a marriage confirmed by honest and worthy witnesses and sealed documents, by despising and vilifying me, your redeemer, and by staining me with vile suspicion as much as you could. You, a man of unhealthy mind, were ashamed to have as wife a widow born to a man of high rank. How much better would it have been if you had been ashamed of breaking your word, scorning the holy and terrible name of God, and with your accursed ingratitude showing how abundant are your vices! I admit that I am not a woman of royal blood. But since from the time I was a child I have been in the company of the daughters, daughters-in-law, and wives of kings, it is not surprising that I have acquired their manners and spirit, and this is sufficient to acquire royal nobility.

"But why say more? I will easily do to you what you with all your power found difficult to do to me. You denied that you were mine, although you were. But I, although I have won, shall willingly grant that you not be mine. Let royal renown be yours, but stained by your treachery. Keep your youthful strength and your fleeting beauty. From now on I shall be satisfied with my widowhood and I shall leave the fortune which God has given me to heirs more honest than those who would have been born of you. Go, then, O unhappy youth, and since you deemed it unworthy to have me, learn to your cost with what arts and deceit you toy with other women. It is enough for me to have been deceived by you once. For this reason I never want to be with you and I think it much better to lead a single life than have your embraces."

After saying this, she went away, and from that time on neither prayers nor counsel prevailed upon her to change her worthy purpose. Roland, confused and repenting his vileness too late, was scorned by everyone. With bowed head, he not only fled his brothers' presence but that of the masses also and wretchedly departed, not daring to ask properly for the woman whom he had treacherously rejected. The king and the other nobles marveled at this woman's lofty spirit and extolled her with great praise. They were not certain whether they should praise more highly the fact that Camiola, contrary to womanly avarice, had redeemed the young man with so much money, or the fact that, once he had been freed and found guilty, she bravely scorned and rejected him as unworthy.

In the 1539 edition there is a chapter inserted here, "Brunhilda, Queen of France," which is not part of *De Claris mulieribus,* but is taken from another work by Boccaccio.

JOANNA, QUEEN OF SICILY
AND JERUSALEM

JOANNA, the queen of Sicily and Jerusalem, is more renowned than other women of our time for her nobility, power, and goodness. It would have seemed hateful not to speak of this woman, and yet it would have been better to remain silent than to write little about her. She was the first child of Prince Charles, the glorious Duke of Calabria and first born of Robert, king of Sicily and Jerusalem of illustrious memory. Her mother was Mary, the sister of King Philip of France. If we seek her parents' ancestors, we will not stop until, through many kings, we reach Dardanus, the founder of Troy, whose father the ancients said was Jupiter. From this family, so noble and ancient, so many famous princes have been born on both sides that there is no Christian king who is not related to it by blood or marriage. Thus, in our days and in those of our fathers no family in the whole world has been more famous than this for its nobility.

While Joanna was still a child, her father died in his youth. Since her grandfather Robert had no children of the better sex, at his orders she lawfully inherited the kingdom at his death. Her inheritance did not extend beyond the torrid zone, or to the North Pole among the Sarmatians, but was between the Tyrrhenian Sea and the Adriatic, from Umbria, Piceno, and the old country of the Volscians to the Strait of Sicily under mild skies. Within these borders, her rule is obeyed by the ancient Campanians, Lucani, Bruttii, Salentines, Calabrians, Daunians, Vestuali,[1] Samnites, Peligni, and Marsi, and by the people of many other lands such as, to mention the largest, the kingdom of Jerusalem, the island of Sicily, and Piedmont in Cisalpine Gaul, which have been usurped from her. In the same manner she is obeyed by those who dwell in the Seventh Province between Narbonian Gaul, the Rhone,

---

[1] This name should be Vestini.

and the Alps, and the county of Folcacherius, and they recognize her as their mistress and queen. How many famous cities are in these provinces, how many remarkable towns, bays, refuges for sailors, shipyards, lakes, mineral springs, groves, forests, pastures, pleasant shelters, and fruitful fields! How many people there are and great nobles, what great wealth, and what an abundance of things needed for life! Certainly, it is not easy to describe all this.

If we examine this kingdom closely, our amazement will be as great as its fame, for it is a mighty kingdom and not usually ruled by women. And what is even more surprising, Joanna's spirit is equal to ruling it, so that she has preserved the noble character of her ancestors. For, after she assumed the royal diadem, she very bravely attacked and cleaned out bands of wicked men, not only in the cities and inhabited places, but also in the Alps and out-of-the-way places, in forests, and in the dens of wild beasts, so that they all fled in fear or withdrew to strong fortresses. They were besieged by soldiers under a noble leader, and the siege of such places was not abandoned until the fortresses had been captured and these abominable men executed. None of the previous kings had wanted or been able to do this. She has so subjected the lands which she possesses that not only the poor but the rich as well can go safely and without care wherever they please, by night or by day. And no less beneficial, she has drawn the great men and nobles of the kingdom from their dissolute ways and has curbed them with such discretion that they have discarded their former arrogance, and those who earlier scorned kings now fear to see the face of this woman when she is angry. Moreover, she is so prudent that she can be deceived more easily by treachery than through shrewdness. She is so steadfast and constant that she will not be easily swayed in her just purposes without reason. This has already been shown clearly enough not long ago by the blows of Fortune which have often struck and buffeted her from every direction. For she has endured the internal struggles of petty fellow-princes and foreign wars which at times were waged within her kingdom. Through the fault of others, she has had to endure

flight, exile, marriage,[2] strict conduct, the envy of noblemen, undeserved ill-repute,[3] the threats of popes, and other things, all of
which she has borne bravely. Finally, her indomitable soul has
conquered everything; this would have been a great deed for a
strong, powerful king, and not only for a woman.

She has a marvelous, charming appearance; her speech is gentle,
and her eloquence pleases everyone. Just as she is majestic and
inflexible when the occasion demands, she is affable, merciful,
gentle, and friendly, so that one would say that she is her people's
companion rather than their queen. What greater qualities would
one seek in a most wise king? And if someone wanted to express
completely the integrity of her character, his speech would be very
long. For these reasons, I not only think that she is noble and of
splendid fame, but an eminent glory of Italy such as has never
before been seen by any nation.

[2] Joanna was married to the following princes: Andrew of Hungary, Louis of
Taranto, James III of Mallorca, and Otto of Brunswick.
[3] It was rumored at the time that Boccaccio was one of Joanna's lovers.

CONCLUSION

AS can be clearly seen, I have reached the women of our time, in which the number of illustrious ones is so small that I think it more suitable to come to an end here rather than proceed farther with the women of today, especially since this work, which began with our first mother Eve, concludes with so great a queen. I know that there will be many who will say that I have omitted numerous famous women, and others who will reprimand me for things for which I may perhaps be justly reproached.

To answer the former in all humility, I confess willingly that I have omitted many. First of all, I could not mention all of them, for time which triumphs over fame has destroyed their names. Nor was it granted me to read about all those whose fame has survived, and memory did not serve me as I wished for all those of whom I had knowledge. Lest they deem me forgetful in everything, however, I want them to believe that I have knowingly omitted many, barbarian as well as Greek and Latin, and wives of emperors and kings. In truth, I considered innumerable women and learned their deeds, but when I took up my quill I did not do so with the intention of writing about all of them. Rather, as I stated at the beginning of this book, I intended to put into it and speak of only a few among the great multitude. As I think I have done this sufficiently well, the objection is unnecessary.

To the others I say that it is possible that some things have been improperly included, and I will easily believe it, for it often happens that a writer is deceived not only by ignorance of the matter but by the excessive love he has for his work. If I have done this, I am sorry, and I ask, for the glory of honorable studies, that wiser men tolerate with kindly spirit what has not been done properly. And if anyone has a charitable soul, let him correct what has been improperly written by adding to it or deleting and improve it so that the work will flourish for someone's benefit, rather than perish torn by the jaws of the malicious without being of service to anyone.

SOURCES OF *CONCERNING FAMOUS WOMEN.*[1]

ABBREVIATIONS

Hyg.	Hyginus *Fabularum Liber.*
Josephus	Josephus Flavius *Antiquitatum Judaicarum.*
Just.	Justinus *Trogi Pompei Historiarum Philippicarum Epitoma.*
Lact.	Lactantius *Divinarum Institutionum.*
Liv.	Livius *Historiarum ab Urbe Condita.*
Ov. F.	Ovidius *Fasti.*
" Her.	" *Heroides.*
" Met.	" *Metamorphoses.*
Plin.	Plinius *Naturalis Historia.*
Serv.	Servius *Commentarius in Vergilii Aeneidos Libros.*
Suet.	Suetonius *De Vita Caesarum.*
Tac. *Ann.*	Tacitus *Annales.*
" *Hist.*	" *Historia.*
Val. Max.	Valerius Maximus *De Factis Dictisque Memorabilibus.*

CHAPTER	SOURCES
II	Just. i. 1, 2; Val. Max. ix. 3. ext. 4; Orosii *Historiarum Adversus Paganos* i. 4; Pomponii Melae *De Situ Orbis* i. 11.
III	Liv. xxix. 10, 11.
IV	Lact. i. 17 (8).
V	Ov. *Met.* v. 341, 391; Hyg. 146, 147, 274.
VI	Hyg. 164, 165, 166; Ov. *Met.* vi. 7, 70.
VII	Hyg. 148; Ov. *Met.* iv. 17.
VIII	Hyg. 145; Ov. *Met.* i. 588.

[1] Boccaccio's sources for many of these chapters are listed in Attilio Hortis, *Studj sulle Opere Latine del Boccaccio* (Trieste, 1879), and in Laura Torretta, "Il *Liber De Claris Mulieribus* di Giovanni Boccaccio," *Giornale Storico della Letteratura Italiana,* XXXIX (1902). A number of inaccuracies in these works have been eliminated.

SOURCES

IX	Hyg. 178; Ov. *Met.* ii. 839; Varronis *De Lingua Latina* v. 31.
X	Hyg. 149, 157.
XI	Just. ii. 4; Orosii *Historiarum Adversus Paganos* i. 15.
XII	Ov. *Met.* iv. 55-166.
XIII	Hyg. 168, 170; Ov. *Her.* xiv.
XIV	Ov. *Met.* vi. 146-312.
XV	Hyg. 15, 74.
XVI	Ov. *Met.* vii. 1-450.
XVII	Ov. *Met.* vi. 1-145.
XVIII	Hyg. 30; Just. ii. 4.
XIX	Lact. i. 6 (9).
XX	Hyg. 151; Ov. *Met.* iv. 743, 792, vi. 119.
XXI	Lact. i. 9; Ov. *Met.* ix. 140; Ov. *Her.* ix; Serv. viii. 291.
XXII	Hyg. 34, 36; Ov. *Met.* ix. 101; Serv. viii. 300.
XXIII	Hyg. 66, 67, 68.
XXIV	Isidori Hispalensis *Originum* viii. 8. 5; Serv. vi. 72; Tibulli *Eleg.* ii. 5. 67.
XXV	Hyg. 277; Liv. i. 7; Serv. viii. 51; Virgilii *Aeneis* viii. 338.
XXVI	Ov. *Met.* vii. 694; Hyg. 189.
XXVII	Hyg. 69, 71, 72, 73.
XXVIII	Pomponii Melae *De Situ Orbis* i. 17; Serv. x. 198.
XXIX	Val. Max. iv. 6. ext. 3.
XXX	Just. ii. 4.
XXXI	Ov. *Met.* xiii. 448; Serv. iii. 322.
XXXII	Hyg. 109, 111; Virgilii *Aeneis* ii. 515-554.
XXXIII	Hyg. 93; Serv. ii. 247; Virgilii *Aeneis* ii. 246, 343, 404, iii. 183.
XXXIV	Hyg. 117, 119.
XXXV	Ciceronis *De Inventione* ii. 1; Hyg. 79, 118, 122, 92.
XXXVI	Hyg. 125, 155; Ov. *Met.* xiv. 248-434; Serv. vii. 190.
XXXVII	Serv. xi. 543, 558; Virgilii *Aeneis* xi. 539-848.
XXXVIII	Hyg. 125, 126; Ov. *Her.* i.

XXXIX	Liv. i. 1; Virgilii *Aeneis* vii. 45.
XL	Just. xviii. 4, 5, 6.
XLI	Josephus viii. 6.
XLII	Plin. XI. xxii. 26.
XLIII	Liv. i. 3, 4; Ov. *F.* iv. 54.
XLIV	Incerti Auctoris *De Praenominibus* vii.
XLV	Ov. *Her.* xv.
XLVI	Liv. i. 57, 58.
XLVII	Just. i. 8.
XLVIII	Plin. VII. xxiii. 87.
XLIX	Josephus viii. 15; ix. 1-7.
L	Liv. ii. 13.
LI	Val. Max. vi. 1. ext. 1.
LII	Val. Max. iv. 4. 10.
LIII	Liv. ii. 39, 40.
LIV	Plin. XXXV. xxxv. 59; XXXV. xl. 147.
LV	Plin. XXXVI. iv. 30-32; Val. Max. iv. 6. ext. 1; Vitruvii *De Architectura* ii. 8; Orosii *Historiarum Adversus Paganos* ii. 10.
LVI	Liv. iii. 44-48, 58.
LVII	Plin. XXXV. xl. 147.
LVIII	Ciceronis *De Natura Deorum* i. 33.
LIX	Just. vii. 6; ix. 5-7; xiv. 5, 6.
LX	Val. Max. v. 4. 6.
LXI	Liv. x. 23.
LXII	Lact. i. 20 (6-10); Macrobii *Saturnalia* i. 10; Ov. *F.* v. 194-212; Tac. *Ann.* ii. 49.
LXIII	Plin. VII. xxxvi. 121; Val. Max. v. 4. 7.
LXIV	Plin. XXXV. xl. 147.
LXV	Val. Max. viii. 15. 12.
LXVI	Liv. xxiv. 25-26; Val. Max. iii. 2. ext. 9.
LXVII	Liv. xxii. 52; Val. Max. iv. 8. 2.
LXVIII	Liv. xxx. 12, 14, 15.
LXIX	Liv. xl. 3, 4.
LXX	Just. xxxviii. 1, 2; Val. Max. ix. 10. ext. 1.
LXXI	Liv. xxxviii. 24; Val. Max. vi. 1. ext. 2.

LXXII	Val. Max. vi. 7. 1.
LXXIII	Val. Max. i. 8. ext. 13.
LXXIV	Val. Max. iii. 8. 6.
LXXV	Liv. xxix. 14; Ov. *F.* iv. 305.
LXXVI	Val. Max. iv. 6. ext. 2.
LXXVII	Sallustii *Catilina* xxv, xl.
LXXVIII	Annaei Flori *Epitome de Gestis Romanorum* i. 38; Val. Max. vi. 1. ext. 3.
LXXIX	Val. Max. iv. 6. 4.
LXXX	Val. Max. iv. 6. 5.
LXXXI	Val. Max. vi. 7. 2.
LXXXII	Val. Max. viii. 3. 3.
LXXXIII	Val. Max. vi. 7. 3.
LXXXIV	Eusebii *Chronicon* ol. 184. 4.
LXXXV	Josephus xv. 2. 3. 7.
LXXXVI	Plin. IX. xxxv. 58; XIX. v. 22; XXI. ix. 12; Suet. Divus Iulius 30, Divus Augustus 17.
LXXXVII	Val. Max. iv. 3. 3.
LXXXVIII	Suet. Tiberius 52, 53; C. Caligula 7, 23.
LXXXIX	Josephus xviii. 3.
XC	Suet. C. Caligula 23, 24, 29; Tac. *Ann.* xii. 1-10, 64-69; xiv. 1-9.
XCI	Tac. *Ann.* xv. 51, 57.
XCII	Tac. *Ann.* xv. 63, 64.
XCIII	Tac. *Ann.* xiii. 45, 46; xiv. 63; xv. 23; xvi. 6.
XCIV	Tac. *Hist.* ii. 53; iii. 76, 77.
XCV	Isidori Hispalensis *Originum* i. 39; *De Scriptoribus Ecclesiasticis* v.
XCVI	Iulii Capitolini *Marcus Antoninus Philosophus* vi; xix; xxvi; xxix.
XCVII	Iulii Capitolini *Opilius Macrinus* viii; ix; Aelii Lampridii *Antoninus Heliogabalus* ii; iv.
XCVIII	Flavii Vopisci *Divus Aurelianus* xxii. 1; xxv. 2-28; xxviii. 3-4; xxx. 1-4, 24-26; xxxii. 4; xxxiii. 2; xxxiv. 3; xxxv. 4; Trebellii Pollionis *Tyranni Triginta* xv; xvi; xvii; xxiv; xxvii; xxx; xxxiii.

XCIX	This legend was preserved by popular tradition until the fourteenth century, when it appeared in written form in chronicles such as the *Chronica Martiniana*. Boccaccio may have been acquainted with the version of the legend found in that work.
C	The sources for this chapter cannot be definitely ascertained.
CI	Boccaccio states in his *Commento a Dante* (II, 434) that he heard of Gualdrada from Coppo di Borghese Domenichi.
CII	G. Villani, *Cronache* IV, 20; VI, 6.
CIII	G. Villani, *Cronache* XI, 108.
CIV	G. Villani, *Cronache* XII, 51, 52, 99, 111, 112, 115.

SELECT BIBLIOGRAPHY

BIBLIOGRAPHICAL NOTE

The following bibliography brings research on *De claris mulieribus* up to date since Guido Guarino's edition of 1963. It is worth noting that the present translation, with its introduction and notes, was completed just on the cusp of the feminist movement of the 1960s and 1970s and well before the beginning of the theoretical turn of the late 1970s and 1980s. Despite this, on its publication Prof. Guarino's was the first complete English edition of this important work and the first to present to a scholarly and general audience Boccaccio's work on famous women. In itself it was a milestone in Renaissance studies that allowed for a generation of scholarly research on, and teaching of, this text.

Another important aspect of the original 1963 edition was the cultural context that allowed such translations to reach a wide audience well beyond the confines of the academic world. This edition was part of a broader scholarly enterprise that fit well into the central position that the humanities and Renaissance studies themselves still played in American culture. Translation as a scholarly enterprise still maintained a high prestige — reflected in such popular series as the Penguin Classics, the Harper Torchbooks, and the Columbia University Records of Civilization — that would only be recaptured in the late 1990s by a small handful of university and independent presses. The introduction, notes and style of this edition therefore fit well into this inclusive spirit.

Much of the research in the following bibliography will offer both new critical approaches to Boccaccio, his work, and this particular text, and also reflect the past generation's work of feminist scholarship on the text of the *De claris mulieribus*, on

Boccaccio himself and on late medieval and early Renaissance views of women. Some scholarship has also focused on what contemporary critics see as Boccaccio's essential misogyny and the misogynistic tradition in late medieval and early Renaissance writing. This bibliography also reflects the large amount of work that has been done on women as agents in both history and in the fields of scholarship and creative writing.

Of particular value for the present edition are two works: the first Virginia Brown's own superlative dual-language edition and translation of the *De claris mulieribus* as *Famous Women*, the first volume of the Harvard I Tatti Renaissance Library (2001), and second the insightful review of this edition by Guyda Armstrong in *Heliotropia* 1.1, with her overview of previous English-language scholarship on the text. Armstrong also provided a detailed comparison between Brown's and Guarino's translations that will be of value to both students and advanced scholars.

One should also note that Guarino was employing the edition of Mathias Apiarius, printed in Bern in 1539, which differs from that used by Zaccaria in his critical edition of the text (1970), from which Brown's English translation derives. The present edition also follows the nomenclature of the 1539 edition as *De claris mulieribus.*

For the complete Latin text and further philological apparatus readers should consult the Brown edition. For ongoing bibliography readers should consult Christopher Kleinhenz's annual "American Boccaccio Bibliography" in *Heliotropia,* an online journal of the American Boccaccio Association, at http://www.heliotropia.org.

• • •

COMPLETE WORKS

Boccaccio, Giovanni. *Tutte le Opere.* Vittore Branca, ed. Milan: Mondadori, 1964–74.

EDITIONS OF *DE CLARIS MULIERIBUS*

Boccaccio, Giovanni. *Libri Johanis Boccacii de Certaldo De Mulieribus Claris gewidmet Andrea Acciaiuoli.* Ulm: Johann Zainer der Ältere, 1473.

——. *De Claris Mulieribus.* Strassburg: Georg Husner, 1474.

——. Heinrich Steinhöwel, ed. *Hie nach volget der Kurcz sin Von Etlichen Frowen: Von denen Johannes Boccacius in Latin beschriben hat. und Hainricus Stainhöwel getütschet.* Ulm: Zainer, 1474.

——. *Der Kurcz syn von ettlichen Frauen.* Augsburg: Anton Sorg, 1479.

——. *Liber De Claris Mulieribus. Epistola ad Andreä de Acciarolis de Florentia Alte Ville Cometissam.* Louvain: Aegidius van der Heerstraten, 1487.

——. Heinrich Steinhöwel, ed. *Von den Erlychten Frouen.* Strassburg: Johann Prüss, 1488.

——. *Le Liure de Jehan Bocasse de la Louenge et Vertu des Nobles et Cleres Dames.* Paris: Anthoine Verard, 1493.

——. *Tractado de Johan Bocaçio De Las Claras, excellentes y mas famosas y señaladas Damas.* Zaragosa: Paulo Hurus, 1494.

——. Vincenzo Bagli, ed. *L'Opera de Misser Giouanni Boccacio De Mulieribus Claris.* Venice: Zuanne de Trino, chimato Tacuino, 1506.

——. *Johannes Boccatius van Florentien, Poeet ende Philosophe, bescrivende van den doorluchtighen, glorioesten ende edelsten Vrouwen ende van haren Wercken ende gheschienissen die si gedaen hebben binnen haren leven in den ouden voorleden Tiden, ende is ghenuechlick om te lesen.* Antwerp: Claes die Grave, 1525.

——. *Libro de Jua Bocacio que tracta de las Illustres Mugeres.* Seville: I. Cromberger, 1528.

——. *Le plaisant Liure de ... Iehan Bocace ... auquel il traicte des Faictz Gestes des Illustres Cleres Dames.* Paris: P. Hermier, 1538.

——. *Ioannis Boccatii insignie opus De Claris Mulieribus.* Bern: Mathias Apiarius, 1539.

——. Heinrich Steinhöwel, ed. *Ein schöne Cronica oder Hystoribuch von den fürnämlichsten Weybern, so von Adams Zeyten angeweßt, was guttes oder böses je durch sy geübt, auch was nachmaln guttes oder böses darauss enstanden. Erstlich durch Joannem Boccatium in Latein beschriben.* Augsburg: Stayner, 1543.

——. Giuseppe Betussi, ed. *Libro di M. Gio. Boccaccio Delle Donne Illustri.* Venice: P. de Nicolini da Sabbio, 1545 (1547).

——. *Boccace Des Dames de Renom: Nouvellement traduict d'Italien en langage Françoys.* Lyon: Chez Guil. Rouille à l'Escu de Venise, 1551.

——. Giuseppe Betussi, ed. *Libro di M. Gio. Boccaccio Delle Donne Illustri: Con vna additione fatta dal medesimo Delle Donne Famose dal Te[m]po di M. Giouanni fino a i Giorni Nostri, [et] alcune altre state per inanzi, con la Vita del Boccaccio, [et] La Tauola di tutte L'historie, [et] cose principali, che nell'opra si contengono.* Venice: de gl'Imperatori, 1558.

——. Heinrich Steinhöwel, ed. *Historien von allen den fürnembsten Weibern, so von Adams Zeiten angeweszt, was gutes und böses je durch sie geübet, auch was nachmals darausz entstanden... Jetzundt zum andern Mal in truck Verfertiget durch D. Henricum Steinhöwel von Weil.* Frankfurt-am-Main: M. Lechler, 1576.

——. Giuseppe Betussi and Francesco Serdonati, eds. *Libro di M. Giovanni Boccaccio, Delle Donne Illustri.* Florence: Filippo Giunti, 1596.

——. *"De Preclaris Mulieribus," That Is to Say in Englyshe, of the Ryghte Renoumyde Ladyes.* Translated from "Bocasse." London: Egerton, Cox and Phillipson; R. Ryan; H.D. Symonds; and W. Richardson, 1789.

——. Donato Albanzani and Luigi Tosti, eds. *Volgarizzamento di Maestro Donato da Casentino dell'opera di Messer Boccaccio De Claris Mulieribus: Rinvenudo in un codice del XIV secolo dell'archivio Casinese.* Naples: Ateneo, 1836; Milan: Silvestri, 1841.

——. Attilio Hortis, ed. *Le Donne Famose descritte da Giovanni Boccacci.* Triest: Rivista Triestina di Scienze, 1877.

——. Donato Albanzani and Giacomo Manzoni, eds. *Delle Donne Famose di Giovanni Boccacci: Traduzione di M. Donato degli Albanzani di Casentino... Edizione terza, curata da Giacomo Manzoni, con note.* Bologna: G. Romagnoli, 1881.

——. Heinrich Steinhöwel and Karl Drescher, eds. *De Claris Mulieribus.* Stuttgart and Tübingen: Bibliothek des Litterarischer Verein in Stuttgart, 1895.

——. Heinrich Steinhöwel and Simon Höpfl, eds. *Des Giovanni Boccaccio Buch: Von den berühmten Frawen: Mit den Holzschnitten der Ausgabe von Joh. Zainer, Ulm 1473.* Munich: Holbein-Verl., Potsdam: G. Kiepenheuer, 1924.

——. Gustav Schleich, ed. *Die mittelenglische Umdichtung von Boccaccios De Claris Mulieribus, nebst der latienischen Vorlage.* Leipzig: Mayer & Müller, 1924.

——. Herbert G. Wright and Henry P. Morley, eds. *Forty-six Lives Translated from Boccacio's* De Claris Mulieribus *by Henry Parker, Lord Morley.* Early English Text Society vol. 214. London: Oxford University Press, 1943, reprint, 1970.

——. *De Las Ilustres Mujeres, en Romance: Zaragoza, 1494. Sale nuevamente a luz reproducida en facsimile por acuerdo de la Real Academia Española.* Madrid: Castalia for Real Academia Española, 1951.

——. Guido A. Guarino, ed. and trans. *Concerning Famous Women.* New Brunswick, NJ: Rutgers University Press, 1963.

——. Vittorio Zaccaria and Vittore Branca, eds. *De Mulieribus Claris.* In *Tutte le Opere* 10. Milan: Mondadori, 1970.

——. Harriet Goldberg, ed. *Text and Concordance of the Zaragoza 1494 Edition of Boccacio's* De las Ilustres Mujeres en Romance. Microform. Madison: Hispanic Seminary of Medieval Studies, 1992.

——. Jeanne Baroin and Josiane Haffen, eds. *Boccace, 'des Cleres et Nobles Femmes': Ms. Bibl. Nat. 12420.* Annales littéraires de l'Université de Besançon, 498, 556. Paris: Belles Lettres, 1993–95.

——. Virginia Brown, ed. and trans. *Famous Women.* I Tatti Renaissance Library 1. Cambridge, MA: Harvard University Press, 2001.

BIBLIOGRAPHY

SECONDARY WORKS

Amendola, R. Natasha. "Weaving Boccaccian Women." *Spunti e Ricerche: Rivista d'Italianstica* 22 (2007): 63–73.

Armstrong, Guyda. "The History of *De mulieribus claris* in English Translation." *Heliotropia* 1.1 (2003): 8 pages, unnumbered. (www.heliotropia.org).

Blamires, Alcuin. *The Case for Women in Medieval Culture.* Oxford: Clarendon Press, 1997.

——. ed. *Woman Defamed and Woman Defended: An Anthology of Medieval Texts.* Oxford: Clarendon Press, 1992.

Branca, Vittore. *Boccaccio: The Man and His Works.* R. Monges, trans. New York: New York University Press, 1978.

——. *Boccaccio visualizzato: Narrare per parole e per immagini fra medioevo e rinascimento.* Turin: Einaudi, 1999.

Brownlee, Kevin. "Christine de Pizan's Canonical Authors: The Special Case of Boccaccio." *Comparative Literature Studies* 32.2 (1995): 244–61.

Buettner, Brigitte. "Les affinités séléctives: Image et texte dans les premiers manuscrits des *Clères Femmes.*" *Studi sul Boccaccio* 18 (1990): 281–99.

——. *Boccaccio's Des Cleres et Nobles Femmes: Systems of Signification in an Illuminated Manuscript.* Seattle: College Art Association, 1996.

Casebier, Karen. "Re-Writing Lucretia: Christine de Pizan's Response to Boccaccio's *De Mulieribus Claris.*" *Fifteenth-Century Studies* 32 (2006): 35–52.

Daniels, Rhiannon. *Boccaccio and the Book: Production and Reading in Italy 1340–1520.* London: Legenda, 2009.

Domanski, Kristina. *Lesarten des Ruhms: Johann Zainers Holzschnittillustrationen zu Giovanni Boccaccios "de Mulieribus Claris."* Cologne: Böhlau, 2007.

Filosa, Elsa. "L'arte del ritratto femminile in Boccaccio: Studi sulla narrativa del *De mulieribus claris.*" Ph.D. Thesis. University of North Carolina at Chapel Hill, 2005.

—. "Petrarca, Boccaccio e le 'mulieres clarae': dalla *Familiare* 21:8 al *De mulieribus claris.*" *Annali d'Italianistica* 22 (2004): 381–95.

Franklin, Margaret. *Boccaccio's Heroines: Power and Virtue in Renaissance Society.* Aldershot: Ashgate, 2006.

Gathercole, Patricia M. "Review of Guido A. Guarino, *Concerning Famous Women (de Claris Mulieribus).*" *Italica* 42.4 (1965): 431–32.

Gittes, Tobias F. *Boccaccio's Naked Muse: Eros, Culture, and the Mythopoeic Imagination.* Toronto: University of Toronto Press, 2008.

Hagedorn, Suzanne C. *Abandoned Women: Rewriting the Classics in Dante, Boccaccio, and Chaucer.* Ann Arbor: University of Michigan Press, 2004.

Heliotropia. An online journal of the American Boccaccio Association. http://www.heliotropia.org.

Holderness, Julia S. "Feminism and the Fall: Boccaccio, Christine de Pizan, and Louise Labe." *Essays in Medieval Studies* 21.1 (2005): 97–108.

Jordan, Constance. "Boccaccio's In–Famous Women: Gender and Civic Virtue in the *De mulieribus claris.*" In *Ambiguous Realities: Women in the Middle Ages and Renaissance.* C. Levin and J. Watson, eds. Detroit: Wayne State University Press, 1987, 25–47.

Kolsky, Stephen. *The Genealogy of Women: Studies in Boccaccio's De Mulieribus Claris.* New York: Peter Lang, 2003.

—. *The Ghost of Boccaccio: Writings on Famous Women in Renaissance Italy.* Turnhout: Brepols, 2005.

Levarie Smarr, Janet. "Speaking Women: Three Decades of Authoritative Females." In Stillinger and Psaki, *Boccaccio and Feminist Criticism,* 29–38.

Lütkehaus, Ludger. *Mythos Medea.* Leipzig: Reclam, 2001.

McLeod, Glenda. *Virtue and Venom: Catalogs of Women from Antiquity to the Renaissance.* Ann Arbor: University of Michigan Press, 1991.

Migiel, Marilyn. "The Untidy Business of Gender Studies: Or, Why It's Almost Useless to Ask If the *Decameron* is Feminist." In Stillinger and Psaki, *Boccaccio and Feminist Criticism,* 217–33.

Müller, Ricarda. *Ein Frauenbuch des frühen Humanismus:
Untersuchungen zu Boccacios* De Mulieribus Claris. Stuttgart: Franz
Steiner, 1992.

Painter, Tara K. "*Exempla Feminarum:* Audience and Purpose in
Boccaccio's *De Mulieribus Claris.*" Thesis (M.A.). University of
Missouri-Columbia, 1995.

Phillippy, Patricia A. "Establishing Authority: Boccaccio's *De claris
mulieribus* and Christine de Pizan's *Le Livre de la cité des dames.*"
Romanic Review 77 (1986): 167–94. Reprinted in *The Selected Writings
of Christine de Pizan: New Translations, Criticism.* Renate Blumenfeld-
Kosinski, ed. New York: W.W. Norton & Co, 1997, 329–61.

Riva, Massimo, and Michael Papio. *Decameron Web.* Brown
University, Department of Italian Studies, 2001–. Internet resource.

Stillinger, Thomas C. and F. Regina Psaki. *Boccaccio and Feminist
Criticism.* Chapel Hill, NC: Annali d'Italianistica, 2006.

Torretta, L. "Il *Liber de claris mulieribus* di Giovanni Boccaccio."
Giornale storico della letteratura italiana 39 (1902): 252–92, 40 (1902):
35–65.

Zaccaria, Vittorio. "Appunti sul latino del Boccaccio nel *De mulieribus
claris.*" *Studi sul Boccaccio* 3 (1965): 229–46.

—. *Boccaccio narratore, storico, moralista e mitografo.* Florence: L.S.
Olschki, 2001.

—. "Le fasi redazionali del *De mulieribus claris.*" *Studi sul Boccaccio* 1
(1963): 253–332.

• • •

This Book Was Completed on June 25, 2011
At Italica Press in New York, New York.
Revisions Were Set in Adobe Garamond.
and in Caslon Open Face. This
Edition Was Produced on
60-lb Natural Paper
in the USA, UK
and EU.

• • •
•

www.ingramcontent.com/pod-product-compliance
Lightning Source LLC
Chambersburg PA
CBHW030754150426
42813CB00068B/3043/J